KEEPING THE FAITH

KEEPING THE
FAITH

John O'Mahony
With
John Harrington

HEROBOOKS

HERO BOOKS

PUBLISHED BY HERO BOOKS
1 WOODVILLE GREEN
LUCAN
CO. DUBLIN
IRELAND
www.herobooks.ie
Hero Books is an imprint of Umbrella Publishing

First Published 2015

Copyright © John O'Mahony 2015
The moral rights of the author has been asserted
All rights reserved

Without limiting the rights under copyright reserved above, no part of this publication may be reproduced, stored in or introduced into a retrieval system, or transmitted in any form or by any means (electronic, mechanical, photocopying, recording or otherwise) without the prior written permission of the publisher of this book.

A CIP record for this book is available from the British Library

ISBN 978-0-9526260-9-1

Printed in Ireland with Print Procedure Ltd
Cover design and typesetting: Jessica Maile
Cover photograph: Sportsfile
Photographs: Sportsfile and the O'Mahony family collection

To my parents, Stephen and Brigid O'Mahony,
and Gerardine's parents, Mattie and Annie Towey

ACKNOWLEDGEMENTS

This book presents my journey in life but, for me, it is more about the people who have accompanied me along the way.

Firstly, I would like to thank Liam Hayes and John Harrington for assisting me in describing my highs and lows, friendships, passions, successes and failures. The telling of this story is due to their vision, talent and professionalism.

John deserves special mention for the careful way the memories have been weaved to cohesion and not least for his willingness to meet at the strangest of times and venues to accommodate the schedule of a rural politician.

Gaelic football has been central to my life.

I am privileged to have worked with some of the greatest players to ever grace Croke Park on championship Sundays, and I thank them for the memories. To achieve any success in sport, the 'players' off the pitch are just as important. To all the selectors, officials and unofficial advisors, coaches, and specialists I have worked with over the years, thank you for your loyalty and support.

Finally, and most importantly, I thank my family and friends who stand behind the stories in these pages. In particular, to my wife, Gerardine and daughters, Gráinne, Niamh, Rhona, Deirdre and Cliodhna, thank you for your unqualified love and belief in good times, and not so good times. And to my brothers, Dan and Stephen, and all in the Towey household, I have always treasured your fullest support.

John O'Mahony,
September, 2015

CHAPTER 1

Growing up in a territorial outpost has a way of making you very protective of the land spreading out behind you.

I was born in Magheraboy, Kilmovee, Co. Mayo in 1953, and my home place is the last house before the border with Roscommon. A few yards away a busy stream that gushes through a v-shaped gully cut deep into the ground divides the two counties.

If you drove by you'd hardly notice it, as it tumbles down a slope between two fields and disappears below the road. But when I was growing up that little stream might as well have been a 10-foot high wall.

On one side there was *them*.

On the other side there was *us*.

We were Mayo, they were Roscommon.

We shared the same passion for Gaelic football, but there was no love lost between us. All that made us different to them was the colours we supported, but that was everything. You respected them. Some of them were your good friends. But a part of you also hated them, and vice versa.

Rivalry is the heartbeat of the GAA and it pumps ever more furiously the closer you get to a county's border. From a very young age I sensed it, embraced it, and was energised by it. Football has always been at the very core of my existence and I just cannot imagine what my life would've been like without it.

The nature of my surroundings helped stoke the obsession, but so did nurture. My father, Stephen O'Mahony was from Drinagh in West Cork and passed on a deep love of football to my two brothers, Dan and Stephen and me. His other passion was road bowling, a popular pursuit in West Cork, but a harder sell in East Mayo.

As I grew older, my father and I had our fair share of disagreements, but the benefit of hindsight made me realise that was because we were both so alike. Even from a young age I was strongly opinionated, and my father would not have indulged me if he disagreed with me. We were equally stubborn and sparks often flew, but they cooled just as quickly.

Another trait I have inherited from him is my work ethic. When I do a job, I want to do it to the utmost of my ability and leave no stone unturned, even if that means I have to make some personal sacrifices along the way.

When I managed county football teams there were plenty of those moments. For example, during my first spell in charge of Mayo I was not there when my daughters, Cliodhna and Deirdre made their First Communions. I just felt that I had to lead by example and I couldn't very well request the players to make a commitment if I wasn't making it myself.

My father prided himself on never missing a day of work, and it was because of that work ethic that he ended up in Mayo in the first place.

Emigration was rampant in Ireland in the 1940s because there was so little work to be found, and the West of Ireland was worse hit than anywhere. The ESRI certainly wouldn't have predicted someone making it all the way up to Mayo from Cork. The East Coast of America would've been a much more likely destination.

My father started out working in Drinagh Co-op and then moved to Tralee where he was a lorry driver before that line of work brought him up to Tuam in Galway. From there he applied for and got a job in Doherty's in Lisacul, Roscommon, which at the time was a thriving shop and egg exporters.

It was here that he met my mother, Brigid Gallagher. Her presence there was just as unlikely or random as his, so it's easy to believe it was their fate to meet.

She was from a very isolated part of the Erris Peninsula in Mayo. There wasn't even a road into their house. You had to go cross-country, through a field and then negotiate a small footbridge over a river to get to it.

Life could be harsh in those days. When her father got sick with what must have been cancer they took him to Ballina so he could get the train to Dublin where he was hospitalised. They did not see him again until he came home in his coffin because going to Dublin to visit him would've been financially and logistically out of the question.

My mother was a quiet woman who would never even visit Dublin in her lifetime, but she had the same determination to better herself that my father did. She did a commercial course that first got her work in the post office in Manorhamilton in Leitrim, before she too ended up in Doherty's of Lisacul.

It was something like the modern version of a department store where groceries, eggs, farm meal and supplies and all that sort of stuff was sold. My mother worked in the grocery shop and my father drove a lorry, going around from house to house collecting and buying eggs.

Eggs were so plentiful at that time that people were able to pay for most of their groceries with the money they received for them. Doherty's graded and tested them on their premises and then sold them on to bigger dealers. My parents must have seen the strength of the business because when they married, and bought a house and small farm across the border in Magheraboy, they set up a one-stop shop of their own.

We sold produce from a small store beside our house that my mother ran but the bulk of the business was done by my father, who set himself up as a travelling shop.

This was in the 1950s when most people would not have had cars of their own, and therefore they struggled to get into town to buy what they needed. So, instead of going to the shop, my father brought the shop to them in the back of a van. He had a set route every week and in the morning would sell groceries. There was a bit of bartering in those days, and people would give him some eggs or other produce they might have in part payment for the groceries. He was then able to sell those eggs to wholesalers.

Each house had their own 'book' so they could buy things on credit and then settle their accounts whenever they could.

There was great trust amongst the people, and as it was a farming community it was natural some households would run up a bill until they'd sell a few cattle and then be able to pay it off.

While my father was selling groceries in the morning he'd also be taking orders for animal feed like Clarinda, Bran, Indian meal or calf nuts. That couldn't be delivered on spec because it was so big and bulky, so he'd take the orders on his morning run and then deliver the animal feed the following morning. In the few weeks leading up to Christmas, when everything got a bit busier, it could be well after midnight when my father returned home.

Running a shop in those days was a very labour intensive operation because practically everything had to be weighed and packed manually. Usually a half ton of sugar had to be weighed and packed at one time into two, three and four pound weights. This would take a full day to do. Other products that had to be weighed and packaged by hand were tea, bread soda, oatmeal, raisins, currants, sultanas, bacon, Indian Meal, barley, crushed oats, bran, and washing soda. We also sold paraffin oil in various measures that were poured out of a 300-gallon tank at the back of the house.

My father was a self-made man but back in the Ireland of the 1950s and 60s you had little choice but to fend for yourself. There was no sense of reliance on hand-outs from the State and you survived or perished depending on your ability to be self-motivated enough to do something for yourself.

I think I learned a lot from my father's attitude and I've always tried to have a similar ethos in life myself. My father's job made him an important cog in the community, and that suited him because he was very much a people person. He was constantly travelling from one house or farm to another, so he knew all the news in the local area and people would look forward to his visit.

There was no Twitter or Facebook in those days, so that's how news was transferred. Occasionally, I'd accompany my father on his rounds, but my older brother Dan was a more willing helper.

I did enjoy it at Christmas, though, when you'd be handing out what were known as the Christmas boxes. Depending on how good a customer someone was, you'd give them tea and sugar, a cake, or some other sort of present. That was the sort of community rapport that existed there, and you always looked forward to doing those Christmas rounds.

As well as having a van for the travelling shop, my father also had a car so if there was any sort of emergency in the neighbourhood and the locals didn't have transport he doubled up as the local taxi man too.

Quite often, the journeys involved bringing people as far as Cobh in Cork to get the ship to America and in later years to Shannon Airport. He also brought people to places of pilgrimage, like Knock and Croagh Patrick.

The car was always fullest, however, on big match days, and one of my earliest memories of him was going to the 1957 All-Ireland football final between Cork and Louth. He always had that allegiance to his home county, but he was just as enthusiastic a supporter of Mayo football.

The car was fully booked for every championship match, and as I got older I made it my mission to be included in these grand adventures.

It took a while before my ambition was realised though, and my brother Dan has a vivid memory of me wailing crying and running after the full car as it bounced down the road on the way to a Connacht championship match without me.

I can only presume I eventually pestered my father so much that he had no choice but to bring me.

The first game I can remember was a Connacht championship match between Mayo and Galway in Tuam in 1961, three days after my eighth birthday. I can't remember exactly who was in the car that day, but I presume my brother Dan and our local postman, Stephen Sheridan were anyway.

Stephen was a good friend of my father's, and over the years they were constant companions on big match days. Others who were often part of a big match day pilgrimage were neighbours like Pa Cafferkey, Tom McCann, and Tommy 'Datler' Griffin.

I did not pick the best day possible to make my 'championship debut', because that particular year there was a massive crush outside the turnstiles of Tuam Stadium. There are side entrances to the ground now, but back then everyone entered through the front. The match was a sell-out, and it was a really frightening experience for an eight year old to be caught in such a crush as everyone squeezed their way into the stadium.

We were sitting behind the goals, and you couldn't really see what was going on down the other end, so I could make little sense of it all. But even though Mayo were well beaten and I'd had a right good fright on the way into the stadium, I knew coming away that I definitely wanted more of this.

Those summer pilgrimages to championship matches became a huge part of my life and were a real coming of age experience for me. It was a gateway into an adult world I would previously have been excluded from, and I relished every element of the day out.

You'd leave early in the morning and there was only one topic of conversation all the way to the match… football.

Back then, there was not nearly so much media analysis of Gaelic games, but there was no lack of it in our car. The previous year's championship performances were minutely dissected and used as the basis to form a judgement on what could be expected this time around.

As a child you are rarely involved in adult conversations, so it was a new and exciting experience to feel like you were part of it in those car journeys.

Match days were all about the little rituals, like the sandwiches out of the boot of the car before the game and the long walk to the ground with the tension rising with every step you took. I loved the tradition of it all, and I suppose it made me appreciate all the more what it meant to the supporters when I later became a county manager.

I knew the sense of wonderment supporters had of what was going on in the team set-up and the deep emotional connection the supporters felt with their team.

This gave me the ability to convey to any group of players I managed the importance of what they were doing, and just how much it meant to the supporters that followed them and even the generations of supporters to come.

I really had an acute appreciation of what it all meant to people, and I believe that any success I've had as a manager has been down in large part to my ability to communicate that to players.

Players often operate in a bubble where the world outside the four walls of the dressing room is a faraway place. You need that to an extent in order to be fully focused. But it is important also to have an emotional connection with your supporters because if you harness it properly it can be a powerful thing.

In my formative years supporting Mayo, we had little to shout about unfortunately. We failed to win a single Connacht title in an 11 year period from 1956 to 1966.

Galway were the 'Kings of the Province' during that period, and also held sway over the whole country when they won three All-Irelands in a row from 1964 to '66. I vividly remember coming out of Castlebar after the 1966 Connacht final defeat to Galway bawling my eyes out and saying we were never going to beat them.

That day we were leading by a point with time almost up, when Galway got a sideline kick. Cyril Dunne took it and the Mayo crowd were already camped on the sideline, ready to invade, so a path had to be cleared for him so he could take a run up for the kick.

But despite the hot Mayo breath on the back his neck, he kicked the ball straight and true over the bar.

Worse was to follow.

Liam Sammon punched a last-gasp winner after a pass from 18 year old Jimmy Duggan who was from Claremorris in Mayo, but had chosen to play for the county of his parents.

Mayo gave me little to shout about for most of the '60s, but their struggles in no way diluted by growing obsession with the game of football.

Even after Mayo were knocked out of the race early year after year, I still kept close tabs on the All-Ireland championship. *The Sunday Independent* used to have a wrap-around colour photograph of the two All-Ireland finalists every year, and soon the walls of my bedroom were plastered with them.

I can remember as a nine year old going into town with my father and brother Dan to watch the 1962 All-Ireland final between Roscommon and Kerry in Denis Egan's pub. It was the first final to be televised, and the pub was absolutely packed even though it was not officially open and no alcohol was being served.

It was shown on a small black and white television, and the reception wasn't great, but it was still a magical experience.

Later, one of our neighbours, Tommy Hayden became the first person I can remember in Kilmovee to own a television, and on a few occasions I plucked up the courage to watch All-Ireland finals there. Tommy had an old-style tape-recorder with a microphone attachment and he'd be conducting interviews for the craic at half-time to get our impressions on the match.

Watching those matches on television, you'd dream of someday getting to watch Mayo play in the stadium. My wish was finally granted in 1967.

Galway were the reigning All-Ireland champions but we hammered them in the Connacht semi final. By then I was so used to seeing Mayo suffer at the hand of Galway that it was almost a surreal experience. Dan and I then travelled to Dublin with my father for the All-Ireland semi final against Meath. In those days it cost an adult 12 shillings and six pence to get in, but I was still small enough to be lifted over the stiles.

That game is remembered in Mayo as 'the day the television broke'.

The broadcast of the match cut out and by the time the signal returned Mayo supporters watching the match on television were horrified to discover that Meath had scored two goals.

That was the margin we lost by in the end, 3-14 to 1-14, and the defeat was blamed by many on the accursed television!

Unfortunately, we're never short in Mayo of something to blame for our failures in Croke Park.

Meanwhile, I was making it my mission to wear the green and red of Mayo myself someday. My brothers and I would kick a football around, and occasionally kick lumps out of one another too, at every available opportunity.

The close quarters stuff would take place in the alley between our house and the shop. Stephen was four years younger than me, so he was given the relatively safe role of goalkeeper as myself and Dan did battle.

Those were the league games; the championship took place in a more auspicious venue.

My father was a busy man, but he'd still find time to regularly take a scythe to the tall grass in the field behind our house so it could act as a serviceable football pitch.

And when Hurricane Debbie blew through in 1961 and flattened our wooden shed along its way, some of the timber was soon put to good use by being transformed into two sets of goalposts.

More of the broken timber was nailed together to make toy electricity poles because our young imaginations were captured by the rural electrification scheme that was being carried out at the time. So, while the ESB crews were putting up their electricity poles, we'd be putting up our toy ones and even spooling thread from one to the next for added realism.

That was only a temporary diversion though, football was the constant one, and that field was where it all began for me.

No one is living in the old family home anymore, but I still go back there occasionally to walk that small plot of land when I want some time to myself to think.

The field seems a lot smaller now, but that is always the way of it when you retrace your childhood steps as an adult. It's overgrown with rushes and yellow 'Buachallan' and the ground beneath your feet is bumped and bruised with humps and water-filled hollows.

To a stranger it might seem like a desolate enough place but, for me and my brothers, it was Croke Park itself.

We'd kick ball there at every available opportunity but the red-letter day of the week was Sunday. That's when we'd be joined on our little home-made pitch by neighbours like the Cafferkeys, the Duffys, the Moffetts, and Patrick Reid, and play for hours on end.

It was my first proving ground as a footballer. Even though it was just kids at play, I still took it seriously because I had a competitive streak from the very start.

I was always striving to better myself as a footballer, and the obsession put down deep roots from very early on. The memory of getting a proper Gaelic football off Santa one Christmas is still a vivid one, and so is the day my brother Dan and I got our first football boots.

We spotted an advertisement for them in *The Sunday Press*. A company in Dublin called Cripps had a special offer and we ordered two pairs.

We waited for our postman, Stephen Sheridan with bated breath for days afterwards. Every day he turned up without them was a massive anticlimax, and when they finally arrived I nearly burst with excitement.

Nowadays those boots wouldn't come close to passing a health and safety check.

The manufacturers clearly just poured some molten plastic into a mould that included the cogs and all. They were dynamite stuff! They'd cut the absolute feet off you but we didn't give a damn. They were our first football boots and we happily took every cut toe and rubbed raw heel that was going, just to feel like proper footballers.

Frustratingly, there was little proper football to be played in Magheraboy Primary School which was just up the road from our house. The school didn't have a pitch, just a yard. It was so small it was mainly soccer that was played because of the danger of breaking windows.

So my first contact with organised Gaelic football was when I went to secondary school in St Nathy's College in Ballaghaderreen. I didn't know it at the time when I first walked through the gates, but it was a place that would influence my adolescent and adult life massively.

Both of them for the good!

CHAPTER 2

I enrolled in St Nathy's in 1966, two years after my brother Dan. We were both there as boarders.

Free education had just come in but my parents still wanted us to board rather than go as day students because they really prioritised our education and wanted to give us every chance they could.

They must have thought that had we stayed at home and just travelled to and from school we'd be distracted by helping with the shop and other things, so they made the sacrifice of letting us go.

It definitely made things easier for me to have Dan there already when I arrived first. It was still a tough transition though, because you'd only be allowed to have visitors for one hour on a Sunday.

When I got home for Christmas for a few weeks midway through my first year there, it was tough going to have to go back boarding again.

I look back on my time as a student in St Nathy's as a positive and character-building one, but there is no doubt it was a very regimented place and creature comforts were few and far between.

You slept in 30-bed dorms and there were communal washing areas where you'd have one shower a week. Each day was scheduled like clockwork by a precise timetable that never deviated. You attended mass every morning at 8.0 am, had your breakfast at 8.30 am, and then there were classes from 9.30 am to 4.0 pm, with an hour-long break for lunch in between. Once classes ended you had sport for an hour, and then study classes between 5.30 pm and 7.0 pm.

You had your tea at 7.0 pm, more study classes from 8.0 to 9.30 pm, and then straight to bed. That was the schedule on Monday, Tuesday, Thursday, Friday, and Saturday.

Wednesday was our sports day; we had a half-day and it was the highlight of the week for me. Then, on Sunday morning, you'd have 'letters study' which meant writing home. There were more study classes later in the day and then that night you'd have the big bonus of being allowed to watch a film on TV.

With the whole school of boarders congregating in the school hall where there was one small TV, there was always a rush for the front row of chairs.

The film would start at 8.0 pm but you had to be in bed an hour and a half later, so you rarely saw the whole film and had to imagine how it ended!

It was a strange existence as contact with the outside world was so limited. In fact, it was actively discouraged because wireless radios were banned. But what I found toughest about my new environment was the food. To put it mildly, it wasn't great.

Breakfast was bread and butter, except on Sundays when there was the luxury of a fry. But it was a mass produced fry so it did not exactly have all the trimmings. The problem was that the food for every meal was destroyed by the overworked kitchen staff being required to feed 150 of us in one go.

Dinner was thin slices of beef that were stuck to the plate by whatever method they had used to heat the meat. If you turned the plate upside down, the beef would stubbornly refuse to obey the laws of gravity.

Along with the meat were potatoes. When they were in season, they'd be good. But, at other times of the year, you could hardly eat them because the strings would still be coming out of them by the time they landed on your plate.

Dessert was semolina or a type of bread and butter pudding that was done in large trays that were lined with newspaper.

More often than not you'd get a piece of the local newspaper stuck to your dessert, but that was a bonus really because it was some contact with the outside world.

At 4.0 pm you'd have cold milk and bread, and for supper you'd have chips and more bread and butter. It wasn't the most nutritiously diverse diet imaginable.

The bread came from Duff's bakery in Ballaghaderreen and the last delivery was on Thursday. That meant by Sunday the bread was stale and hardly edible. On the Monday night though it was fresh from the ovens, hot even, and we used to eat all around us.

There were prefects coming out of the kitchen with extra bread on the Monday night to feed the masses, and you'd go to bed stuffed.

In many ways it was a tough environment, and I've met a lot of people who would not have great memories of the place, but that is not the case for me. I made some really loyal friends for life, and I learned a lot about leadership by being given the opportunity to captain school teams.

It also gave you the ability to live with people, see the benefit of community, and have the corners knocked off you.

There was some rough and tumble and you'd occasionally get a few clips because corporal punishment was part of the curriculum at the time. For example, being caught with a pot of 'black-market' jam that was smuggled in would earn you six slaps.

It was a tough and regimented place at times, but in my experience it was never an abusive one. Maybe some people were able to cope with it better, and it certainly helped me that I had an older brother there.

It was formative, definitely, but formative for the good.

I think you needed an outlet to cope and I had a major one in football which became the centre of my universe throughout my time in St Nathy's. I loved Gaelic football for the sheer joy of playing the sport, but it certainly helped too that it made life in St Nathy's a little bit easier in a variety of ways.

Making it onto a school football team earned you a place in the elite of the school's social pecking order. There was a special table reserved for the team at meal times and, on the morning of a match instead of the normal breakfast, you'd get a boiled egg. Little things like that made a big difference, believe it or not.

If you were playing a match against a school like Summerhill, in Sligo, you'd effectively be gone from school for the day. And, when you returned to school after a match, you could be back late enough to miss a study class which was another nice perk.

There were three school teams… juvenile, junior, and senior.

The juvenile team played up to the under-15 grade so there were second years and some third years on it, but I was determined to make it in my first year in college. I also took a calculated approach to achieving my objective, and reckoned my only chance of doing so was as a goalkeeper. So I put myself forward as one even though I had no experience in the position. Maybe there was not a long line of alternative candidates, but I impressed sufficiently in trials to get the jersey.

From second year on, I made the full-back line my home.

I didn't have lighting pace or any great skill but I had a good bit of size and strength and I was determined. I was ambitious, but I was realistic too, so I knew my best chance of successfully making teams in the coming years was as a no-nonsense defender.

Wednesday was always the highlight of the week because that was when the senior football team in the school would train and have a fully-fledged match. Thirty players were required, but there weren't 30 on the senior panel so a few were called up from the junior team to make up the numbers. Even when I was only a second year I made it my mission to be involved in these matches.

I'd follow the captain or vice-captain of the team around with my chest out and let them know in no uncertain terms that I was available for selection.

By the time I was 16, I was captain of the school's junior team, and that earned me some more privileges. On the evening before a match, the captain and the vice-captain were brought up to the room of Fr Michael Joyce who was training the team at the time to help with picking it. It was nice to feel that much involved in the process, but what was even better was the fact that you were served tea and sweet cake.

Even if your opinion wasn't really being heeded all that much, you'd be keen to draw out the discussion as long as possible if it meant getting an extra slice of cake.

I got a kick from those conversations and I suppose that was my first taste of team management to a certain degree. Even then I was already interested in the tactics of the game, and had a copy of Joe Lennon's famous book, *Coaching Gaelic Football*.

I revelled in the responsibility of being team captain, and was always keen to influence guys to train and play as hard as possible. The satisfaction of being involved in a common cause definitely shaped me as a person, and is something that is still the driving force in my life today.

My time in St Nathy's also served to heighten my appreciation of the rivalries that are the lifeblood of the GAA. Because it was a Diocesan School, you'd have lots of lads there from Roscommon and Sligo, as well as Mayo. There were some fierce arguments because we were all warmed by the heat of the rivalry and did our best to stoke it as much as possible.

We'd all try to gain whatever edge we could over one another, no matter how preposterous.

On one particular Sunday, Roscommon beat Sligo and Galway beat Mayo in the Connacht championship. The Rossies had the bragging rights that day, while ourselves and the Sligo lads had to make do with arguing over which of our teams was worse.

One Sligo fella, Peter Brennan felt he had definitive proof that Mayo were the worst of the lot. After all, our match against Galway was the first of the afternoon which meant they exited the championship before Sligo did, and were therefore the inferior team.

The innocence of it! But those were the lengths you would go to in order to get whatever edge you could. Football was what gave us our different identities, but it was also the glue that bonded us together. Even though we were effectively cut off from the outside world, we'd find ways and means to slake our thirst for football knowledge.

Transistor radios were banned, but they were regularly smuggled in and provided our main source of information on how our respective counties were doing in the league or championship.

On Sunday afternoons in a study class you'd secretly listen to the radio through an earphone to get updates on matches. Then, that night, you'd hide under the blankets of your bed and tune into Seán Óg Ó Ceallachain for the day's results.

When I was in fourth year, Mayo unexpectedly got to the league final against Down and a few of us were determined to tune in for the match even though it coincided with a study period. The radio wasn't mine, but I got my hands on it and a set of earphones so I could listen to it quietly and then pass updates about Mayo's progress around the classroom.

Mayo scored four goals that day and won a great match, which was a really pleasant surprise at the time. Despite my best efforts, I can only presume that the lads and I in the class got a bit too vocally exited by it all because, when the Dean came into our classroom, he quickly rumbled what was going on and the radio was confiscated.

Listening to match reports on the radio might have been frowned upon, but the teachers in the school were hugely positive about developing us into the best footballers we could possibly be.

One of our teachers, Father Tom Lynch, an uncle of my future wife, Gerardine, had a big influence on me in this period. He taught me history when I was in fourth year and was someone we looked up to because he trained the school's Hogan Cup winning team in 1957. We'd always ask him about that win because he had scrapbooks with match reports and photographs that he could be persuaded to produce.

Father Lynch had a great knack for story telling, and the way he described their historic All-Ireland win just fuelled my obsession to become a champion footballer myself. Football was a very different sport back then than it is now. Our trainers were brilliant in their own way, but there was no in-depth analysis or tactical innovation.

By the end of my school days I usually played corner back, and in those days the game was simply about winning the ball when it came into your area and then kicking it as far as you could.

This idea of keeping possession simply wasn't part of the game. Football at that time was a very basic sport really.

In fairness, our small training field in St Nathy's didn't exactly lend itself to tactical innovation. It was little more than a bog, and even though you could have a wash yourself after training, your togs and jersey were only washed once a week. All you could do was throw them on the radiator and let the mud dry. They would nearly be standing up by themselves afterwards.

By second year I was full back on the juvenile team that beat St Jarlath's of Tuam in the Connacht final which was a major achievement for us because they had such a tradition of success. I captained the junior team to a Connacht title two years later, but failed to achieve my dream of winning the Hogan Cup with the senior team in my Leaving Cert year.

St Jarlath's beat us by a point in the Connacht semi final that year, and I really felt at the time like it was the end of the world. Even to this day it would still be a personal disappointment that we failed to win the clean sweep of juvenile, junior and senior Connacht titles, and that I never got that chance I craved to play for a Hogan Cup.

That is the nature of sport, it is the defeats that often leave a more lasting impression that the victories.

It was while I was in St Nathy's that I also began my club football career.

There was no actual club in my own parish of Kilmovee, and the rule at the time was that if there wasn't a club in your parish you could play with a club of a parish that bordered yours. Myself and Dan would've been making a name for ourselves in St Nathy's, so Ballaghaderreen were keen for us to join them.

We were also eligible for the Aghamore club, so there was a bit of a tug-of-war for a short while, but eventually Ballaghaderreen seemed the obvious choice because we went to school there.

It was a decision I have never regretted since because Ballaghaderreen GAA club has been a massive part of my life.

St Nathy's had strengthened my appreciation of how important rivalry is to the GAA, and my association with Ballaghaderreen has amplified it even more. The town has always had a complicated identity. The club plays in the Mayo championship and its players are only eligible to play for the Mayo county team.

But the town is actually geographically part of Roscommon, so some club members would regard themselves as Roscommon supporters rather than Mayo supporters.

John Dillon, the one-time leader of the Irish Parliamentary party at Westminster, MP for East Mayo, and a native of Ballaghaderreen, is believed to be the man responsible for the town's complicated identity. It was 1898, the local authority boundaries were being redrawn, and the story goes that Dillon wanted the town included in Roscommon where rates were lower than in Mayo. He got his way, and with the stroke of a pen Ballaghaderreen was cut adrift from the rest of the county.

The GAA club, which had been founded 14 years previously, refused to budge, though.

The club members insisted on continuing to play in the Mayo championship and providing footballers for Mayo rather than Roscommon. So now you have the unusual situation where some of the club's members would root for a player like Andy Moran when he wears the Mayo colours, but regard themselves as Roscommon supporters first and foremost.

In recent years, seven or eight of my friends from Ballagh would play cards once a week during the winter months. Four of them are hard-core Roscommon supporters, while the rest of us are seriously committed Mayo supporters.

The slagging can be fairly ferocious depending how well or poorly our respective counties are going, and there's never any shortage of debate. Those of us living in the town who support Mayo would do so with extra fervour because we'd regard ourselves as very much on the front-line.

You almost have to proclaim your allegiance all the more because the town is associated with Roscommon as well as Mayo. When I was playing with Ballagh you'd occasionally have someone say to you, 'ah, sure you're only a Roscommon man'.

It was usually done in a good spirited way, but you'd be still setting them straight fairly quickly!

Once I made the decision to join Ballaghaderreen, success came quickly. Along with Dan, I was part of the county minor championship winning team in 1968 when I was 15 years old.

Then, in 1972, we achieved what must be the unique accomplishment of winning the county under-21 title, the county intermediate title, and the county senior title all in the one year.

The intermediate title should have been played in 1971, but the father of our club secretary, Pat Dooney, died so it was postponed until April, 1972. Then, having won promotion, we also won the senior championship at the very first attempt and the county under-21 title too, which was a fair achievement.

It was a hectic time for me on a lot of different fronts, both sporting and personal.

I fulfilled the ambition of my young life by pulling on the Mayo jersey as a county minor in 1970 and '71. And, after completing my Leaving Cert in '71, I made the big decision to enrol in Maynooth College to study to become a priest.

CHAPTER 3

The decision to study for the priesthood was not something I rushed into or did on the spur of the moment. It was very much a personal choice and one I had thought deeply about.

It is very difficult for anyone that young to be fully convinced about what their vocation is in life, but I felt there was an onus on me to give it a chance and see if this was mine.

It was a gut decision, and perhaps I was partly swayed by the fact that a number of my close friends from St Nathy's had chosen the same path. So, too, had Dan two years previously.

It wasn't as if I had this ambition for years that I wanted to become a priest, but I also felt I would deny myself something if I did not explore it as an option. That is not to say either that I was taking it for granted or being in any way flippant about the commitment I was making. There was no pressure on me to go, and there was no pressure on me to stay.

But, after two years, I knew the priesthood was not the life for me.

Once any doubts started to come in, I wanted to confront them quickly rather than glide along. I had genuine reasons for studying for the priesthood, but I'm not sure anyone could possibly be certain if it is for them until they give it a chance.

I went into it for genuine reasons, and I left it for genuine reasons. I did not want to continue unless I felt I was fully committed to the way of life. It was time to move on. I knew if I stayed I would wonder every day whether I was making the right decision, and that sort of self-doubt proved that deep down I knew it wasn't for me.

One of the factors that influenced me was the authoritarian and hierarchical nature of the Church. I could not buy into all of their decisions and practices. I remember coming home at the weekends and having fairly intense debates with my father over what I perceived to be the Church's excessively authoritarian outlook on life.

'Well if you have such a problem with it then,' he eventually exclaimed, '... why the hell are you studying to be a priest?'

You couldn't really argue with that, and it was not long after I made my decision to leave. Ending my training did not mean leaving Maynooth because I continued to do my Arts degree as an external lay student.

The nature of my studies might have changed during my time in Maynooth, but football was a constant.

My first year there coincided with Maynooth's first year in the Sigerson Cup. We had a very committed group of players who were passionate about making their mark. We also had the benefit of being coached by Malachy O'Rourke, who has since left the priesthood but at the time was a lecturer in the college.

He is an uncle of the current Monaghan manager who bears the same name, and was way ahead of his time in terms of his coaching, tactical innovation and man-management.

He influenced me massively in terms of my understanding of the game from both a playing and management point of view, and remains a very good friend. Malachy was the first trainer I had ever heard suggest there's no reason why a corner back should not be as capable of getting a winning score in a match as a corner forward.

That really resonated with me because as a corner back myself I was much more used to a limited rather than expansive role in the team. You patrolled your patch in the full back line, did all you could to prevent the corner forward getting his hands on the ball, and when you won it yourself you rarely did anything more ambitious than kick it as far down the field as you possibly could.

But Malachy did not believe that a player should be in anyway straitjacketed by his position.

He wanted us to both attack and defend as a team. So when we lost the ball the forwards were expected to funnel back and play as auxiliary defenders. And, when we won it back, the defenders had a licence to bomb forward and join in the attack.

That might seem like a statement of the obvious now in terms of how best to play football, because it is the guiding principle of the modern game. But in 1972 it was truly revolutionary.

I had never once before been given the licence to go on an overlapping run from corner back, and this new sense of freedom was hugely refreshing. It made me realise that I wasn't just a stopper or a hatchet man; I could develop my skill as much as any other player on the pitch.

And because I now had the licence and self-confidence to become much more involved in the general play, I became a much fitter and more effective footballer.

I was also becoming a smarter one. Just because you were allowed to get forward as a defender did not mean you went on all sorts of brainless runs. To make Malachy's version of 'Total Football' work, there had to be a lot of understanding and communication amongst the players.

If I went on a run forward someone had to cover for me, and all over the pitch you had guys interchanging positions fluidly until the move died or ended with a score.

And if it died and the ball was turned over you were not vulnerable to a counter-attack because a teammate had moved in to fill the space behind you when you ran forward. That style of play was a really marked contrast to the static and regimented game I had known before coming to Maynooth.

Malachy was also extremely inventive in terms of the type of training he did, and was open to using all sorts of different resources. He often brought a big boom-box to training that had Irish music blaring out of it. And as he sped up the music you also had to speed up whatever drill you were doing.

He had us running through freshly ploughed fields or charging up hills carrying logs of timber over our shoulders to improve our endurance. He also brought us to Laytown beach to go running up the sand dunes and on those sessions he really pushed us to the limit.

On one of those trips he asked me to take charge of the training for 20 minutes. Here I was, just 19 years old, and I was being trusted enough to take charge. It shocked me, but it also got me thinking.

That was typical Malachy.

He was a very inclusive coach who wanted his players to think for themselves and welcomed an exchange of ideas. For young men like us, who were maybe more used to an authoritarian approach, it was hugely inspirational to feel like your opinion was valued in that way. I soaked up everything like a sponge. I think maybe Malachy saw that I shared his passion for the thing which was why he pushed me forward to take charge of the occasional session.

Thanks to his influence, I began looking at the game with an even more analytical eye.

Playing as a corner back gave me a good vantage point in that regard, and definitely fed into my view of the game as a manager in later years. As a corner back you have to win your individual battle, but you are very much dependent on what's happening in front of you. If the men further out the field are not doing their job, then you will be under the cosh and it is the most unforgiving place possible because you are totally exposed.

From corner back you have a good view of the whole pitch opening out in front of you. If a link in the team's chain is weak or breaks, you can quickly see where the trouble is originating and what sort of consequences there will be.

As a corner back, also, you can never afford to switch off. You take in every single aspect of the play, and I think that really gives you a good understanding of the game and how best it should be played. It also encourages you to develop leadership skills. If you are in the corner and are not in constant communication with everyone around you then you are not doing your job.

A corner back has to bollock his team-mates to get them to do the right thing, because if they don't it is quite often the same corner back who is left looking stupid and shipping the bulk of the blame.

My understanding of the game took a quantum leap forward while I was in Maynooth.

I didn't just learn from Malachy how to became a better footballer, he also played a massive part in my development as a coach and manager. Much of what I learned from him formed the foundation of my own philosophy on the game, and his methods and ideas are as relevant now as were back then.

We were quietly confident the combination of Malachy's coaching along with the quality of player we had in our panel would see us make a big impact in our first year playing Sigerson football. But our chances of doing so were scuppered by an unlikely set of circumstances.

It was 1972, and after the Bloody Sunday massacre in Derry on January 30, politics, rather than football, suddenly became our focus.

Tomás Ó Fiaich, the future Archbishop of Armagh and Primate of All-Ireland, was a Professor of History in the university at the time, and spoke out strongly against the atrocity.

Emotions were running high, and Malachy decided we needed to make a statement by joining an organised public march on the British Embassy on the Wednesday before our Sigerson Cup match against UCC

We started out from Maynooth and walked the 20 or so miles to the British Embassy in Merrion Square. But, by the time we got there, it had already been set on fire by protestors.

That march to Dublin drained us physically. When we played UCC three days later in the Sigerson Cup we couldn't muster a gallop. The following year we were determined to make amends when we played UCC in the Sigerson Cup semi final. We hammered them, but in doing so I think we sowed the seeds of our defeat against UCD in the final.

Instead of easing up in the second half against UCC and emptying the subs bench, we played hard until the last whistle which was suicidal because the final was the following day.

They had a galaxy of county stars like John O'Keeffe from Kerry, Eamon O'Donoghue from Kildare, Kevin Kilmurray from Offaly, and Laois' Enda Condron, and were managed by the highly regarded young coach, Eugene McGee.

We pushed them close, but ran out of steam and were beaten by four points in the end. It was devastating, because we had all put so much into it.

I like Eugene McGee as a person now and I'm good mates with him. But if you do not know him well he can come across as a bit aloof, and that was certainly the opinion I formed of him after that match.

We were absolutely devastated, yet rather than be gracious in victory he said something to us that made me want to absolutely open him up. I dealt with the disappointment of it all by drowning my sorrows afterwards. We didn't have much, but it was the first time I had ever taken a drink.

The following morning we were meant to be up for mass in the college at 7.30 am, but along with a few of my mates from the team I didn't make it. We were all hauled in and read the riot act by Father Joe Delaney, the Dean of Discipline.

He eventually came to me.

'Don't worry about it Father,' I told him, '... I'll be leaving in a few weeks' time.'

I had decided I had come to the end of the line as far as training for the priesthood was concerned, and, in fairness to Father Joe, once he heard that he was very kind. Deciding to become a lay student had the side benefit of making it that bit easier for me to fulfil my ambitions as a footballer.

Because, even though being coached by Malachy O'Rourke was making me a better player, studying for the priesthood could make it a little more difficult to play football outside of the college.

When Ballaghaderreen reached the county final in 1972, Dan and I had a bit of a predicament because there was a religious retreat on in Maynooth and that meant none of us were allowed leave the college.

Obviously there was no way we could miss the county final, so we hatched a plan to make good our escape.

One the morning of the match, myself and Dan walked out of the college after mass along with two of my classmates, Donie Brennan and Michael Marren. We walked down as far as the bridge where we were met with a car driven by Tommy Towey from Ballaghaderreen, my future brother-in-law, who was also a seminarian in Maynooth.

In those days seminarians had to wear soutans, which were long, black gowns that were buttoned down the front.

Dan and I hurriedly unbuttoned our soutans and gave them to Donie and Michael who simply put them on over their own and strolled back into the college.

The game was on in Crossmolina at three o'clock, so time was tight, but we still had to get mass along the way somewhere because we wanted the Lord's blessing ahead of the big match.

We pulled in to Enfield and by luck there was an old priest saying mass in the church there. He had it said in just 15 minutes, and we blessed him all the way to Crossmolina for his speed. Our next dilemma was how could we possibly get away with playing this match without the President of Maynooth finding out?

We figured we'd never get away with it if our names were in the newspaper. So we got out club chairman, Father John Doherty, to give a couple of false names, John and Dan Moloney, to the local media.

The Moloney brothers played their part in a historic win for Ballaghaderreen over Claremorris, but afterwards there was no time for celebration.

We jumped straight back into the car, drove back to Maynooth, and under cover of darkness climbed over the wall and back into the college. At that moment it felt like the perfect crime, but we had forgotten one obvious flaw with our plan.

Father Joe Spellman, who was a Professor of Theology in Maynooth, was a Ballaghaderreen man too and would obviously have been aware that we had won the county final.

It only dawned on me the following morning when I met him between lectures and he asked how I was, and congratulated me on our great win.

After he walked away I realised this could bring our house of cards crashing down on top of us because Father Joe sat around the 'cabinet table' with the President.

The potential leak had to be plugged, so I raced up the old circular stairs that led to his quarters and confessed to him that we didn't have permission to go and play the match. He just smiled broadly and assured me not to worry, that he had no idea whatsoever that Ballaghaderreen had just won a county title, so he wouldn't be mentioning it to anyone.

Studying for the priesthood also made it a little bit more difficult for me to fulfil my ambitions of playing county football.

By the time I enrolled in Maynooth, I was in my second year playing for the Mayo minor team. We had been beaten in the 1970 Connacht final by a talented Galway team that went on to win the All-Ireland that year, but in '71 we gained vengeance.

I was given the job of marking their star forward, John Tobin and was under strict orders to stop him by whatever means necessary.

In those days you'd have anything up to 10 selectors with a county minor team. I presume this was because you'd have fellas from all over the county without their own transport, so having that many selectors from every corner of the county meant they could bring along the players with them.

Before that match, one of our many selectors took me aside and basically told me to soften up Tobin before a ball had even been kicked. He told me I was the only man for the job, and I was the sort of footballer who always wanted to do my job well.

When Tobin came into me he was wearing a pair of white boots, which would not have been common at all in those days, and that just fired me up even more. So I drew a kick on him before the ball was thrown in and took the legs clear from under him.

There was a big shout from the crowd, but thankfully the referee didn't see anything. After the match, when I thought about what I did, I cringed, because it really was an awful thing to do.

It taught me a lesson for life, that when you're managing young players you need to be careful about what orders you give them.

As a manager you have a responsibility to do whatever you can to win a match, but you should draw the line at asking players to do crazy stuff like that. Before a big game, if you're young, it's very easy to be influenced. So that was something I was always cognisant of in later years as a manager.

By the time I was in Maynooth the following winter, Tobin was in UCG, and we played them in a match. Before it started, I went over to him and apologised for what I had done.

I just felt terrible about it, and in fairness to 'Toby', he accepted my apology.

We knew after beating Galway in '71 that we were a good team because they were reigning All-Ireland champions. So it was no major surprise really that we went on to beat Roscommon in the Connacht final and then reached the All-Ireland final where Cork provided the opposition.

The problem for me was that, by then, I had enrolled in Maynooth which meant I was in danger of missing out on the All-Ireland. The first years started classes at the beginning of September, and once you were in you couldn't get out so I had to train on my own for four weeks.

I hadn't played particularly well in the semi final, so the prospect of not being able to train with the team for the month before the final made me fear I'd lose my place. There was no guarantee I would even be allowed out to play in the match.

But when I went to the President of the College he gave me permission. One of the selectors picked me up from Maynooth and I met up with the team at the Ormond Hotel at noon on the day of the match. Thankfully, I kept my place, and we won. I was not exactly hugely involved in the contest though, because I only had one touch of the ball and that was the last kick of the game.

I was allowed out from Maynooth again the following day for the post All-Ireland final reception, a tradition that no longer exists. Both the winning and losing All-Ireland senior and minor teams were brought for a meal in the Hibernian Hotel on Dawson Street. We also watched a full replay of the previous day's All-Ireland senior final at the RTE studios.

Afterwards our team bus pulled into Maynooth on the way home to Mayo and I was dropped off and returned to my cloisters.

I had always imagined an All-Ireland win would involve a triumphant return to Mayo, but it was still a hugely satisfying achievement. Mayo had never really come close to winning a senior All-Ireland when I was growing up, and now here I was winning one myself.

Suddenly all sorts of possibilities opened up in front of me, and the dream of someday seeing Mayo win the Sam Maguire Cup was overtaken by the ambition of lifting it myself.

Winning that minor All-Ireland gave me a higher profile and was the start of a really prolific stage of my playing career. The following year, 1972, I won those three county titles with Ballaghaderreen and made both the county under-21 and senior teams even though I was still only 19.

After the County final win I was approached by the county secretary, Johnny Mulvey who asked for my address.

In those days you'd be sent a card to invite you to join the county senior panel, so I knew what it meant and I was walking on air afterwards. Once I got back to Maynooth the post was checked every morning until finally the precious invitation arrived.

It was a big deal, not just for me, but for my circle of friends who were all GAA mad.

Paddy Henry was already playing for Sligo himself by that stage, and it was a cause for celebration if any of us were called up. We were a very tight bunch, and before I left Maynooth I was determined to win the Sigerson Cup with friends. But, alas, it wasn't to be.

We hosted the final weekend in 1974, and Malachy revolutionised the thing really because he made it much more of an event than it had ever been before. The previous year when we had been beaten in the final down in UCC, there hadn't even been a reception of any kind for the two teams afterwards.

Malachy thought that was a disgrace, so he put forward a plan to the GAA's Higher Education Authority on how it should be better run and they gave him the green light to effectively organise the whole thing. He got Ulster Bank on board as sponsors and arranged an official launch, an exhibition game between Maynooth and an Allstar team, and a post-match banquet for the two finalists.

Everyone involved in football in the college put a massive effort into making it a big success. But that also meant that we were not as focused on our own team, and so we didn't reach the same level we had the year previously.

I never got to lift the Sigerson Cup, but at least my brother Dan did.

He completed his training for the priesthood, so he was in Maynooth for a couple of years longer than I was and captained the team that won the college's first and only ever Sigerson Cup in 1976.

I was delighted for him, and all the more because Maynooth beat yet another star-studded UCD team managed by our nemesis Eugene McGee in the final. That Sigerson Cup was not the only piece of silverware that Dan would collect in his time in Maynooth of which I will always be envious.

What every footballer in Maynooth craved was to be part of a winning Class League team. Every year in the college had their own team, and we all played one another in a league format after which the top two teams contested the final.

It was crazily competitive and taken extremely seriously. There were seven teams; the six years of those studying for the priesthood and a seventh team made up of external and lay students.

The teams drawn from the higher years had the advantage of being older and more experienced, but the disadvantage was a smaller pick because students would opt out of the seminary along the way.

When I was in second year we had a really talented team, and were dead set on winning the league. We had Paddy Henry (Sligo), Tom Bardon (Longford), Mick McElvaney (Longford), Louis Walsh (Donegal) and Donal Brennan (Sligo), and we were all playing senior county football at the time, and we had plenty of other fine footballers as well.

Dan was two years ahead of me and, as fate would have it, both of our teams reached the final.

I was captain of mine and he was captain of his. But before a ball was even kicked, there was controversy. Tony O'Keeffe from Kerry had previously been in Dan's class but had left Maynooth and then returned that year to do some course or other. Because he was no longer studying for the priesthood, we felt he should be playing with the 'externs' team as he was now a lay student.

But, instead, he was given permission to play with what had been his own class. We put in an objection, but it was overruled. There's some irony there because the same Tony O'Keeffe later became the chairman of the GAA's Central Competitions Control Committee.

By the time we met them in the final, I was absolutely raging over what I perceived to be a massive injustice. I was completely wound up over it, lost my focus, and had a stinker of a match.

I was so busy fucking everyone out of it during the game that I totally forgot to play football and the guy I was marking scored two goals that won Dan's team the match.

It felt like losing a Connacht final, and there was a fierce row after the final whistle. It didn't turn physical, that was my only saving grace, but I spared no-one the sharp edge of my tongue.

Walking off the pitch I continued to let everyone know what I thought of them in not very complimentary language. I was going for maximum effect!

Dan tried to calm me down, but I told him where to go too.

That hurt him, but I didn't care at that stage.

It was a big event, and there were a few hundred people watching including the College President, Tomás Ó Fiaich, so I had a fine audience for my theatrics. When I look back on it now, I cringe. The impetuosity of youth! But at the time I was absolutely raging and I was not about to either forgive or forget in a rush. Even the following day when I met a College Professor, Sean Freyne, who was a friend of Malachy O'Rourke's, I gave him a tongue-lashing too for good measure.

I wouldn't speak to Dan for three or four weeks afterwards, and he was wise enough not to bring the cup home to Ballaghaderreen because that would've been the last straw altogether.

We can joke about it all now and I deserve any ribbing I get, but it was no laughing matter at the time.

I suppose it illustrates just how seriously I took the bloody thing at that stage. Losing that match in the manner I did taught me a valuable lesson. But had you suggested it at the time I would not have given you charitable hearing.

I have always had a temper, but I found out the hard way that you're no good to anyone on a pitch if you cannot keep your cool.

I had my ups and downs in Maynooth both on and off the pitch, but when I look back on my time there I only take positives from the whole experience.

There were valuable life lessons that helped me grow as a person, and I gained a trove of football knowledge that stood me in good stead for future years and still does.

CHAPTER 4

From a distance, I had viewed county football as the pinnacle of the game, but when I scaled that peak I soon realised that the vista was not all I imagined it would be.

I was being exposed to the highest standards of team training and man-management in Maynooth at the time. However, when I first joined up with Mayo I quickly discovered that their standards of best practice were not nearly so evolved. County football was a completely different world back then to what it is now.

There was no collective training whatsoever until the three or four weeks before the first round of the championship.

And if you were beaten in the first round, your commitment for the year, outside of simply playing matches, amounted to little over a month of training, which is some difference to the situation today.

Through the winter and for the vast majority of the league campaign you were expected to do your own training, especially if you were living outside the county. Whenever possible, I'd get a lift to matches with my teammate, Willie McGee who was living in Dublin but sometimes I'd have to thumb my way home to Mayo.

The only time you'd find out whether you were on the team or not was when you'd get the newspaper on the Tuesday or Wednesday.

I had come from the culture fostered in Maynooth by Malachy O'Rourke where you were encouraged to have an input, so I naively thought my opinion would be just as valued in the Mayo senior team.

We were trained at the time by Father Martin Newell who had been successful as a trainer of the St Colman's College teams.

He had us training indoors at St Colman's and told us that he was going to get us as fit as was humanly possible. It was around this time that Kevin Heffernan was making a name for himself as Dublin manager by building his team around big, strong men whom he got ferociously fit.

Fr Newell was now espousing the same philosophy. He was right to, really, but I still felt obliged to pick a few holes in it.

I pointed out that Dublin were about more than strength and fitness. Jimmy Keaveney wouldn't get out of the way to warm himself, but he was a brilliant footballer and their key forward. Even though Kevin Heffernan might have been putting it out there that Dublin were fitter, faster and stronger than their opponents, he was clearly also accommodating someone who gave them something different.

I could tell by the way Fr Newell looked at me that he wasn't too impressed because I wasn't an established player and here I was perking up and questioning his rationale.

I'm sure some of my older teammates were raising their eyebrows too. But, as far as I was concerned, I was making the perfectly rational point that when you train a group of players a 'one size fits all' is not necessarily the best way to go. I was always thinking about the game. But, depending on your perspective, I was either an upstart or a deep thinker.

Self-confidence came easily to me because, when I first joined up with the Mayo senior team, I was on a hot streak of success. It was not long before I hit a speed bump and learned the hard way that senior county football can be an unforgiving crucible.

On the back of our County final victory I was one of six or seven Ballaghaderreen players who featured in the early rounds of the league in the winter of '72.

We started with an uninspiring draw with Westmeath, and then suffered the indignity of a home defeat against Fermanagh. The confidence placed in the Ballaghaderreen contingent was seen as misplaced by many.

I was still managing to hang onto my place by the time the championship came around, and my debut was a sweet one because we beat Roscommon in the Connacht semi final.

Much of my youth in Magheraboy had been spent in the football field behind our house beating Roscommon in my imagination. To do it in real life, in my first ever championship match for Mayo, really was a dream come through.

We were beaten by Galway in the Connacht final, but earned some honour by mounting a late comeback that fell just short.

It was some consolation that we then beat a Galway under-21 team featuring many of the senior players in the provincial final.

The subsequent All-Ireland semi final against Tyrone in Dungannon had to be held up for an hour because the man I was marking, Tommy Woods, was hauled in by the RUC before the game. There was a massive crowd in Dungannon that day and the news about Woods only made the atmosphere all the more tense.

At one stage during the game a bottle came flying in from the crowd. It was hot stuff. We got out of there with a draw and won the replay in Carrick-on-Shannon to set up an All-Ireland final date with Kerry.

That Kingdom team contained future stars of the game like Mikey Sheehy, John Egan, Paidi Ó Sé, Ger Power, Jimmy Deenihan, Paudie Lynch, Ger O'Keeffe and Mickey Ned O'Sullivan.

It says something of our own quality that we were ahead by three points with just 10 minutes to go, but they then hit us with a late goal and flurry of points.

The following year, we made amends by beating Dublin in the semi final and Antrim in the All-Ireland final after a replay. There was a huge ambition and sense of self-belief among those under-21s that we would be a serious force at senior level for years.

But, ultimately, that generation of players would not even win a single senior Connacht championship.

Too much was expected of us too soon. Eleven of the 1974 All-Ireland winning team played in the 1975 Connacht senior final, and that was too many young players to bring through together at once. Then, when we did not make the expected immediate impact, many of us were discarded rather than given the time to learn the ropes at senior level.

That was the category I fell squarely into myself, unfortunately and a senior county career that had started so promisingly ended fairly brutally.

Even though I had performed quite well in the 1973 Connacht final, I found myself out of favour for the 1973-74 league campaign. I was doing my final exams at the time, so I went to one of the selectors to explain that might possibly hamper the commitment I could make.

I was hoping he'd say something supportive.

'Not to worry, John… you'll still be in our plans,' or something like that?

Instead, he said I should look after the exams, and that attitude told me in no uncertain terms that I was out of favour.

My stock rose again on the back of our All-Ireland under-21 win that year, so I was back in the team for the 1975 campaign. But going into the Connacht final against Sligo, I felt that there wasn't huge confidence in me from the management.

There is nothing worse than thinking that when you're a young player, especially when you play in such an exposed position as corner back. When I began managing teams, if I was ever in doubt about a player I would not select him because I knew from my own experience it is just not fair.

If you're picked and you know the management are almost waiting for your first mistake to substitute you, then it puts you under massive pressure.

We drew with Sligo and I held onto my place for the replay but never felt secure in it. And, sure enough, when I was beaten for the first couple of balls by my man in the replay I was hauled off after just 13 minutes.

It was a humiliating experience.

What made it worse was that it was the last time I would wear the Mayo jersey, so we did not part on good terms. Famously, Sligo went on to beat us that day to win only their second every Connacht title. It was a great day for Sligo, but it was regarded as one of the darkest hours for Mayo football, and the fall-out was significant.

A lot of the young players on the panel like myself were deemed not up to scratch on the basis of that defeat and were simply discarded, while others who got another year's grace were given their marching orders when Mayo then lost to Leitrim in the 1976 championship.

I was never officially told by anyone that I was finished as a Mayo footballer. I just heard it through the grapevine, and it was confirmed when I was not called up for the 1975-76 league campaign. From my own personal point of view, the way it was handled was unnecessarily blunt and it also felt too arbitrary.

There was no guidance as to what I was doing wrong or what I could do differently in order to improve in the areas the management team felt I was lacking, and my mood was not helped by the fact that my place at corner back on the Mayo team for the 1976 championship was taken by my brother, Dan.

He had captained Maynooth to the Sigerson Cup earlier that year so his stock was high.

I was thrilled for him that he got the call-up, but I still could not bring myself to watch them play Leitrim in the first round of the championship. I wasn't a marquee player so perhaps I did not have the natural ability to make it anyway.

But I'd love to have been exposed to the type of training I did with Malachy O'Rourke in Maynooth over a period of time at county level because perhaps then I could have unlocked my full potential. I am not saying Mayo would've been more successful in the 1970s if they had invested more time and effort with me, however there were definitely a number of players like me who were successful at underage level but who then suffered because of a lack of patience and long-term planning by management at the senior grade.

The thing of coming together just three weeks before the championship for collective training meant there was little in the way of continuous assessment.

If you won your first couple of matches and had a long summer, then the chances were the team would be given the opportunity to evolve naturally and you could have a long career. On the other hand, if the summer ended early then the probability was that everything would start from scratch again the following year.

There is no doubt we allowed a lot of talent to wither on the vine in the 1970s.

The Kerry under-21 team that narrowly beat us in the 1973 All-Ireland final provided the bulk of the side that went on to win the 1975 senior All-Ireland and another four in-a-row between 1978 and '81.

I am not saying we could have matched arguably the greatest team there has ever been, but there is no doubt but that at the very least we should have been winning Connacht titles in the same period.

Apart from Ger Feeney, none of our All-Ireland winning minor and under-21 teams had long careers at senior level. All things considered, we fell a long way short of our potential.

Perhaps things would've been much different had we beaten Sligo in 1975, and that generation of young players may have blossomed with that first senior Connacht championship won, and gone on to win many more. It was not to be, though, and instead Mayo went through a barren period that saw them fail to win another provincial title until 1981.

The positive from a personal point of view was that the whole experience was pivotal in shaping my career in management.

Not only did it propel me into that sphere at a relatively young age, it also helped form some of the core principles of my philosophy on the game and emphasised to me that in management you really need to support the people who need that support the most.

Over the years I have seen that if you give that to players you can significantly boost their confidence levels by interacting with them and showing you believe in them enough to want to make them better.

Maybe I was really not good enough. Though I still like to think that if someone had shown more belief in me my county career could have been a longer and more successful one.

CHAPTER 5

Many people spend much of their lives looking for their place in the world and some never discover it.

I'm fortunate that I found everything I wanted from life right on my own doorstep. The three pillars of a happy existence are family, work and play. Before long, I had that triumvirate set on rock-solid foundations.

While I was still in school in St Nathy's I had struck up an innocent romance with a girl from Ballaghaderreen called Gerardine Towey after a happy quirk of fate had brought us together at a club dinner dance one Christmas.

There had been an awful flu in the town that same winter and Ger ended up taking the ticket of someone who was unable to go that night.

That was the first meeting, so to speak, and until our romance was interrupted by my time in Maynooth, we exchanged letters and met occasionally. I was not long back in Mayo before we picked up where we had left off, and by 1978 we were married.

Ger is just as fanatical about the GAA as I am. That's a good thing too, because life with me would be unbearable if she wasn't.

We had got engaged in the Christmas of 1977 and one of the first things I did afterwards was ring the County Board secretary to find out the championship fixtures for the following summer, so the wedding wouldn't clash with a big game.

Ger knew from the very start that football would always be a very big part of our lives together. She and our five daughters, Gráinne, Niamh, Rhona, Deirdre and Cliodhna were always hugely supportive of me when I was a county manager and are pillars in my life once again since I entered the political sphere.

All of my daughters are just as passionate about sport as I am. Gráinne represented Ireland in athletics, Niamh played Ladies football for Kildare and Westmeath, Rhona played in an All-Ireland final for Armagh, Deirdre won an O'Connor Cup medal with UL, and Cliodhna captained St Nathy's College basketball team to All-Ireland victory.

It was a sports mad house really, and I have lost count of the amount of times that Ger went above and beyond the call of duty to facilitate my passion for football.

One story, perhaps, illustrates Ger's dedication to the cause better than any other.

When Ballaghaderreen were a man short for an over-40s tournament I played in, she went so far as to tog out for us so we had the full complement. She mustn't have done too badly either, because as far as I recall we won the tournament and Ger got a trophy for her troubles.

She has deserved a good few more medals along the way too because football has had a monopoly on my time for much of our married life.

I was no longer a county footballer by the time we started dating seriously and were then married, though I had quickly moved to fill that vacuum by maximising my potential at other levels of the association.

Not playing for Mayo meant I now had the time to throw myself into doing all I could for Ballaghaderreen, both on and off the pitch. I became secretary of the club in 1975, and by the following year I was also player-manager with the senior team.

I always had an interest in coaching and tactics, and now here was the opportunity to put my ideas into practice. I soon found that I got a great kick out of coming up with game plans and coaching a team to execute them, and even though we were beaten in the County semi final, it was agreed by many that we were playing with a certain method.

I had tried to bring a fresh tactical approach and implement a lot of the lessons that Malachy O'Rourke had taught me in Maynooth.

We worked on things like a short kick out strategy that was seen as innovative at the time. The common practice was for the goalkeeper to just boot the ball down the field as far as he possibly could, but I wanted us to bring a more thoughtful approach.

We wanted to retain possession as much as possible and keep teams on the back foot by attacking as a team. This meant our corner backs had as much licence to get forward as our wing backs and midfielders.

As well as taking charge of the senior team, I also found myself training the club's under-14, under-16, and minor teams. I was juggling a lot of balls, and it became hard to handle them all.

Eventually, the club chairman, Jim Fleming, told me I needed to step back and put a more complete structure in place rather than try to do everything myself. There's always a danger of thinking 'nothing can be done here without me', but that attitude is wrong and self-defeating.

Of course I took Jim's advice on board and pared my responsibilities down to being chairman of the club's underage structure and trainer of just one of the underage teams. That year, 1975, was also the year that I returned to St Nathy's as a teacher after completing the H Dip.

I had been doing a few hours there while I was still studying in UCG, and once I got my degree I was lucky enough to get a full-time job. I taught geography and history and also immediately involved myself training school teams.

I believe that a career in teaching also helped me develop some of the traits you need to be a successful manager, and in both roles your communication skills are important. The classroom is quite like a dressing room in many aspects.

In a dressing room you have to be able to get your players fully tuned in so you can get your message across, and that is exactly what I was also trying to do every day in the classroom. A background in teaching definitely helped prepare me for management, but the benefits went both ways.

Because I trained school teams I developed a much better understanding of what made many of my pupils tick. They also saw me in a different light too, and I'm sure it humanised me to a certain degree and made them more receptive to me in the classroom.

Sport was our common interest. The odd time on a Monday morning to break the ice I'd read out a match report in the class and we'd have a short discussion on the big results of the weekend. I knew this was the sort of thing that the boys appreciated, because once upon a time I was sitting where they were and enjoyed the same interaction.

When I was a pupil in St Nathy's, we were taught Irish by a Father Giblin who'd often bring in the paper on a Monday and read us out some of the match reports and then let us discuss them for five minutes afterwards.

We were all mad keen on sport so this was manna from heaven.

And you'd do more for Father Giblin afterwards, because you appreciated that sort of interaction a lot. It's amazing now how often many of my past pupils bring up those discussions whenever we meet.

Thanks to football, many of my pupils got to know me in a different way and I think respected me more which made my life easier. In the same way that teaching becomes easier and more rewarding if you bring your pupils with you, you are also more likely to be a successful manager if you adopt that sort of approach.

I never went into a dressing room for the first time and told the players I was going to show them how to win a Connacht title or an All-Ireland title.

I always first asked them what they wanted to achieve? And, eventually, someone would say they wanted to win that sort of major silverware. Once that ambition had been aired, I would then ask all the players what it would require from them to achieve it? What sort of obstacles would we need to clear from their path?

So, right from the very start, the players feel they have a real stake in what we are doing. With that comes an extra responsibility to give it absolutely everything they have.

The more you feel a part of something the more you want to sign up for it, and I think it is important to have that culture in a county dressing room now more than ever because the demands on players are so extreme. Players are training six or seven days a week, and I know some teams are even being forced to literally sign codes of conduct.

That is crazy.

If you require your players to sign some sort of covenant then it surely means you do not trust them in the first place. A manager who cracks a whip excessively hard might get results in the short term, but eventually players who are dictated to rather than encouraged to be self-motivated will rebel. You can't just put everyone in the same box or get them to sign a contract that covers everything. It is important to have freedom of expression and spontaneity within every team dynamic.

If the county game keeps going down this path then I can see a situation where it will frighten off people.

It should be enough to come to a verbal agreement with a group of players that 'we are all in this together' and 'fully committed' to the same cause.

The manager has to be the ultimate authority in any dressing room, but if he constantly uses the stick rather than the carrot then he is not encouraging other leaders to emerge in the group.

Every team will have setbacks along the way and there is only so much a manager can do to lift a team when it is down. If you do not have leaders in the team who will, in those moments, drag the rest of the group with them then you don't have a hope.

Empathy is an important quality to have as a manager, just like it is when you are a teacher.

To a large extent both jobs require you to treat everyone equally, but you have to recognise too that in education or sport a 'one size fits all' approach will hinder your ability to unlock a group's full potential.

Every group is made up of individuals with their own quirks who may require a little bit of leeway now and then in order to get the best from them. It is a tricky balancing act though because the last thing you want is for the rest of the group to think any individual is a 'teacher's pet', because that sows the seeds of resentment.

Trying to get it right isn't easy. But, if it was, everyone would be a successful manager.

If you have a panel of 30 players you have to treat them equally, but also persuade them all as individuals that they are the most important player in the panel. You have to be able to hone in on each one. And convince each man or woman that you have a special interest in them.

That means having a detailed knowledge of who they are, and where they come from?

I always made a big effort to know who a guy was married to or who he was dating, as well as the first names of his parents, and his children if he had any?

I was constantly doing that sort of homework. It is human nature to be flattered if someone shows that they know some factual piece of information about you that you haven't told them yourself.

You go away quietly impressed, and with that bit more respect for the person who has made time for you.

If you are interested in one of your players on a human level rather than just what they can do for you on a football pitch, then you will find they will do more for you on that pitch.

I regularly phoned players to just ask them how they were doing? If everything was going okay on the work front? And if there was anything I could do for them in that regard?

Over the years I have heard a number of players refer to the fact that they found that motivational because they knew they meant more to me than just the number they wore on their backs every Sunday.

I was in no way putting on an act. I genuinely did care about every player I ever managed. The manner in which my own county career ended so brutally gave me a natural empathy with players and a desire to help them achieve.

And I soon realised that unlocking an individual's potential and maximising the ability of a team was something that gave me a massive buzz.

My breakthrough success in management came in 1981 when myself and another local teacher, Brother Philbert took charge of the Ballaghaderreen under-12 team that won the County 'A' title.

I could still name that entire team.

I have found going through life that early experiences and memories are more hardwired than recent ones. We played Ballina in the semi final and it was a very close game that we would not have won perhaps were it not for a piece of good fortune.

Gerry Clarke was our club secretary at the time, and that day he was doing umpire behind one of the goals. A high ball was hit in to our big full forward, James Towey, and it looked like it was going over the bar.

Gerry shouted to him to let it go.

But, unfortunately, the poor ladeen in goal for Ballina thought he was talking to him and allowed the ball to sail straight into the back of the net.

Gerry apologised to the goalkeeper, and explained he had been talking to our full forward. He then promptly raised the green flag.

We won the game narrowly and then caused another upset by beating Castlebar in the final. It was a hugely satisfying experience, and all the more so because it justified all the effort we had put into our Bord na nOg structures and the links we had developed with primary schools in the area.

By this time I had also taken up refereeing.

I refereed minor finals in Mayo and was also beginning to referee senior games. I even won a Connacht 'Young Referee Award', so I suppose I was being lined up for bigger things down the road. Though once I got a taste for success in management, it took over completely and the refereeing went by the wayside.

In 1982 I managed Ballagh's under-21s to the County final and that enhanced my credentials. I can only presume it was on the strength of that achievement that the then Mayo senior manager, Liam O'Neill recommended I take charge of the county under-21 team.

Liam had brought a new professionalism to the Mayo set up and he obviously wanted to influence who would take over after him whenever he decided the time was right.

I had never imagined I was to be fast-tracked into management at that level so early in my career, but once Liam sounded me out I immediately told him I'd love to be involved. It all happened very quickly and unexpectedly, but I instinctively knew that this was a glorious chance to really make a mark.

CHAPTER 6

I was a deep thinker on the game all my life, so the chance to manage the county under-21 team was the opportunity to test all my theories and beliefs at the highest level.

When you coach a club team you have to make the best of what you have and sometimes make a silk purse out of a sow's ear, but at county level you're going to have a much better pick of high quality players and that means you can implement tactical plans that might have been beyond most club teams.

I had a very clear picture of the sort of football that I wanted to play with that Mayo team, and I knew I had players who were talented enough to execute it, like John Maughan, Ger Geraghty, Eddie Gibbons, Kevin McStay and Peter Ford. They were not just talented footballers, they were natural leaders as well.

Many of them proved that in later years by also going on to manage at a very high level themselves.

What I also found when I started working with a higher calibre of player was that they challenged you and questioned you more. I welcomed that and I encouraged them to give their opinion in team discussions because I saw it as being helpful rather than a threat to my authority.

Players are more likely to implement something if they believe in it themselves, and they are more likely to believe in it if they feel they had a part to play in its formulation.

I was only 30 myself and still playing club football, so it was easy for me to relate to the players.

From the very start, I was conscious of a line I could not afford to cross.

I wanted the lads to be comfortable enough around me to allow me to get inside their heads and find different ways of motivating them. Yet, at the same time, I also had to project myself as an authority figure, rather than being just one of the lads.

I also had to prove quickly that I knew my stuff despite my lack of experience as a manager.

Driving to my first training session I was feeling both nervous and excited about what lay ahead. From the very start I wanted to get a grip on the thing, and let the players know they were going to be doing everything to a very high standard. I even spent £1,400 of my own money on a top of the range video camera and recorder because I felt video analysis could be a really helpful tool.

My brother, Stephen would set it up on top of the press box or some other vantage point and operate it for all our matches. There was slow-motion and replay functions I could use when I would play the video back for the players and I'd often get Pat Coen, who was one of my students in St Nathy's, to put a commentary over it.

It was very rudimentary compared to the video analysis done now, but back then it was ahead of its time and it definitely helped me a lot.

The players appreciated it too. Not only did it illustrate the things they were doing well and the areas they needed to improve on, it also showed we were taking this thing very seriously.

I knew the group of players I had inherited was a talented one because most of them had been part of a Connacht championship winning minor team three years previously. At the same time, I also wanted to cast the net as far and wide as possible to ensure we had the best team possible on the field.

Nowadays talent identification is a much simpler process because the best players in the county will have come through development squads and have had their progress marked along the way.

There was no such system in those days and it was possible for some very talented players to be overlooked. I knew of one such player in my own club, Noel Durkin, who I was convinced could be my secret weapon that year.

He had never played minor for the county but I knew he had the quality to be a real star of the game if I could get him playing.

Noel lived in the last house inside the Roscommon part of the parish and all his friends were Roscommon supporters, so playing for Mayo would never have been really high on his agenda.

He was a shy fella too, and when I first approached him about joining up with us he just sort of laughed quietly.

'Ah I might… I might,' he replied.

We started training in March, and, even though I couldn't persuade him to come in at that stage, I was not going to give up on him because I knew just how big an addition he would be. Three weeks before our first Connacht championship match against Leitrim I managed, finally, to get him to come in.

But, because he was so shy, he did not express himself fully and fell some way short of the quality he was producing at club level. I still started him against Leitrim, although he hung back and did not make much impact on the match.

I did not want to be accused of favouritism to a clubmate, so I took him off with 10 or 15 minutes to go.

'Sure… I told you I didn't want to play,' he said to me on the sideline, and he didn't come in for the team meal afterwards.

I was still not going to give up on him.

I knew his potential, so I quickly tracked him down the following day and persuaded him to stick with it. We were up against Roscommon in the Connacht final. They were reigning champions and had reached the All-Ireland final the previous year.

We hammered them, 1-19 to 1-6, and Durkin proved his worth by kicking three points from play.

That earned us a shot at Kerry in the All-Ireland semi final, and it looked like we were going to blitz them too when we scored 2-1 in the opening stages, but we failed to score again for another 41 minutes and looked in dire straits when Padraig Brogan was red-carded.

That, luckily enough, only seemed to fire our lads up and they scored 1-5 without reply in the final 14 minutes to win the game, 3-6 to 0-7.

We played Derry in the All-Ireland final and looked home and hosed when we led by six points late in the second half.

But they hit three quick points in-a-row and then in the last minute Damien Barton somehow smashed a free-kick to the roof of the net from 15 yards out to snatch a draw.

It was a real sickener.

We had to go up to Irvinestown for the replay. It was the first time an All-Ireland had been played in the Six Counties, so we knew they'd have massive support and it would be a tough place to win.

I quickly realised this was my first serious test as a manager. Replays are won by the mentally stronger teams, so I had to set a good example in that regard. It was my job to raise everyone's morale even though we had thrown away a match we really should have won.

I made it known that I believed playing in Irvinestown was a blessing rather than a curse.

Everyone was going to say we had missed our chance, and here was an opportunity to prove them all wrong. I did wonder though were we mentally in the right place when Padraig Duffy informed me, when we got to Irvinestown for the replay, that he had forgotten his boots.

Thankfully Padraig's absentmindedness was not a bad omen, and we ground out a hard-fought three point victory after coming back from four down.

I would occasionally look back on that video and it was pretty dour stuff, but when you come out on the right side of the result you do not give a damn. It was a hard-hitting match with no quarter given or taken by either team and we had to survive the sending-off of our captain, Eddie Gibbons in the final minutes.

Because of that they wouldn't let Eddie lift the cup after the match, so that honour fell to our vice-captain, Ger Geraghty.

I still insisted on Eddie giving the acceptance speech because he was a great guy and we wanted to acknowledge his importance to the group.

Thankfully no GAA official tried to prevent him from saying his few words, and common sense prevailed.

I was delighted for the players because they had given such a great commitment. It was also hugely satisfying personally. My county management career could not have gotten off to a better start, and that victory gave me the platform to do all that I did afterwards.

I knew how lucky I was and it made up for the disappointment of my county career being cut short.

Even though I had thrown myself into other roles in the GAA afterwards, the hurt of being rejected by Mayo as a player had stayed with me. It stopped feeling so raw after that under-21 success. I never got to fulfil my dream of winning a senior All-Ireland as a player, but managing an All-Ireland winning Mayo team was a fine compensation.

A massive Mayo crowd had travelled to Irivinestown and there was great jubilation after the match. We stopped off in Sligo on the way home for food in the Park Hotel, and it seemed as though every supporter who was at the match came in there with us.

We all travelled home together to Mayo in a massive cavalcade and Ballaghaderreen was the first port of call, like it always is for Mayo All-Ireland winning teams.

That was a special moment, especially as Noel Durkin was the Man of the Match in the All-Ireland final replay.

It had taken a lot of time and effort to persuade him to join up with us that year, and that only made it all the sweeter. I stayed on as under-21 manager for one more year and we won the Connacht championship again in 1984 but were beaten by Cork in the All-Ireland final.

I knew now that the next step for me was to manage the county senior team, but I was willing to be patient.

Liam O'Neill was doing a good job with them, and in 1985 Mayo were unlucky to be beaten in the All-Ireland semi final replay by Dublin. I'd have to wait a while for my chance to come.

In the short-term, I focused my energies on finishing my own playing career on a high.

When I won my county senior championship medal in 1972 as a 19 year-old I thought it would be the first of many.

We had a talented young team that I assumed would only get better and better, but unfortunately it would be another 13 years before we would even reach the final. Along the way there was a lot of talent wasted, and we failed to fulfil our obvious potential.

Circumstances didn't help us in so far as a lot of our players were in the army or gardai. It was the time of border duties, and they were spread out all over the place, so it was hard to get any sort of cohesion.

We started to get competitive again in the mid-80s though, and after we won the county league in 1984 I knew the following year's championship was probably my last chance of winning a county senior medal again.

I was training the team, as well as playing full back, and I was determined that no stone would be left unturned in the quest of winning the title.

Frank Kelly was one of the club's most talented players and even though he was working in England at the time he would plan his summer holidays with Ballaghaderreen's championship matches in mind. He'd come into our dressing room after a match and we'd always be saying to him he'd be a massive addition to the cause if he wasn't in England.

He had been a sub on the All-Ireland winning Mayo under-21 team of '73 even though he was only 19, so he was a serious talent. When he was home for Christmas myself and our team manager, Christy McCann decided to look him up and try to persuade him not to return to England.

We drove out to his home place which was five or six miles out in the countryside. When we got there, his father told us that Frank had cycled into town for a few drinks.

It was a snowy night. As we begun the drive back towards Ballaghaderreen, we noticed there was a track in the snow that we figured had been made by Frank on his bicycle.

We followed the tracks all the way into town and, sure enough, they led to the pub where Frank was supping.

We managed to persuade him that now was the time to make one last big push for the county title. By the start of the 1985 championship he was back home and integrated. He had been playing in England for a good few years where the football was brutally tough and had taken a toll.

His knees would not have passed an NCT, so we sorted out two operations to make sure he would be at full throttle for the championship. It looked like we had all our ducks in-a-row, and when we got to the county final against Ballina, I was sure we would win it.

Disaster struck, however, when one of our midfielders, Seamus Quinlan had a serious accident that ruled him out of the match. He worked in the Shannonside powdered milk plant in the town and he fell into a drier that had huge blades at the bottom of it.

He nearly lost his arm but was lucky in a way because, if he had fallen into the drier at a different spot, he could have been cut in two.

Seamus was a big loss for us and his absence meant Noel Durkin had to move from the half forward line to midfield, which dulled our attacking edge. We still should have won the match. But it was one of those days where a lot of things went wrong for us and we ended up losing by a ridiculous scoreline, 4-2 to 1-10.

We were by far the better team but we let in four soft goals. Losing in that manner was a bitter pill to swallow.

I knew in my heart that I would never have another chance to win a county title, and to this day the memory of that match is a raw one. I played on at club level until the 1988 championship, but by then I was gone past it.

If you play in the full back line your career rarely ends on a high, and my last game was a painful experience when played Knockmore in Charlestown one day.

Padraig Brogan, who I had managed on the 1983 All-Ireland winning under-21 team, gave me a right roasting. Normally retiring from club football leaves a massive gulf in your life, but there was little chance of me having too much free time on my hands.

That's because 1988 was also the year I was appointed the Mayo senior team manager.

CHAPTER 7

When Mayo had a poor year under Liam O'Neill in 1986 there was speculation that I would get the job. I was never going to challenge for it though because I had too much respect for the man.

But when he decided his time was up after the 1987 campaign, I let it be known that I wanted the job.

The players from the 1983 All-Ireland winning under-21 team were coming into their prime, while veterans like Willie Joe Padden, Dermot Flanagan, TJ Kilgallon, Anthony Finnerty and Martin Carney still had a lot to give.

I knew there was a potentially very good team there, but also that the window of opportunity to combine two different generations of players to the best effect was closing fast.

When I was offered the position the first request I made to the County Board was that I be given the power to pick my own selectors.

I wanted to bring in the complete backroom team that worked with me when we won the under-21 All-Ireland, but the board insisted on making the appointments themselves. At 34, I was still very young to be a county manager, and I got the feeling they thought I was too inexperienced to be given a completely free rein.

I was not happy about it at the time, but I'd have to admit that they appointed very solid people.

Seamie Daly, in particular, was a vital guiding light for me. He had trained the Mayo team that won the Connacht championship 1967 and '69, and the league in 1970 and was hugely experienced. He was someone that had been through it all and led from the front before, but was now happy with a role as a selector and determined to give me every bit of help that he could.

I benefited from his presence because he was around the block long enough to know how best to deal with the County Board, whereas that was all new to me. I was able to grow up faster as a manager with him by my side. He was hugely loyal and utterly dependable, and over time we became very good friends.

My other three selectors were Christy O'Haire, Charlie Collins and County Board chairman, Mick Higgins. Christy had been part of my under-21 management team, so I was happy with his nomination.

And, even though I did not know much about Charlie Collins apart from the fact he had led Mayo to a Vocational Schools All-Ireland title, it soon became apparent he was another quality operator.

He was around the same age as me and was very knowledgeable about physical training so he immediately brought a lot of value to the thing. We have been life-long friends ever since. So even though I did not get to pick my selectors, I got lucky.

I needed good men with me, because I soon found out that managing a senior county team was a totally different world than being in charge of an under-21 side.

My reign had started promisingly with two wins and a draw from our first four matches of the 1987-88 league, but then we suffered three defeats in a row after Christmas. That consigned us to a relegation semi final match against Armagh that we lost by two points.

By now I sensed that the players were starting to doubt me. Worse again, I was even beginning to doubt myself.

I remember coming home to Ger after that defeat to Armagh feeling really sorry for myself and questioning what I had gotten myself into?

I had some cheek really to be coming to her with a sob story. It was the day after she had come home from hospital after the birth of our youngest child, Cliodhna, and had not gotten much help from me when it came to changing nappies and all the other extra duties suddenly in front of us.

I got a more sympathetic hearing than I deserved. She consoled and cajoled enough for me to stop the whinging and just get on with the job.

I was really feeling the pressure.

It was only my first year in charge but I knew that if I did not win the Connacht championship then my management term could be aborted very quickly. The defeat to Armagh meant we were faced with the daunting prospect of playing Kerry in a relegation play-off in Ennis.

We performed well, but ended up losing by three points and went down. My reign as Mayo manager could not have gotten off to a worse start, but I did my best to rally the troops in the dressing room afterwards.

I looked them all in the eye and told them that we were going to go on from there to win the Connacht championship.

That was not something I said in any way disingenuously. I knew there was a lot of potential in the team and the players themselves knew it too. They had underachieved since winning the 1985 Connacht title, and there was a real determination within the group to finally show their true colours.

I could sense it. So even though being relegated from the league was a major disappointment, I was still convinced we could bounce back. We had three months to prepare for the first round of the championship and I knew that what we did in that period of time would make or break us.

Because we had played so many league matches before and after Christmas, there had been no opportunity to do some really heavy training as the players needed to be fresh for the weekend.

But the three-month gap between the end of the league and the start of the championship gave me the perfect opportunity to crack the whip.

Because Leitrim and Sligo were our first two matches in Connacht, I knew we could afford to put a training plan in place that would have us peaking for a Connacht final. I was not taking Leitrim and Sligo totally for granted because as a first year manager you have to err on the side of caution, but I knew we did not have to be at full throttle for the first round.

In the late 80s it was still possible to gain an edge on many of your rivals by being ferociously fit, so I made that my first objective.

There's a fine big beach between Kilalla and Ballycastle called Lacken Strand, and this was where we started the process of pushing the players to their absolute limit.

The players were warned what we were going to do, and why we were going to do it, because I always felt that you needed to plan everything as meticulously as possible and make the players understand why it was worthwhile.

Every time we went out to Lacken I got Charlie Collins to draw out an exactly measured running course on the sand that made the best of all that the beach had to offer.

The course took the players across hard sand, soft sand, heavy wet sand, and up and down sand dunes. Every possible muscle in their legs was being tested. It was tough going but there was a feel good factor to the work because the players knew it was money in the bank.

Our challenge match results during this period weren't great, but we were more concerned about long-term goals than short-term ones. The training sessions on the beach were easy compared to those we did on our own version of Heartbreak Hill.

There are houses built on it now, but back in the late 80s there was a grassy hill in the centre of Castlebar called Baines' Hill.

It was extremely steep, and you would struggle to walk up it never mind run it. One part of it was almost sheer, and the lads would seriously suffer when trying to get up it. It was a brutal workout, but a very effective one. Because on the way up you were working your thighs, and going downhill you were engaging the hamstrings.

I felt it was even more beneficial to us mentally than physically. Suffering hardens the mind, and I could see our players become more determined and resolute.

My own experience of playing for Mayo convinced me that we could also make big gains if we made an effort to get the players eating more healthily.

During my short time on the team we were treated after training to big steaks, greasy chips, glasses of 7-UP, and as many Clubmilk bars as we could eat. It was dynamite stuff.

We'd be eating all of this at 10.0 pm too, so we were doing the wrong thing altogether.

It wouldn't have taken much of an effort to improve on that regime, but I was determined we would get the best fuel possible into the players

Ger, as a Home Economics teacher, was a big help in terms of putting together dietary plans for all the players. She also made healthy fruit smoothies and brought them to training sessions along with bags of whole fruit. And, whenever we stayed overnight anywhere for a match or a training camp, she would get in touch with the hotel and make sure they could provide the players with healthy food.

At the start of the year, to begin with, I brought all the players down to Thomond College in Limerick for fitness testing.

Everything was measured, including their body fat, speed, and endurance, and then we brought them back a few months later again to see how much progress they had made. They had all significantly improved their scores, so that reinforced the belief in their minds that what we were doing was working.

As the championship drew closer, it was starting to look like things were coming together nicely. The players were fit and focused. The morale in the camp was much better than it had been at the end of the league.

But the nature of county management is that just when you think things are going smoothly, you usually hit a few pot-holes.

Three weeks before our first championship match we had a challenge game against Longford.

John Maughan, our centre back, came to me before the game and told me that he had decided to get surgery on a niggling knee injury that had been bothering him for some time. The top surgeon, Brian Hurson had already done a couple of successful knee operations for us and I was keen for John to go to him.

But John was in the army at the time and told me that he was going to get it done through them. I pointed out that the championship was only three weeks away, but he was confident he could be back training in a couple of weeks.

He went out and played that match against Longford, but unfortunately it was the last time he would ever play for Mayo.

Whatever surgery he had obviously did not work out well for him. Even though he put himself through the wringer in the following years to get back to full fitness, he was never able to get the knee right again.

He was a huge loss for us. He had been a key man in the All-Ireland winning under-21 team, he was our full back and a really important leader in the group. He was the only really natural centre back we had in our panel too, so he was always going to be hugely difficult to replace.

Dermot Flanagan would do a good job for us there in 1988, but it was not his best position and he did not look fully comfortable there. And, unfortunately, I would spend much of my first stint as Mayo manager trying to find someone who was a natural No.6.

Despite the loss of Maughan, we still beat Leitrim easily by 1-13 to 0-4 in the first round. But, shortly after the game, we suffered another setback.

Padraig Brogan scored 1-2 for us that day, but we subsequently found out that he had been out drinking on the Friday night before the match. That was an unacceptable breach of discipline and I knew that the other players on the panel were looking at me to see how I would deal with it.

Padraig was a very talented footballer, but as a manager in my first year in charge of the team I knew I had to take a strong line, or else my authority would be undermined.

It was a hard decision to make.

When Seamie Daly agreed with me that it was the right thing to do, I knew for sure that it was.

We brought Padraig back into the panel again in 1989 and for a short while things seemed to be going well, but when there was another breach of discipline we had no choice but to let him go for good.

It was a crying shame because he had everything in his locker to be a great footballer for Mayo. When he played on the 1983 All-Ireland winning under-21 team he was still a minor. His potential was massive, but unfortunately for him and Mayo he would never fulfil it.

We had another easy win over Sligo in the semi final which set us up for a Connacht final date with Roscommon. Defeat was unthinkable for me.

I was from Ballaghaderreen.

The town was adorned with Roscommon as well as Mayo flags.

That brought extra pressure for me personally. The stakes couldn't have been any higher really.

The banter was great between the genuine supporters on both sides, but I did not fancy being on the wrong end of it for the best part of the year. Roscommon had a very good team at the time. Men like Tony McManus, John Newton, Seamus Killoran and Paul Earley were skilful footballers and powerful athletes.

However, because of where I lived, I knew all of those Roscommon players like the back of my hand.

I was expecting a war, but it turned out to be a strangely comfortable seven point win. I still couldn't relax until the final whistle, but at no time did we really look like losing the match.

We had the luxury of being able to bring on Willie Joe Padden and Jimmy Bourke in the second half who both made big contributions.

Willie Joe was carrying a knock but I was always going to bring him on at a time when the game was in progress because I knew he'd give everyone a lift. He was an heroic figure for the Mayo supporters, and had that rare quality of being inspirational in almost everything he did on the football pitch.

Sure enough, when he came on in the second half the place shook, and Roscommon shrank that little bit more. Jimmy made an even bigger impact after his introduction. He was a cool character and changed the whole course of the game when he went in at full forward.

The reason he hadn't started was because he was one of those players that always took some time to get to peak fitness. He hadn't the quickest pair of legs in the game, but usually beat his man to the ball because he was gone before him.

The ability to read the play and to instinctively be in the right place at the right time is a great gift as a footballer, and Jimmy had it. He would never outpace his man. Instead, he usually out-thought him.

The Roscommon full back that day, Pat Doorey had been dominating our full forward Tommy Morgan, but when Jimmy came on he just couldn't handle him, and the rest of our forward line prospered from his presence and intelligence.

Martin Carney was another of the older contingent in the panel who came up trumps on the day by scoring four points. He had previously been a corner back, but I knew he could do a job in the forwards for us because he was a deep thinker on the game and would be able to adapt.

He was more badly needed in attack than he was defence.

We definitely lacked some natural scoring forwards. Noel Durkin was good for two or three points every game, but he was more of a player who would make it happen for others with his running and vision.

So Martin was pressed into action as a forward and he turned out to be a very good one. Not only did he deliver on the field for me, he was also a hugely valuable presence in the dressing room. We would never have bounced back from relegation in the league had the leaders in the team not had the drive and belief to set the example. Along with players like TJ Kilgallon and Dermot Flanagan, Martin was superb in that regard.

I had told the players in the dressing room in Ennis, after the defeat to Kerry, that we would win the Connacht championship and they had justified my faith in them.

I got the feeling I had justified myself to them too, because the vibe in the aftermath of the win over Roscommon was that it came because we had put such a savage effort into our training.

There is nothing more satisfying than achieving something when you work really hard for it, and we had definitely done that. It was a proud moment for me personally to win a Connacht championship in my first year in charge, but not long after the final whistle I was immediately focused on the All-Ireland semi final.

We were up against the reigning All-Ireland champions Meath, but I felt we had a great chance of winning it.

Maybe the players did not share my confidence, because they only started to really play once the game looked like it was over as a contest. We were down by eight points to two at half time after a disastrous first half that saw us miss some easy chances from both play and free-kicks, and we had Jimmy

Bourke forced off with an injury.

A Liam McHale goal gave us a lift in the second half, but we were still seven points down with 10 minutes to go.

We kept battling to the end though. Larry Finnerty got a goal and then it looked like McHale had another but it was ruled out for a square ball. Of course I'm biased, but I really didn't think it was a square ball. McHale was moving into the square and had the jersey torn off him on the way. So even if it was square ball it was a penalty first.

In the immediate aftermath I felt deflated because we had not played to our potential though I did not stay that way for long and my spirits were lifted on the Monday evening when I met up with a group of senior players

They told me that their overwhelming feeling was also that we had not done ourselves justice, and that they felt the team was capable of achieving bigger things.

Winning what was just the county's third Connacht title in 20 years was acceptable to most supporters and the County Board, but the players and I knew we could do more.

There and then, we began the preparations for 1989. We promised we would leave no stone unturned in the quest to bring Sam Maguire back to Mayo.

CHAPTER 8

The nature of our defeat to Meath in the 1988 All-Ireland semi final convinced me that our team was mentally weak and beaten before a ball was even kicked. I knew, by the end of the year, that strengthening the team psychologically had to be a priority.

At the time it was almost hard-wired into Connacht teams that they wouldn't win All-Irelands and would be lucky to even reach one. We really felt it was time to rip up that script and write a new one.

Frank Noone, a wing back on the team, was developing Delphi Adventure Centre where companies would bring their employees for team-bonding sessions.

He told me he had met at guy at one of these sessions who might be able to help with the team's mental preparation. His name was Bill Cogan. He was Scottish, and worked in human resources with Digital in Galway.

He had no knowledge of football, but his speciality was challenging people mentally and giving them self-confidence. I met up with him, and he really impressed me, and I decided to bring him on board with us.

Today most county teams do some sort of work with a sports psychologist, but back then it was totally taboo.

I'm not sure if it had really been done before, and I knew that if word got out they would send for the men in white coats. Therefore, Bill's work with us was kept a secret, and it is a testament to how tight the group was that his involvement never became public knowledge.

I wanted to begin our preparations for the 1989 championship with a bang because our league campaign had ended with a whimper. A defeat to Cavan in Ballina had ended our promotion hopes, and as I walked off the field that day my ears were ringing with the booing from the Mayo supporters.

A few months previously they had been telling me that I was a genius for winning a Connacht title.

Now I was a dunce.

That is Mayo supporters for you.

They can switch very quickly from the brightest of optimism, to dark pessimism, and there is rarely any middle ground between these contrasting emotions.

Those boos in Ballina that day were harsh and made me angry, but you have little option but to insulate yourself from that sort of negativity. It just made me all the more determined to really lift things ahead of the championship.

We arranged a weekend away in Dublin, in The Burlington Hotel, that started with a challenge match against Meath in St Vincent's GAA club on the Friday evening.

We won the game and let the players go for a few drinks that night, and then the following morning we brought them together for a team meeting. Bill Cogan told me we should start the day with a real bang.

We brought in Mick Doyle, who had coached Ireland's Triple Crown winning team of 1985, to give a speech about what it takes to win at the very highest level in sport. When I introduced him I made it clear what our mission was that year.

We were aiming to win the All-Ireland.

The year previously we had been nearly men, and Mick Doyle was well qualified to tell us what it took to turn nearly men into winners. The Ireland rugby team at the time would usually win two matches in the then Five Nations, but then lose two just as quickly, and fall short of silverware.

Here was a man who had dealt with players with a history of falling short, and he had managed to break through that glass ceiling.

He spoke brilliantly. There was plenty of practical advice, but also jokes and amusing stories that had all of our lads in the palm of his hand. When Mick had finished, I introduced Bill Cogan and explained how he was going to help us over the coming weeks and months.

He did his first session with them, and the players were extremely receptive. That encouraged me because it proved they too were willing to do whatever it took to win the Sam Maguire Cup.

Even something as simple as saying out loud in that group setting that we wanted to go all the way that year was empowering

Obviously you're taking a slight risk too, because this is still only Mayo and there are a lot of hurdles between the first round in Connacht and the All-Ireland final. However, I really felt we needed to verbalise our ambition if we were ever going to have the self-belief necessary to go and achieve it.

We broke up into groups, and the topic of discussion was what it would take for us to become All-Ireland champions?

What were the targets we needed to set and reach? And what were the obstacles we had to remove from our path? Why had Mayo not even reached an All-Ireland final since they last won it in 1951?

Why were Connacht teams consistently losing All-Ireland semi finals?

It all had to be confronted because that was the only way I felt we could change the county's history of underachievement. Everything was written up on boards and all the issues raised were discussed and debated.

This was not just an exercise that the players took part in. Team management and the County Board officers present were also involved. The message I was putting out was that we had to all buy into this thing, because the only way we could possibly achieve the dream was to have everyone pulling in the same direction together.

There was great feedback from everyone on the day and there was a real sense that our unity of purpose was being strengthened by the exercise.

I felt driving back home from Dublin that Saturday evening that we had really kick-started our campaign and that it was important to sustain the momentum the weekend had generated. Everyone was in agreement that more nights away together like the one we had in The Burlington would be hugely beneficial, but the problem was we did not have the finance to do that.

So, I went on a fund-raising trip to London that was organised by a friend of mine, Hugh Conway, who was a fanatical Mayo supporter.

He took over an Irish centre in Camden Town and organised a function that I spoke at. We made four or five hundred pounds which was enough to pay for another trip away for the team, this time in the Old Head Hotel down in Louisburgh in Mayo.

This enabled us to build on what we had done in Dublin, and it gave us even more momentum. It was not a matter of me imposing this; everyone involved wanted it. We were setting standards, and making more demands of one another.

Boldly declaring that we were going all-out to win the All-Ireland title and that nothing else was good enough put us under more pressure, of course.

But I welcomed that pressure.

I wanted to get to the next level and the only way I felt it would be possible was if that was something we demanded of ourselves, rather than something we all just hoped for.

I had the feeling, in 1989, that it was possibly now or never. The elder statesmen of the team like Willie Joe Padden and Martin Carney were coming towards the end of their careers and would be hard to replace

That year the Connacht champions were facing the Ulster champions in the semi final, which gave us a greater opportunity of getting to an All-Ireland final because Ulster football was in the doldrums too. Players like Padden and Carney did not need any encouragement to squeeze the last few drops out of their playing careers.

I had a role to play in drawing more out of the younger players in the team who still had room for improvement. Liam McHale was someone I put particular focus on. Even though he had been an inexperienced player in 1988, he was still one of our best.

He took the fight to Meath on his own at times in the All-Ireland semi final in what was a real coming of age performance. He was one of the most physically gifted footballers I had ever seen, but he was a complicated enough character and it took me a while to get to understand what made him tick.

Basketball was obviously another passion of his so I was always trying to steer him more in the direction of the football. I used to run camps for children in the summer and got him involved with those. It was immediately obvious he had a gift for coaching. He'd have the youngsters eating out of his hand.

When the Connacht Council decided to set up a programme to send GAA coaches around to schools, I knew he was an ideal candidate.

I sorted that with the County Board and told Liam he could have his pick of schools in the Ballina area. Liam was interested, but told me he didn't think he'd be able to do it because he had no transport. After our good run the previous summer there was a bit of sponsorship going around, so I managed to get someone to stump up for one of those little vaneens you could put gear, balls and bollards in.

I was fairly chuffed with myself, but when I broke the good news to Liam, he just laughed.

'But, John... I can't drive!'

He had my heart broken at that stage but he was the sort of fella you just couldn't get mad with. So, in the end, we got someone to drive him. Liam was not the type to offer the solutions himself, and you always had to keep on his case.

That was not simple though because there were no mobiles in those days and he was not an easy man to contact. He was living at home and whenever you'd ring it was usually his mother or his sister, Marion who would answer. And when you'd pass on the message it was usually one of them who'd eventually get back to you rather than Liam himself.

He was not doing it out of badness or anything. He was just an incredibly laid-back guy and it was a challenge to get inside his head.

He was so big, strong, and skilful that at times he just made the game look ridiculously easy. Because it came so easily to him, I did not want him to think he could just play at his ease and coast through matches. That would still have made him one of the best players on the pitch, but I knew if he really applied himself then the sky was the limit.

I stayed on his case. I kept pushing him, and pushing him, not in a dictatorial kind of way, that would've been counter-productive.

My philosophy has always been that a player will achieve more if he is motivated from the inside out, and it was my job to tell him just how good he could be, and then challenge him to fulfil that potential.

I told McHale that he had all the tools he needed to be the best midfielder in the country and, as the year went on, I could see he had the ambition himself to become that player. Soon he was driving the thing on himself and becoming one of our key leaders, rather than someone you felt you had to crack the whip with.

Another player I knew was absolutely essential to our cause in 1989 was Noel Durkin.

But the problem was that after the '88 campaign he had moved to London because he was on low wages locally and the economy over there was beginning to take off.

I did all I could to keep him at home, but eventually I had to compromise and agree with him that he could go in the autumn and then return to the panel in time for the championship.

A date had been arranged for him to fly home and I had the tickets bought, but then I got a phone call from Noel early one Saturday morning. He told me he was going to America.

I asked him to come home and talk it out with me at least and, if he decided he really did not want to stay, that I would pay for his ticket back to London and he could go on from there to America if he wanted.

I knew that if I got him home then I had a good chance of twisting his arm and persuading him to stay. He was absolutely vital for us, and was worth the effort. He came home and I went down to his place in Edmondstown and we had a long chat about it all and, thankfully, I was able to persuade him to stay.

Unfortunately, I was not able to work the same sort of magic with another player who might have made a massive difference in 1989.

Ger Geraghty had been vice-captain on the 1983 All-Ireland under-21 winning team, but after playing for the county senior team the following year he moved to America. I really felt he could be the key to us winning the Sam Maguire Cup in 1989, so I plagued him with phone calls to Chicago and tried to persuade him to come home.

I even got him a job locally, and eventually in January of '89 he rang me to say that he would come back the following April and join up with us. I was over the moon because it really felt like the most important part of the jigsaw had fallen into place.

Ger was a superb footballer who could have played anywhere across the half forward line or in the middle of the field for us. He was a left-footer and had a rare mixture of athleticism and skill. He was a natural leader too, the sort of player who would grab the game by the scruff of the neck when it was there to be won.

The weakness of that Mayo panel was that we did not have an abundance of natural forwards, and Ger would've definitely given us more of a scoring threat. But, unfortunately for us, shortly after he had agreed to come home he met a woman in Chicago and fell in love.

That changed his whole perspective. By April, he had decided to stay put in America rather than return to Ireland. The woman, Carla eventually became his wife, so from his own point of view he definitely made the right decision.

Years later I was over in Chicago in 1998 with the Sam Maguire Cup and some fella came up to me and said, 'You don't know me, but I know you!'

'I used to be Ger Geraghty's flat-mate,' he explained. 'You used to be ringing at all fucking hours of the night... t'was many a cursing I gave you from a distance!'

I could only laugh. I was always conscious of trying to get Ger on the phone before he left for work at seven in the morning, but clearly his flatmate had no reason to be up that early.

Not getting Ger Geraghty was a massive opportunity missed, but we were definitely fortunate that Michael Fitzmaurice had come onto the scene. In 1988 the lack of a specialist free-taker really hurt us in the All-Ireland semi final, but Fitzmaurice filled that void.

He was captain of the minor team that won the All-Ireland in 1985 and had great mental strength for someone so young. He would come early to training every day and work on his free taking with Seamie Daly.

Michael had this wonderful ability to strike a ball perfectly with his left foot, and it was all technique rather than power. He could take them from distance as well as close in, so he was an invaluable addition for us.

Kevin McStay was also developing into a really fine forward which added further to our firepower, and as the Connacht championship approached I was in a very positive frame of mind.

Our team building weekends had gone brilliantly, and I could sense a real belief in the squad that this was going to a big year for Mayo football.

CHAPTER 9

All of our lofty plans very nearly came unstuck in the Connacht semi final against Galway when the best we could manage was a draw in Tuam.

Mayo football seems to attract superstition, and our failure to win the match was blamed by many on the infamous 'Tuam Jinx' which stretched back all the way to 1951.

Our provincial success the previous year had raised expectations, but when we failed to beat Galway we were castigated by the local press. Much of the commentary was over the top, even if it was a game we should have closed out but didn't.

It was a fairly controversial match too, because Kevin McStay received a bad dig off the ball. Kevin was forced to go off and at the time it was thought he had a broken jaw. An x-ray later showed it had not been broken, but the incident was still a hot topic afterwards.

No suspension was handed down in time for the replay, and we felt that a major injustice had been done.

In a situation like that you can use those things to your advantage. The message we were putting out to the lads was there was only one way to pay Galway back, and that was to give them a good beating in the replay.

With emotions running high, it was hardly a surprise that the second match was a tense affair with some hard-hitting on both sides.

We won well in the end, 2-13 to 1-8 even though Sean Maher was sent off in the first-half.

We were a good deal better in the replay victory over Galway than we had been in the drawn game, but we were still falling someway short of our potential.

I was starting to worry that perhaps everyone in the camp was so focused on the ultimate goal of winning an All-Ireland that they had taken their eye off the steps required to get that far.

When we had our team meeting the day before we played Roscommon in the Connacht final I wanted to make sure that everyone was fully tuned in for the task at hand.

I had briefed our captain, Jimmy Browne, that I would be throwing out a rhetorical question about what it would mean to win two Connacht titles in-a-row?

At that point Jimmy was meant to pipe up and say a few inspirational words. But, before he had a chance, another player, Michael Collins, rose to his feet. I nearly had a canary at this stage because I knew Michael was very disillusioned about not being in the team.

He had struggled against Brian Stafford in the 1988 All-Ireland semi final and had lost his place on the team.

Coming into that Connacht final he felt he had done enough to win it back at the expense of Peter Forde. When I had told him earlier in the week that Forde was holding onto the jersey he was extremely annoyed. I was afraid he might voice that frustration again. The last thing we needed the day before the match was negative emotion in the dressing room.

But instead Michael was inspirational.

He admitted he was desperately disappointed not to be playing, but that he was one hundred per cent behind Peter Forde, and would do his utmost to help us win a Connacht championship if he got a run as a substitute.

It was a fantastic moment, and I immediately abandoned the meeting because I knew Michael's gesture had struck the perfect chord.

But even though I felt we were primed to give a much better account of ourselves than we had against Galway, we once again failed to fire on all cylinders.

We kicked some terrible wides, and the game ended in a 0-12 to 1-9 draw. It was hugely frustrating because we felt like we were back in the old rut of not maximising our potential.

The focus of most of our team meetings was about finding a way to unlock the potential greatness in the team, but it seemed as though we were no nearer to locating that key.

We would've lost had our goalkeeper, Gabriel Irwin not made a super save in the dying minutes from Paul Earley.

It was Gabriel's championship debut because our regular goalkeeper, Eugene Lavin was injured. Gabriel played so well he held onto his place, which was hard luck on Eugene because he was a brilliant goalkeeper himself.

We did a fitness test with Eugene the day before the match in Ballyhaunis. He had been struggling with a muscular injury in his leg, and I thought he had come through the fitness test fine.

But, in fairness to him, he came to me afterwards and said he just did not think it was right and that we should select Gabriel instead. I thought it was a very honest thing to say. Considering how things worked out with Gabriel holding onto the jersey, you would understand if Eugene was a bit peeved.

But, instead, he gave Gabriel his full support and the two continued to push one another in training. That did not just reflect well on Eugene, but on the camaraderie as a whole in the panel.

Two other players who came to the fore against Roscommon that day were Peter Forde and Jimmy Browne. They were up against two superb forwards in Paul Earley and Tony McManus, but they won those crucial individual battles.

Peter's form hadn't been great coming into the game and my decision to stick with him would not have been universally praised. However, I was never likely to drop him because I had more faith in Peter than most men I managed. He was a true leader, but a quiet one; not the sort of fella who would be shouting too much in the dressing room.

Instead, he led by his actions and the calm sense of authority he radiated.

He was an All-Ireland boxing champion in his youth, and he had a really confident way of holding himself and was always in great shape and very focused. When we had first brought in Bill Cogan to work with the players, Peter asked me what we needed him for?

Peter was so mentally strong himself he had no need for someone like Bill. Unfortunately, not every player on the panel was as self-assured. If they had been, I wouldn't have seen a need for Bill Cogan myself.

Much like Peter, Jimmy Browne was another player who had a fairly bulletproof level of self-confidence. He really brought into our vision of aiming high and believing we could be the best, and that was one of the reasons why I made him the team captain. His own self-belief was very apparent in the way he played the game as a corner back. He was very attack-minded, and always wanted to be out in front of his man.

That attacking style fed into my philosophy as a manager because, since my days being coached by Malachy O'Rourke, I believed the last line of your defence could also be the first line of your attack.

Jimmy had a lot of pace and he would always be tearing out of defence with the ball and getting the team on the front foot.

If anything broke off the half backs he'd be onto it like a flash and flying down the pitch. It was an inspirational example for his teammates, and had the added benefit of firing up the crowd. More importantly, as far as that drawn Connacht final was concerned, his pace and positivity meant he was beating Tony McManus for most balls that came their way.

That was vital because McManus was such a lethal forward that if he got his hands on the ball at all he would make something happen.

The reason both Peter and Jimmy had to be on their toes that day was because our midfield was being dominated, and a lot of traffic was flowing towards our goal. We were badly missing the inspirational TJ Kilgallon who had suffered a knee ligament injury in a league match against Louth and still was not one hundred per cent fit.

He made a big impact when he came on as a sub though, and I decided we could not do without him for the replay.

Centre back was still a problem position for us. Even though TJ was our best midfielder, he was also our most adaptable and had the ability to do a good job there. At that time we had four powerful men who all regarded midfield as their favoured position, TJ Kilgallon, Willie Joe Padden, Liam McHale and Sean Maher.

Four into two doesn't go, but they were all such good footballers that they had to be accommodated somewhere.

So for the replay against Roscommon, TJ was at centre back, Liam McHale and Sean Maher were in the middle of the pitch, and Willie Joe was at centre forward. Maher was the least adaptable of the quartet so he had to play in the middle, and McHale had developed to such an extent that his athleticism was wasted anywhere else on the pitch.

So, Willie Joe was pushed into centre forward, and his size, strength and fondness for running straight at goal made him a serious weapon in that position. The influence of that quartet gave us a much better grip on the middle third of the field in the replay than we had in the drawn match.

Kilgallon, especially, made a big difference. He was one of those players who could organise everyone around him and by doing so enable them to raise their level. He also had the ability to do the right thing at the right time and keep his cool when others around him were losing theirs.

Because of that he saved Sean Maher from a certain sending off in the replay and, by extension, probably saved us too. Eamonn McManus had been edging at Maher all day, and eventually Maher reacted by absolutely creasing him in the ribs.

I think he may even have broken a rib or two because Eamonn was absolutely dying on the ground after the belt. Mickey Kearins was the referee.

Before Kearins decided what to do, Kilgallon walked up to him.

'You'd want to keep an eye on McManus,' said TJ.

'... he's at Maher all day.'

Even though Maher could have been sent to the line, suddenly Kearins had a different picture in his head and in the end did nothing about the incident.

It was another ferociously contested match, but we looked like we had chiselled out a hard-fought win when we led by four points with three minutes remaining. Roscommon fans were streaming out of the ground at that stage, but there was plenty of fight left in their team.

They kicked over two frees. Then they won a penalty in injury time that

Tony McManus calmed slotted.

That looked like the end of us, and now it was the turn of Mayo fans to head for the exits. However, then came a moment I truly believe would not have happened without all of those intensive team meetings we had been having with Bill Cogan all year.

One of the core principles we had been working on in relation to the team's mental strength was its ability to react positively when something negative happens.

You will always have set backs in games.

The important thing is how you immediately react to them?

When McManus scored that penalty, Gabriel Irwin rushed to pick the ball out of the net and take a quick goal kick.

From there, we went straight down the field to score what looked like a winning goal from substitute Michael Collins but, for some unknown reason, Mickey Kearins called back play and gave us a free in instead.

Moments earlier I'd have gladly taken the draw. And my predominant emotion was still relief when Michael Fitzmaurice pointed it.

The manner in which we kept fighting right to the end proved to me that all the work we had put into our mental approach had paid off. In the past, if a Mayo team had conceded an injury time goal like that to Roscommon in Hyde Park they'd have said, 'fuck our luck'.

The towel would have been thrown in.

When the final whistle blew there was nearly as much pandemonium outside the ground as inside it. The Roscommon and Mayo fans who had left early rushed to get back inside, though others only realised that the game had gone to extra time when they got to a pub down the town or turned on their car radio.

Neither team returned to their dressing room before the start of extra-time.

We gathered in a huddle and, after I said a few words, Frank Noone took centre stage. He had been forced off in normal time with a serious knee injury that turned out to be a badly ruptured cruciate ligament.

Even though the leg was half hanging off him, he limped into the middle of our circle and spoke inspirationally.

I was sure we were going to drive on from there, although we were on the back foot in the first half of extra time as Roscommon outscored us by four points to one. When we then hit seven wides in the second half of extra time, it was starting to look like were going to kick ourselves out of it.

Once again, we proved we were now a mentally tougher team as we scored 2-1 in the final couple of minutes to win an epic contest in fittingly dramatic fashion.

On the outside I was trying to stay calm. But, on the inside, I was absolutely buzzing. Beating Roscommon was always something special because of the nature of the rivalry, and to do it like this only added to the sense of achievement.

We could have become yet another Mayo hard luck story.

Instead, we changed the narrative. We refused to accept anything other than a happy ending. It really felt like a coming of age moment, and by now I was more convinced than ever that we were going to end the county's long wait for Sam.

CHAPTER 10

The All-Ireland semi final against Tyrone could not have been better set up for us. They had played Kerry in the 1986 All-Ireland final and led at one stage by seven points before losing in the end. It was seen as a missed opportunity in Tyrone.

In the run up to the All-Ireland semi final against us some of their players were even interviewed wearing t-shirts emblazoned with the slogan 'Unfinished Business'.

They were assuming they had a God-given right to another All-Ireland final and that played right into our hands. Not only were they underestimating us, they also gave us fuel to ignite the fire in our bellies.

I was confident coming into the match because we had come through some really tough battles in Connacht and I knew that they would stand to us. Our only cause for concern was the knee injury that had ended Frank Noone's season.

He was a really classy, attacking wing back and one of our foremost leaders, so he was a big loss. However, his absence opened the door for Michael Collins who had been so disappointed not to be chosen at full back for the Connacht campaign instead of Peter Forde.

Wing back was not his most natural position because he lacked a bit of pace, but he came in and did a great job for us. The team as a whole had developed a much harder mental edge, and it really came to the fore in the semi final.

Even when Eugene McKenna scored a goal for Tyrone and they went 1-5 to 0-6 ahead, I never got the sense our players doubted for one moment they were going to win the match.

Liam McHale, in particular, was absolutely outstanding against Tyrone. Some of his high fielding was so spectacular that there were audible exclamations of wonder from the crowd. He was no longer coasting through matches because everything came so easily to him.

He was pushing himself to his limits to see just how good he could become and it really was an impressive sight to behold. Neither were we just playing better as individuals, we were gelling more as a team than we had in '88 as well.

The emergence of Michael Fitzmaurice as a free-taker was also proving more and more important as the stakes grew higher and the margin for error shrunk. It was a hard-fought match against Tyrone.

In the second half, when it mattered, we were the team with the greater self-belief, fitness, and skill to go and win it.

It always helps in those sort of matches to have a true warrior on your side, and we certainly had one in Willie Joe. He received a bad gash on the head late in the second half and our doctor, Frank Davey performed whatever stitching he could on the sideline before putting a special gauze cap on him to help stop the bleeding.

The sight of him running back onto the field, a bloodstained warrior coming back for more, really lifted the crowd. They, in turn, lifted the players.

Willie Joe's bravery and toughness sent out the message that this Mayo team was something different.

We were no soft touches anymore.

We were a properly hard-edged group of players who would do whatever it took to be winners. That bloody-minded determination combined with some great football just blew Tyrone away in the final 10 minutes of the match as we scored six points in-a-row to run out 0-12 to 1-6 winners.

To watch those points fly over was thrilling for every Mayo person in the stadium, myself included. When the final whistle blew, the explosion of emotion that greeted the win was incredible. Noel Durkin fell to his knees and started kissing the ground. He had come close to walking away from the team, but now his decision to stick around had been justified in the best way possible.

All of us felt a similar sense of justification. We had put in a massive effort, and everything we achieved could be traced back to the weekend away together in The Burlington Hotel the previous May.

We had set a goal that I'm sure almost everyone outside the group felt was overly ambitious. The difference was we had gone and proven we had the mental resolve to pull it off.

Our county had become more associated with failure than success, and we really felt like we had broken through a formidable barrier. The scenes in the dressing room were crazy. Even though my instinct was to calm the thing down, I soon realised there was little chance of that happening.

We had reached the county's first All-Ireland final since 1951, and it was only right the achievement be celebrated.

We went back to The Ashling Hotel that night and had a hell of a party. All year, my slogan had been 'Keep the Faith'.

Whenever I spoke to the players or even the media, that was my message. As the year progressed, supporters even started bringing banners to matches with those words written on them.

KEEP THE FAITH

It had all the more resonance now that we had achieved what we set out to do at the start of the year and overcome all sorts of obstacles on our way.

The memories of being booed off the pitch after being beaten by Cavan in the league and the criticism in the local press after we drew with Galway all came flooding back as I surveyed the joyous scenes in the hotel.

That negativity had been all washed away, and there was an incredible feel good factor in the room. A lot of the players continued the celebrations at the

Belmullet Fair for a couple of more days but, by the Monday morning, I was already planning our assault on the All-Ireland final.

We had five weeks to prepare for the match.

Because I was a teacher and was off for the summer holidays, I was able to totally focus all my energies on it.

We did not train in the week immediately following the win over Tyrone. I used that time to hold a series of meetings and plan our preparations down to the finest detail. I soon learned though that we were all operating outside of our comfort zone because the entire county had gone mad.

There were a few thousands supporters at most training sessions, and the hype had gone through the roof.

At the time there were two old dressing rooms, side by side at the McHale Road end of the ground in Castlebar, and we divided our panel between both of them. People liked to stand in the area between both dressing rooms to watch our matches, and one evening I couldn't get from one dressing room to the other because there was such a crowd.

There was massive interest in the team too from the local and national media, and I needed to get a grip on the situation by having a press event for the media and an open day for the supporters on the same day.

The idea was that the media would leave us alone after this one day where they'd have access to all the players, and that the supporters would also give us a little more peace after an organised event.

Press days were very much in their infancy back then, and ours was not nearly as limited and censored as they tend to be now.

All the players were on the pitch doing a few laps or sprints for the photographers, and the journalists had the licence to grab whoever they wanted for a few words. Not all of our players liked this idea though. Noel Durkin had never done an interview in his life, and had no intention of doing one now.

He legged it out of the ground, and ran across the road to Martin Carney's house.

Martin's wife, Gina was our team physio. Noel reckoned feigning a suddenly tight hamstring was his ticket away from the bedlam of journalists and supporters.

After that manic open day we decided it was time to get out of the county for a while and have a team weekend away like we had at the start of the summer in Dublin.

There was so much goodwill in the county towards us now that it was easy to raise the funds necessary. There were all sorts of auctions for signed jerseys, and I'm pretty sure Willie Joe Padden's blood-stained gauze cap from the All-Ireland semi final was sold to the highest bidder at least 10 times.

Our team doctor, Frank Davey had a good stock of them, though I'm not sure where he got the blood to give them a more authentic look!

We decided to spend our weekend away in Brian McEniff's Great Northern Hotel in Bundoran, though it quickly became apparent that was a poor choice. The word spread. It didn't help either that half the Gardai in Donegal are from Mayo.

Phone calls were constantly coming from journalists to the reception looking to talk to me and the players. It wasn't as controlled an environment as I'd have liked.

It was still a positive weekend. We got Mick Doyle back in again to give another talk to the players. There was a real sense that the journey that had started in The Burlington Hotel in May had now reached the destination we had dreamed it would.

My brother, Father Dan also came up to Donegal with us and said a mass for the team. Before matches I have always incorporated a mass into our team preparation.

I'm not one for imposing religion on anyone, but there is definitely something spiritual about being involved with a GAA team because you are all on the same mission together. A mass brings a unity of purpose to things and draws everyone together in a quiet moment of contemplation and reflection.

Even if some are not listening to a word the priest is saying, I think players source a really positive energy from being in an environment with their teammates where they are all silently contemplating the challenge ahead.

Preparing for a senior All-Ireland final was a new thing for all of us, and I was very conscious that the unique pressure of the situation would affect certain players more than others. Bill Cogan played a big role in this regard. He was at every training session and his job was to identify any player who was getting distracted.

Then they were quietly taken aside and he'd have a word with them to help them get refocused.

Everything was being watched closely. It wouldn't be natural if lads weren't getting distracted because this was a whole new experience. The closer the match came, the more the hype was cranked up. The local radio station, Midwest Radio, played a big role in this escalation of excitement.

It had only been launched that year, and the first match commentary was the replay of the Connacht final. Right from the start, the station recognised that the Mayo team was a vehicle for its success. They were keen to have as close a relationship as possible and the County Board recognised the fundraising potential in such an arrangement.

On the Thursday night before the final, Midwest broadcast a big fundraising rally for the team training fund live on radio with three or four hundred special guests.

There was to be a discussion of the match afterwards with tickets for the game up for grabs and they wanted some of our players to take part. I was conscious of facilitating the County Board as much as possible. I brought our team captain Jimmy Browne along.

It was a great night for the fans, but I did not enjoy it because I knew it was a distraction for our players.

I did not want to be a control freak either. I was very conscious of trying to insulate the players as much as possible from the hype and excitement around them. In one sense it was great that the county was behind us to the extent that they were, but it was not making my life any easier.

I knew we could not afford further distractions like that on the weekend of the All-Ireland final itself, and I decided we had to stay somewhere our supporters would not be able to find us.

Connacht teams that reached the All-Ireland semi finals and finals had traditionally stayed in The Ashling Hotel.

I decided we would instead book The Grand Hotel in Malahide. It was out of town and secluded, and I also liked the fact that it was associated with Kerry All-Ireland winning teams.

I went up to Dublin and discussed everything with the manager of the hotel about the sort of bedrooms and meeting rooms we'd need, as well as the team's dietary requirements. Usually hotels like to advertise they are hosting an All-Ireland final team, but I insisted that our booking there was to remain a secret.

And, in fairness to the hotel staff, they managed to keep a lid on the whole thing.

Our County Board chairman, Mick Higgins once rang the hotel to query something, but the receptionist coolly informed him that the Mayo team was not staying there.

It was a great test of how seriously they had taken my request for secrecy, and they passed it with flying colours. Rather than get a train or a bus to Dublin we decided to fly from the newly opened airport in Knock.

At our team meeting in The Burlington the previous May we had made the mission statement that we would fly back into Knock with the Sam Maguire, so this was the first leg of that journey as far as we were concerned.

That sense of being on a mission was reinforced by a motivational video that the RTE television reporter, Tommie Gorman put together for me.

I had gotten to know Tommie first when he had worked with the *Western Journal* newspaper. I had written the local notes for the paper and over time we became good friends.

Tommie is a native of Sligo, but he took a big interest in what I was doing with Mayo. Eventually he came to me and said he'd like to help me in some way if he could. He effectively became my video analyst and an unlisted member of my backroom team. Not just with Mayo, but later with Leitrim and Galway too.

After every championship game I would source the match video from RTE and sit down with Tommie and pick out what we did well and poorly.

He would then package these clips together and I was able to give the players the sort of feedback I felt was most relevant.

For the All-Ireland final, he travelled around the county shooting footage of the places that would mean something to the players and give them a sense of just how much everyone was behind them.

He even got the Sam Maguire Cup, put the Mayo colours on it, and then went out to Knock airport to video a Ryanair flight landing.

All of his footage was set to music, and when the whole thing was packaged together it was the perfect motivational tool to get the players in the right frame of mind on the eve of the match.

Flying out from Knock from a practical point of view was important too because it was a much faster way of getting to Dublin, and it was great promotion for the new airport.

As soon as the media heard we were flying to Dublin, they wanted to be on the plane too. The County Board were keen to accommodate them. I dug my heels in.

The only concession I agreed to was to do an interview outside the plane with RTE's Jimmy Magee.

Frank Noone and John Maughan were also interviewed. They were both injured and unable to play in the final, so I put them forward for a lot of media duties in the days and weeks leading up to the game in order to shield the players who were involved.

Despite my ban on media travelling with us on the plane to Dublin, one journalist, Declan Lynch of *The Sunday Independent* did manage to work his way on board. We had allowed photographers to travel with us, and he masqueraded himself as one.

He wouldn't have been known to us at the time, so when he boarded with a camera around his neck we weren't to know he was actually a journalist rather than a photographer. Sure enough, he had a big exclusive in *The Sunday Independent* which hit the streets of Dublin that Saturday night.

That annoyed me, but otherwise the decision to fly to Dublin worked well. We were in Dublin quickly, and the turnaround at the airport was handled speedily too. When we got to the Grand Hotel in Malahide, it was an oasis of calm.

That night I totally believed that we were mentally in the right place and had somehow survived the crazy hype of the previous five weeks.

We were ready to go.

I just couldn't wait for the following day to come.

CHAPTER 11

The most difficult task for any manager is picking a team for an All-Ireland final. Every manager is so keenly aware how much it means to every player to be involved in the match, and taking that opportunity away from him is a really tough decision to make.

In the 1980s a manager was allowed a match-day panel of 21, and that was even tougher to pick than the starting 15.

At least if someone didn't make the team he could console himself with the possibility of coming on as a sub, or of having the chance to win a medal even if he didn't play. But, if you have been part of the extended panel all year and are then told that you will not make the cut for the match-day itself, then it must be devastating.

For the '89 All-Ireland final, the Mayo team mainly picked itself. The only conundrum I had was whether to start Anthony Finnerty or use him as an impact introduction.

He had started the drawn Connacht final but did not make much of an impact so he was on the bench for the replay. He was massively influential when he came in that day, kicking a goal and a point, so he was back in the team for the All-Ireland semi final against Tyrone.

Once again, though, he failed to set the world alight in that match. I figured that maybe he was a more dangerous weapon coming off the bench.

Larry, as he was known to the lads, was a gifted footballer, but at times he would frustrate me because I knew there was more in him than he was getting out. He was a great man to have involved though because he was very much the joker in the pack and was usually involved, some way or other, in whatever slagging was going on.

His nickname was 'Fat Larry'.

Clearly he did not take any offence at that, because he opened up a chipper in Carraroe in Galway that he named 'Larry Romhair's'. He was happy to poke fun at himself as well as everyone else, and it is important to have someone in the group who can put a smile on people's faces.

He never missed a genuine opportunity to do that either, and his comic timing was usually spot-on.

At one of our group sessions with Bill Cogan we were looking for people to come up with suggestions about how we could improve our game. Because we had made a point of making those sessions inclusive, there were a couple of members of the County Board executive there, but I wanted the contributions coming from the players rather than from them.

On this particular day, a County Board officer decided to give his tuppenceworth on how we could improve our play and he suggested we should be drop-kicking the ball a lot more.

I wasn't sure how I should respond to a suggestion I thought was ridiculous without sounding patronising, but thankfully Larry came to the rescue by breaking into the chorus of *Drop-kick me Jesus through the Goalposts of Life*. The place exploded with laughter, and we were able to quickly move on without injuring anyone's pride too much.

I didn't mind the joking as long as he took himself seriously on the football pitch, and I was always pushing him to be better. It seemed as though you always got more of a reaction from him when he was dropped to the bench, and that is why I thought he could do more damage for us as a sub than a starter against Cork in the All-Ireland final.

It was difficult to break the news to him, but Larry was better equipped than most to deal with it because of his bubbly personality. I knew he was disappointed. I also knew we could count on him to have a big impact if and when he was called upon.

On the morning of the match, I could only sense positive vibes from the players. We had been beating the drum that this was an occasion to be relished rather than feared, and they really seemed to have bought into that mind-set.

Coming in to Dublin from Malahide, we could have taken a relatively quiet route that brought us in around the back of the stadium, but I always believe you should never try to protect a player too much, and that it is important to expose him to the reality of just how important the journey we are on together is.

The bus driver was instructed to bring us on the most crowded route down through Drumcondra, and past Quinn's pub where the place was absolutely thronged.

We had a Garda motorbike escort and one of the outriders was Rory Duffy, who I had taught in St Nathy's, so I felt this was a good omen. The Gardaí on those escorts definitely enjoy the experience as well and add to the sense of occasion with the skilled way they clear the traffic in front of them.

It really creates the sense of being men on a mission.

'Clear the way… we're coming through!'

It's almost a passage through the Red-Sea type of scenario. We had worked on visualisation techniques all year with Bill Cogan, and one of them was what this journey would be like so the players were well prepared for it. That experience was a really spine-tingling one for me, and I'm sure for the players too. The noise and energy from the Mayo fans when they realised it was the team bus coming through was absolutely electric.

It really drove home the fact that we were all on this big adventure together, and by the time we got to Croke Park we were fit to burst from our skins.

We were underdogs because our opponents Cork had been in the 1987 and '88 All-Ireland finals. But we had no fear of them. We had forensically examined their tactics and personnel, and we felt we matched up well against them in every respect.

Perhaps, in hindsight, we paid too much attention to their strengths and should have focused more on ourselves.

I had drummed into our players that we could not give frees away because Larry Tompkins was so deadly accurate. But our defenders became so obsessed about not conceding frees that it took the edge from the usual physicality they brought to their game and instead of really getting stuck into the Cork forwards, like they had the Tyrone forwards in the semi final, they stood half a yard off them and were much looser.

I would not blame them for that. The mistake was mine to put such an emphasis on not conceding frees to Cork.

Going into the game we felt we would be able to overpower them in the middle of the field, but we did not get the dominance there we hoped for. Liam McHale tried his heart out, but he just didn't hit the same heights he did in the semi final win over Tyrone. One miss from close range, after he had done brilliantly to power his way through the Cork defence, summed up his frustrating afternoon.

The loss of Jimmy Bourke to injury in the first half was another bad blow.

He was knocked unconscious after a collision with a Cork player and swallowed his tongue. Thankfully, our doc Frank Davey got to him quickly and managed to retrieve it. Jimmy was a big loss, because just before he was injured he was starting to get on the ball and conduct our whole forward line in that understated way of his.

Despite all that, it was still a match we could have and probably should have won. Larry Finnerty came on for Jimmy Bourke and scored a goal early in the second half that put us a point up.

We were starting to really dominate possession and come forward in wave after wave, however we kicked three bad wides at a time when a few more scores would really have given us tremendous momentum.

Finnerty had another goal chance 20 minutes into the half but his shot screamed past the post.

I would not blame Larry for the miss. It was a difficult chance, and he only deserves credit for the impact he made in the second half. At that moment Cork were teetering. They had lost the two previous All-Irelands and I could see self-doubt suddenly infect their play.

Even on the sideline I could sense a growing panic in their management team that gave me a lot of encouragement.

We had them on the cliff-edge, but we could not apply the final push. That was, and remains to this day, a massive regret. Ultimately, we just weren't clinical enough, and when they came back off the ropes they were able to take the sort point-scoring chances that we had missed.

Perhaps that Mayo team fell short because we just didn't have enough natural scorers. We rushed our shots. We lacked the composure in the vital moments of the match. That in no way lessens the pride I had in the team. They proved their mental strength by producing a big performance on the day. Unfortunately, it just was not quite enough.

When the final whistle blew it was hard to deal with because we all fully expected to win the match.

I was absolutely devastated.

We had worked so hard to change the whole culture and mental capacity of the county and it really felt like we were on a mission that would only end in success.

Our supporters were very gracious. The attitude was that we had done the county proud, and that 'you have to win one to lose one'. In my heart, I knew that was an easy statement to make on the night of an All-Ireland final.

I was thinking back to the massive effort we had made to bring the team so far, and I realised it would not be easy to get all the jigsaw pieces back into place the following year. My sense of foreboding only increased when we got back to Mayo and were greeted by an incredible homecoming as over 10,000 people welcomed us at Knock Airport.

It was an incredible sight to see people standing 10 deep at the fence surrounding the runway. But I knew this was a problem.

We were being feted, even though we had failed.

I was afraid the players would be lulled into believing they had scaled the mountain, when the reality was that we had come up short. Even though we had lost the All-Ireland, we were still expected to do a tour of the county. It was hard to say 'no'.

The supporters were showing such love and loyalty to the team.

My emotions were all over the place, and that only got worse when we came into Ballaghaderreen and I got the bus to drive past my home place in Magheraboy. I wanted to go past that little field where it all began for me and

I was hoping too that my mother would be outside and would see the bus go past. She had always been a hugely supportive influence behind the scenes, and I knew she would be proud of me.

She wasn't there when we went past on the bus. I drove back to the house myself the following day.

I ended up getting an awful shock, because that was the first time I noticed she was developing the early signs of dementia. She was asking me about the match but she was confused and the things she was saying weren't quite adding up. It was apparent that her memory was slipping, and that realisation was a really poignant and sad moment.

Unfortunately, her health diminished very quickly after that and she passed away the following year.

When someone you love, someone who has been unwavering support that you have taken for granted all your life is suddenly gone, it leaves an awful gulf.

My mother was a quiet woman who didn't even visit Dublin in her lifetime, but she was a real rock for me, for my brothers, and of course my father.

She was the woman who washed my togs. The woman who lit candles for me every time I was involved in a big match. It's virtually impossible to sum up the loss you feel when such a reassuring presence in your life is no longer there.

CHAPTER 12

There was an expectation within the county that we were simply going to continue building on the progress we had made in 1988 and '89, and deliver the All-Ireland title in 1990.

Our early league form before Christmas further fanned those flames of expectancy because we won our first three games against Tyrone, Monaghan and Roscommon.

The game against Roscommon drew the biggest crowd ever for a league game in Ballina. People were literally hanging from the rafters, and there was a carnival atmosphere in the ground when we beat them thanks to an injury time point.

That fact that it was kicked by a Ballaghaderreen man, Noel Durkin and was the only time we took the lead in the whole match only added to the satisfaction. The reality of the situation though was that we were still surfing the adrenalin of our All-Ireland appearance.

It eventually ran out when we suffered a surprise defeat to Antrim, and our season nose-dived fairly spectacularly from that point on.

We subsequently suffered two more defeats, against Meath and Louth, that ended our promotion hopes. The players looked mentally tired. The same will to succeed that had driven us forward the previous year was just not there.

They had been feted as heroes after the All-Ireland final and it was no surprise that some lads lost their focus a little.

They were being pulled left, right, and centre to open up shops, present medals, and do all sorts. I think one or two even dressed up as Santa Claus for a couple of events around Christmas time.

What the lads didn't realise was that the adoring public who wanted a piece of them that winter would be the first to criticise them after our early exit from the Connacht championship.

I hoped that a team holiday before the start of the championship would refresh us and act as the same sort of launch-pad that our weekend in Dublin the previous year had been. Instead, it was a total disaster.

We went to the Center Parcs holiday resort in the Midlands in England where I hoped the team would bond again by having a bit of craic together. There were water-sports activities, restaurants, and bars all under one roof, and the plan was that we would do everything as a team.

The trip was built around a match in England that the GAA had organised and which was meant to be something along the lines of the old annual Wembley tournament.

We played Cork in Brentford FC's ground. The match was even publicised on local TV and radio over there. It turned out to be a complete dead duck because they charged £15 for tickets which was a lot of money at the time, and only two or three thousand people turned up.

What was worse from my point of view was that the Mayo diaspora living in England were inviting our players here, there, and everywhere, so there was no sense of unity or purpose.

The previous year I had left The Burlington Hotel buzzing about our championship prospects. After our trip to England, I felt the complete opposite. A bad situation was made worse by injuries to key players, as Noel Durkin and TJ Kilgallon were both ruled out of the Connacht semi final against Galway. They were two massive losses.

Our heads just weren't right that day and we could have no complaints about our two-point defeat.

Reaching the '89 All-Ireland final had been a brilliant high, so getting knocked out of the championship in our very first match the following year was a terrible low.

The big lesson I took from it was that simply replicating what had worked in the past is never good enough. You have to be constantly evolving, and I had not freshened things up enough. Ahead of the 1991 campaign I knew I needed to bring in some new faces, and bolster the team in areas that it was weak.

Centre back was still our main problem position, so I decided to take what I knew would be a controversial approach to solve it.

The Galway centre back, Tomás Tierney was a teacher in Westport and I heard he had fallen out with the county management. Tierney was a player I had massive respect for, but he was not exactly the most popular man in Mayo.

Asking him to play for Mayo was always going to be a risky manoeuvre. However, I knew he would be a tremendous asset.

It helped too that senior players, TJ Kilgallon and Peter Forde had played Sigerson football with Tierney in UCG. They were friends with him off the pitch, and had huge respect for his ability on it.

I didn't want to be seen poaching a player from Galway. So when I made contact with Tierney, I told him we'd love to have him but only if there was no avenue for him to return to the Galway panel. I told him that if he agreed to play for Mayo he would come straight in as our first-choice centre back, so he knew from the very start that I appreciated his ability.

He agreed to join us, and I knew that his commitment to the cause was a full one because that was the sort of character he was. Tierney was the sort of guy you'd want beside you if you were going to war. He was tough, ruthless, and always gave it one hundred per cent. He really was the piece we had been missing for the previous three years.

I knew getting him on board was a massive coup for us. I have no doubt either we'd have won the All-Ireland final if we had him at No.6 against Cork.

We were also strengthened by the emergence of Colm McManamon, Paul McStay and Tony Morley. Colm had been playing in the Australian Football League with Geelong but returned home following the death of his father.

We made huge efforts to keep him and thankfully they paid off. Colm was a huge addition. He was six-foot plus, strongly built, and was a brilliant ball-carrier because he had an engine that would go all day.

Meanwhile, McStay and Morley were two talented forwards who together gave us a keener cutting edge in attack than we had previously. As we prepared for the 1991 campaign I got the feeling that we were back on track and building for something exciting again.

Everyone realised we had screwed up in 1990 and there was a real determination in the group to make amends and set out on another big adventure.

We hammered London in the first round, and next up was Galway in the Connacht semi final. There was a lot of tension surrounding the game because Tierney was now playing for us, and the man who had cut him loose from Galway, John Tobin, was their manager.

We beat them easily.

Tierney was superb.

We went into the Connacht final against Roscommon full of confidence and looked like edging a ferociously fought contest when Liam McHale put us a point up in injury time.

But then, the referee Pat Egan awarded a free to Roscommon that was in no way a foul at all in my opinion, and from around 60 yards out a 19 year old Derek Duggan pinged the ball over the bar for a dramatic equaliser.

We lost the replay by a point. It was a devastating defeat because we had done huge work to rebuild the team. Seven players were playing their first Connacht final, and if we had won it then I'm convinced that team would've gone from strength to strength. The self-belief would've soared.

After the game I went down to the Abbey Hotel and I immediately sensed that the mood of the County Board executive officers had swung again me.

It was more what they were not saying than what they were saying, and at that point the writing was on the wall. I wanted to stay on for a fifth year, but I felt the only way to do the job properly was on my terms, which meant having the power to pick my own selectors.

My backroom team had done a great job for the previous four years, but I felt it was time to change the dynamic slightly. When I made this known to the County Board executive, I was bluntly told me that I could not pick my own men.

I went to the next County Board meeting and stood up from the floor and read out a short letter explaining that my request had been refused and that I viewed this as constructive dismissal.

It was clear I didn't have the support or confidence of the County Board executive. I felt I had no option other than to step down.

If there was any bad will towards me, and I felt there was, then the team didn't need to be carrying that on its back as well. The problem with Mayo is that it is an insecure county and the mood, far too often, is very much influenced by the last few results.

Even though I felt I had done a good job in 1991, bringing through a lot of new players, and bedding in a new team, there was little recognition of that. It was extremely hurtful because it was so public and I had put so much into the thing only for it to end badly.

Afterwards, a number of clubs came to me and said they wanted to nominate me again when the County Board started the search for a new manager.

I was happy enough for my name to go forward, but the County Board didn't even interview me which clearly underlined my gut feeling that they no longer had any confidence in me was the correct one.

What stung the most was that, even before that County Board meeting where I had read out that letter, I heard they had already made an approach to Brian McDonald about the position. Mayo is a great county for rumour and I have no definite evidence that they spoke to McDonald while I was still technically manager, but the fact that he was subsequently appointed suggests it did happen.

The whole experience made me realise that county management is a ruthless business.

No matter how much success you have, you can nearly be always guaranteed that it will end in tears. I reflect on those four years in charge of

Mayo between '88 and '91 with a mixture of satisfaction and regret. We won consecutive Connacht titles for the first time in 38 years, and I was proud of the way we had successfully changed the culture of underachievement that had held Mayo back. But, our inability to deliver the Holy Grail of an All-Ireland senior championship was obviously a huge source of regret, and still is to this day.

I often think that had I taken charge a year earlier and had the chance to work with the older players in the panel for a longer period of time then, by 1989, we would have been the best team in the country.

After '89 those older players were on the wane. It was always going to be difficult to climb the mountain again.

CHAPTER 13

The phone call from Leitrim came right out of the blue.

It was July 1992, and I had just picked up *The Irish Press* newspaper in my local shop. As usual, I went straight for the sports pages and one of the first headlines I read was 'Eugene McGee in line for Leitrim Job'.

PJ Carroll had just stepped down after four years that saw the team raise their standards, but keep coming up short against their neighbours, Roscommon. I had just finished reading that article when our house phone rang. It was Tony McGowan, the Leitrim County Board chairman. He asked me would I consider putting my name forward to be the county's next manager?

I told him I had just read that McGee was their man. Tony replied that Eugene's was one of the names in the hat, along with Peter McGinnity from Fermanagh.

Managing a county other than Mayo had never really entered my head up until then. I just told Tony to go through whatever processes they were going to go through, and then come back and talk to me if they were still stuck.

I didn't want to say… 'Jaysus, yeah… I'll meet ye straight away'.

But, over the next couple of days, I actually thought about the prospect of managing Leitrim. The more I thought about it, the more I was attracted to it. I had discovered that management at the highest level was the next best thing to playing at the highest level.

I had won an All-Ireland under-21 title, two Connacht under-21 titles, and two senior Connacht titles and, by now, I had definitely caught the management bug, big time. Tony had told me straight out that he thought I was a good candidate for the job because I had won those two Connacht titles with Mayo.

Leitrim had claimed their one and only provincial title in 1927, so winning the Connacht championship was their Promised Land.

Tony was a supremely positive man and he saw no reason why Leitrim could not do it. They had won an All-Ireland 'B' title and a Connacht under-21 title during Carroll's time in charge, and he was convinced they had the necessary talent.

I felt it was a realistic target for them too. Even though Roscommon had consistently gotten the better of them, it was usually because Leitrim made a hero out of their goalkeeper, Gay Sheerin.

A few days later Tony rang me back and told me the job was mine, if I wanted it? I'm sure that if Eugene McGee had said 'yes' they'd have given it to him because of the heroic All-Ireland he had won with Offaly. But he was so busy with his newspaper work and he could not commit the time.

I agreed to meet them for a talk, but did not want word getting out in either Mayo or Leitrim about it. We settled on the Forest Park Hotel in Boyle for our sit-down.

I had lunch with Tony, County Board secretary Tommy Moran, and vice-chairman Eamon Tubman. What I wanted to find out was whether they were really passionate about getting me on board?

They made it clear that they were. After that, the next thing to do was to meet up with some of the senior players in the panel and gauge their mood. Once again, the Forest Park Hotel was the venue, and this time I sat down with Declan Darcy, Mickey Quinn and Shane Heslin.

They were hugely positive too, and made it very clear they were deadly serious about winning a Connacht championship. It was impossible not to be sucked in by their enthusiasm. Despite my best plans to keep these talks quiet, word inevitably got out.

That summer I had been coaching the Michael Glavey's club team in Roscommon, and one of their players spotted me in the hotel and also recognised the Leitrim lads.

It wasn't long before I got a call from another one of the Glavey's players wishing me well and hoping I'd get the job.

Now, it wasn't exactly Alex Ferguson sitting down with Real Madrid, but with the GAA grapevine being the wonderful thing it is, I should have known I wouldn't be able to keep it all under wraps. Anyhow, by then I had decided that I wanted the job, but before shaking hands on it I wanted also to suss out the lie of the land in Leitrim.

I got a list of all the players in the county who were in the frame for the senior panel, and a list of the venues where they trained. I drove around and inspected every single place. I knew there was a lot to be done, but the enthusiasm of everyone I spoke to convinced me that this could be a good fit.

My big worry was how it would be perceived in Mayo if I went outside the county to manage a provincial rival? At the end of the day, I didn't want to be seen as being in any way disloyal to Mayo.

I valued Seamie Daly's opinion higher than anyone else's, so I visited him in Mulranny and asked him what he thought?

He asked all the obvious questions. When I assured him I was really up for it, he told me I would be stupid not to take the opportunity if I was not wanted for management in Mayo. He figured it would re-energise me. Once I got his blessing I knew I was making the right call.

I gave the Leitrim County Board my final decision.

The one thing I was always going to insist on was the power to pick my own selectors, something that had been denied me in Mayo, and the Leitrim County Board were quite happy to give me that backing.

I wanted two people who knew Leitrim upside down and inside out, and settled on Joe Reynolds and Ollie Honeyman.

Joe was a former county player who won a Connacht under-21 title with Leitrim in 1977 and was still playing junior football and very much involved with his club. Ollie had been a member of the panel for the championship that year in 1992 and hadn't contemplated retirement, but I still wanted him to be part of the management team. He told me that he did not want to hang up his boots just yet.

I told him he could combine playing with the duties of being a selector. The way I figured it, with Ollie still part of the playing group I'd have the inside line on what the mood in the dressing room was at all times.

There was never going to be any favouritism, and I admired the way there was no conflict or tension when he was unable to force his way into the starting team for the championship. Ollie continued to train as hard as any of the other lads and also made a really valuable contribution to the management team.

Joe was first class too, and it quickly became apparent I had chosen very well. They were both absolutely loyal to the cause, and had an in-depth knowledge of every player in Leitrim. Joe and Ollie were my right hand men. But I was also keen to set up a wider management group.

I wanted to avoid the pitfalls that had opened up beneath me at Mayo when my relationship with the County Board developed a 'them and us' dynamic. I wanted to bring everyone along with me and have them all know what was happening rather than feel like they were in any way excluded or disenfranchised.

We set up a wider management group made up of myself, Ollie, and Joe; the County Board chairman, secretary, vice-chairman, and treasurer; the team doctor; and Declan Darcy's father, Frank who helped train our Dublin-based players.

I also brought Bill Cogan on board again, and before every meeting he would draw up an agenda.

He was the chief facilitator, but we passed around the chairmanship of the group to different people on a regular basis so everyone knew this was a democracy. The only thing not up for discussion was team selection. That buck stopped with me, Ollie and Joe.

The wider management group looked after everything else to do with our preparation; weekends away, training and playing venues, nutrition and expenses for the players.

I explained to everyone that if we were to break down the barriers that had prevented Leitrim from attaining success in the past then we needed to work together to eliminate all of those obstacles. Everyone involved in that wider management group had very defined roles that best suited their particular skill-set.

They were all asked to write down how they felt they could best contribute, and then they were given tasks that fell within the parameters of their personal skill-sets. At regular intervals we would also ask them to write down what they felt they could contribute, but weren't currently doing.

So, if someone felt they could help in any area, I was immediately made aware of it. Trusting them to do that job further strengthened the bond we had with one another.

I knew the only way Leitrim could catch up on the more traditionally successful counties was to do everything better than their neighbours, so that is what I set out to do. Setting up that wider management group proved really beneficial, because it brought everyone along together and really unified us under a common cause.

There were plenty of differences of opinions, but because the way in which they were aired was so structured we were always able to quickly find a way to solve any problems.

I insisted on having a County Board officer at every training session. If there was ever any sort of logistical crisis that needed to be sorted, someone was there to do that.

The other thing I set in stone was which County Board officers could travel on the team bus, and who could be in the dressing room on match days.

I did not want a scenario where, if we started becoming successful, every County Board officer would suddenly be piling onto the bus and the players would be wondering where the hell they were all coming from?

So, at the start of the year, the officers who would travel with us were named, and thereafter they had to travel with us to every single match we played, not just the big ones.

That way there were no unusual comings or goings, and we established a pattern that everyone was comfortable with. I wanted us to make a strong statement about our pride in being the Leitrim county football team.

Our team bus carried a big logo in the front window that read 'Leitrim '93'. There were Leitrim flags on the mirrors.

We were perceived as the poor relations in the province but we wanted to show we were proud of who we were, and that we would not be bowing down meekly to anyone in future. We wanted to send out a statement about our ambition and professionalism in every way possible, and on match days the players dressed in uniform rather than their usual civvies.

When we started off, that just constituted t-shirts with the Leitrim colours and crests, but as the year went on the players got more and more gear. The message being sent out was that the players were being rewarded for achievement. And, as anyone who has ever played for or coached a team knows, there's nothing players love more than new gear.

Early on in the year, when we played a challenge match against Tyrone, the players arrived in cars and a couple of different mini buses that belched black smoke out of the exhausts.

The whole thing just needed a big lift.

Therefore, for championship matches I insisted on a team coach. A new one, registered that year if possible, not a banger.

If we were staying in a hotel I insisted on the County Board booking us a good one. If you want players to be winners, you need to treat them like *winners*.

'Stay five star… Play five star.'

That was my motto.

I wanted our players to have the best of everything, but I also wanted them to give me and their county their absolute best.

Anyone who was not going to buy in totally to what we were trying to do was surplus to requirements. Initially, I had planned to have 30 players on my panel, but when there were a couple of early breaches of discipline those players were cut and I made do with a relatively small panel of just 26.

Although it was a hard decision to make, because I was already working with the smallest pick of players in the country, I knew I could not afford to have any bad apples in the group. By getting rid of them I was sending out a message, loud and clear to the rest, that only those who were fully committed to the cause were going to be on board for this journey.

George Dugdale was one man I definitely wanted involved. He had not played in the 1992 championship because he had just married and had taken up a teaching job in Cavan. There were rumours that he was going to declare for Cavan.

I knew he was the sort of quality operator we could not do without so I made it my mission to persuade him to make the commitment. This was an era before mobile phones though, and his new home in Cavan did not have a house phone yet. The only means of contact I had for him was his address.

I wrote him a letter telling him we needed him and that I wanted to sit down with him as soon as possible. A couple of weeks later I still hadn't received a reply. I decided to drive to Cavan to track him down. Eventually, I found the flat he was living in and within a couple of minutes I knew my journey had been worthwhile. He actually had the letter still on his kitchen table and immediately apologised for not getting back in touch with me.

George was a very self-motivated guy who was a fitness fanatic and when I explained to him how seriously we were going to be taking the thing his enthusiasm was obvious.

In order to further strengthen the panel we started to look outside the county for players who could improve us.

A rule had come in at that time that allowed weaker counties like Leitrim to recruit players from stronger counties, if their parents were born in Leitrim. So we put up notices in every clubhouse in Dublin advising players they were eligible to play for us if either of their parents were from Leitrim.

In this way we recruited Jason Ward for the 1993 campaign. Ciaran McGovern came on board in 1995, and a number of underage players were also unearthed by that recruitment drive.

Our panel was small, but we had a lot of quality players. Younger lads like Declan Darcy and Colin McGlynn had won a Connacht under-21 medal in 1991 and there were some quality older players there too like Mickey Quinn, Paul Kieran, Liam Conlon, Padraig Kenny, Pat Donohue and Joe Honeyman.

The raw ingredients were there. It was up to me to get the blend right, to make them good enough to win a Connacht championship.

CHAPTER 14

When you talk *big* you have to back it up with your actions. From the very start, I put a big emphasis on our league performances. Other counties could possibly use the league primarily to build up fitness and try different players without worrying too much about the result, but not Leitrim.

My mission was to create a culture of high standards and achievement. Every single league match was specifically targeted as an important game to win. Before every game we set targets of what we hoped to score and concede in the match, so that afterwards it was very obvious whether we had achieved our goals or not.

Even during the league, every team we played was scouted extensively.

The man who helped me most in this regarded was Brendan Harvey, a Leitrim native who was living in Dublin. He never got to see Leitrim play in the league because, instead, he was always watching whatever team we were due to play the following weekend.

He would compile an extensive report on their performance with the strengths and weaknesses listed of all their players, and what they did and didn't do in the previous game.

When we presented all this information to our own players it was another indicator for them that we were taking this thing very seriously and raising the bar. Brendan's espionage would become more and more detailed as time went on, and even occasionally underhand. Getting his hands on recent videos of our next opposition became one of his specialities.

I won't name the counties in question, but he would contact the County Board secretary pretending to be a supporter and spin a yarn about an Uncle in Australia who would love to get his hands on a video or two of the county team in action.

He may have even gone so far as to suggest this 'Uncle' was in poor health, and that this was one of his dying wishes. There was all sorts of stuff going on, and the more invasive and underhand it was, the bigger kick myself and Brendan get out of it.

It was all done in good humour, though. It's not like we were getting our hands on any national secrets; it just meant we could prepare better.

Brendan would even go to watch opposition teams train and provide me with a detailed report on what players were being tried in what positions. Because he would not have been known that well outside of the county, he was usually an anonymous face who I'm sure our opponents simply presumed was a keen supporter of their own county.

During my time with Leitrim we played in Division Two of the league and came up against quality teams like Cork, Down and Tyrone.

Down won All-Irelands in 1991 and '94, but we managed to beat them in the league and also drew a great match against Cork in Carrick-on-Shannon. We were always very, very competitive. Because we were putting it up to these big teams, our players were really starting to believe we now had no reason to fear anybody. Just like I had in Mayo, we kick-started out championship preparations in 1993 with a team weekend away.

We had a match on the Friday evening and then Saturday was dedicated to meetings where we asked one another what it was going to take for us to be successful? What obstacles needed to be removed from our path?

The players, management, and County Board officers were all mixed together and then divided into groups.

Those groups all had brainstorming sessions where absolutely everything was confronted, from delayed expenses, to the type, intensity, and punctuality of training we were doing.

Then each group nominated someone to come forward and speak in front of the collective about what issues they had identified. On the back of that, there was further debate and discussion. It really broke down barriers between players, management and County Board officers.

That night, the players were rewarded for the hugely positive contribution by being allowed to let their hair down. We were all in the same room together having a few drinks and the craic was mighty. At one stage the players held a mock County Board meeting where our wing back, Gerry Flanagan was the star of the show.

Gerry's disciplinary record was notoriously poor and the joke was that he had plenty of experience of going before a committee to explain himself.

One of the most famous convictions on his lengthy rap-sheet was the day he decked John Maughan with a box in the 1997 Connacht championship. Maughan was Mayo manager and ran onto the pitch in those famous shorts of his when a melee broke out.

I'd say Gerry could hardly believe his luck when he saw those tanned legs coming in his direction.

Gerry was called up before the disciplinary committee, and the Leitrim County Board secretary, Tommy Moran made sure he had him well coached before he sent him into it. Tommy told him to go in and immediately apologise. But to say he only shoved Maughan, rather than punched him, so that the seriousness of the offence would be downplayed.

Good plan.

However, when Gerry was asked by one the committee members whether he had hit Maughan hard, he could not stop himself grinning.

'Well… I was happy enough!'

Despite being tutored to the last, Gerry still could not help but take pride in the clean connection he had made with John Maughan's jaw. He ended up getting the maximum suspension going.

When we had our mock disciplinary board meeting that night with the

Leitrim team, we decided to turn the tables and put Gerry on the right side of the law for a change.

He was given the role of County Board chairman, and our actual County Board chairman, Tony McGowan, was the sinning player up before him. It was the ultimate role-reversal. Gerry brought the house down because he was such a natural comedian. Needless to say, Tony ended up with a lengthy suspension for all manner of crimes.

As important as the meetings we had held earlier in the day were, there is no doubt that the more old-fashioned bonding exercise of having a few pints together is still one of the best ways to bring a group of men together.

That night, however, one of the lads ended up having a couple of pints too many and there was a bit of damage done to one of the rooms.

We had a team meeting the following morning where the incident was brought up. I asked the players how they were going to deal with it? Off their own bat, the players collected a few bob from everyone on the panel. It was sorted.

I remember coming home that day saying to myself that these guys were starting to think in a different way.

Throughout the league our panel was effectively split in two with the Dublin-based players trained by Frank Darcy in Dublin, and the rest of the lads training with me in Leitrim. But, as the championship approached, the whole group also trained collectively together in Kells, in Meath.

It was roughly halfway between Dublin and Leitrim, and the secretary of the club, Patrick Lynch was very helpful, so it was a good base.

In one way it is not ideal to have to train outside your own county, but because meeting in Kells required another big commitment from all of our players it just seemed to bond us together even more.

Our morale was high coming into the 1993 championship, and my next task was to put the best team I possibly could out on the field.

That did not simply mean just putting our best players in their best positions. I knew if we were to beat Galway we had to come up with a formation and tactics that neutralised their strengths, while also maximising ours as much as possible.

Mickey Quinn was Leitrim's most high-profile player at the time, the county's only ever Allstar and a renowned midfielder. But I decided to reinvent him as a full back which was seen as a questionable enough call at the time.

The priority for me was to bed down a strong spine to the team, and there was no outstanding candidate for the full back position. Seamus Quinn had emerged as a really talented 18 year old corner back, but I felt he was still a bit too raw to be entrusted with the No.3 jersey.

I had two other fine midfielders in the shape of Pat Donohue and Jason Ward, and I believed we could cope with no longer having Mickey in the engine room. And with Declan Darcy at centre back, George Dugdale at centre forward, and Colin McGlynn at full forward, we now had a really strong spine to the team.

Coming into that Galway match we had gone through the A, B, and C of literally every scenario that could happen.

The strengths and weaknesses of all of their players were minutely dissected and plans were put in place for neutralising key men like Tomás Mannion, Gary Fahey and Ja Fallon.

Liam Conlon scored a goal for us after three minutes and we then missed a penalty not long afterwards. Neither event raised or lowered the team's blood-pressure because both were scenarios we had discussed before the match. After 20 minutes it was clear from the body language of our players that they were gaining self-belief. Our game plan was frustrating Galway.

We were winning key battles all over the pitch, and the decision to put Mickey Quinn at full back was looking like a sound one because he was neutralising the threat of Kevin Walsh.

Galway came with a strong surge either side of half time that propelled them into a four point lead, but again, this was a scenario that we had discussed exhaustively before the match. I had put it to the players that too often in the past Leitrim teams had folded in this very situation.

It was as if they were happy to have put up a good fight for as long as they had, but were now going to once again meekly accept their status in the pecking order of Gaelic football?

They always had the obvious argument of having far less resources than a county like Galway, so it was no shame to be beaten by them. But, this time we had all promised ourselves that we would not fall back on such a weak-minded excuse.

That day Leitrim refused to be beaten.

To see them play with such a raw mental strength was an amazing experience because we had all put so much effort into creating that mind-set.

Another scenario that we had run through before the game was the likelihood that the game was going to be a very tight one and would probably come down to one of our players winning a ball that simply had to be won.

In that situation you need a leader to step forward, and we had one in Pat Donohue.

A Ja Fallon free had just tied the game for Galway with time almost up, but from the resulting kick out Donohue won the high ball and played a great pass to Aidan Rooney who kicked the winner.

For Leitrim fans it was an unfamiliar sight to see their team have the self-belief to beat Galway with a last minute winner.

As I said to the players afterwards, we simply executed what we had previously planned. That was not being arrogant, but you nearly had to convince them to become arrogant in order to get to where you wanted to go.

Changing the traditional Leitrim mind-set was always going to be my biggest job, and it was a challenge that really excited me.

Here you had the weakest team in the country in terms of playing resources, and one that had not won a serious piece of silverware since 1927. At that time most people in the county seemed to be satisfied by moral victories. Running a big team close was seen as an achievement, rather than a failure.

When that has been the pervasive culture in a county for a long time it is not an easy job to get the players to alter their own mind-set and really believe they are capable of much better.

As an exercise in getting the players to start thinking differently earlier in the year I had cut out a load of newspaper headlines from previous years that heralded Leitrim defeats in the championship.

ANOTHER DARK DAY FOR LEITRIM
TAME EXIT FOR LEITRIM
These were the standard judgments.

I found a big wooden board somewhere that had an advertisement for Jacobs on one side and was clear on the other. I photocopied and enlarged all of those depressing headlines and sellotaped them on the clear side of the board which was about half the size of a door. There were no power-point presentations in those days.

I asked the players what headlines they would like to create for themselves and they came up with many.

GREAT HOPE FOR LEITRIM'S FUTURE
That was one of the positive ones.

I just shook my head.

'Lads… ye're still not fucking winning!'

Getting them to actually have the self-confidence to write something really positive took some time.

After we beat Galway I cut out all the headlines from the national newspapers and stuck them up on the board.

The biggest of the lot stood out. It was simply worded.

MIRACLE MEN
Another clipping proclaimed that Leitrim were now ready to follow in the footsteps of the Clare and Donegal teams of 1992, and the Derry team of 1993, and join the aristocracy of football.

The theme in almost all the same newspapers before the match was that we were lambs to the slaughter. But now here we were reborn… as lions. The headlines that our players had thought of writing were insignificant to the ones that they actually got to read.

I really hammered home the point that they had ripped up the old script and written a new one for the county of Leitrim.

It was the first time Leitrim had beaten Galway in Tuam since 1949, and I only really appreciated the significance of the achievement the following day when I saw it was front page news in the national newspapers.

I had failed to win there as Mayo manager. I had to put up with all of that annoying talk about the 'Tuam Jinx'. So it was hugely satisfying to go there as Leitrim manager and lay that ghost to rest.

It was no happy accident either. The only reason we had come out on the right side of a one-point game was because we had made such a monumental effort and had ticked every single box possible. Perhaps the reason we did not then beat Roscommon in the Connacht semi final was because the players did not realise that a county like Leitrim has to tick all those boxes, every single time they played.

Just because we had done it once did not mean we could coast along and keep reproducing it without making the same manic effort.

Maybe beating Roscommon was another, higher, mental hurdle that we were not quite ready to leap just yet.

Roscommon had beaten Leitrim for the three previous championships in-a-row, so it is possible there was some sort of mental block there that we had not yet managed to totally flush out. It was still a match that we could have won, but the turning point was the moment that Gerry Flanagan was sent off for an off-the-ball altercation with Don Connellan after 53 minutes.

There were no yellow cards in those days and I was not aware at the time that Gerry was given his marching orders, because it happened on the far side of the pitch and the sun was in my eyes.

The next thing I saw Gerry walking up around the goals and then down the sideline towards me.

'Where are you going?' I asked him.

Gerry told me what had happened. I used the choicest language I could to express my displeasure. We were always going to need everyone on the field and Gerry was a massive loss. We only lost by two points despite playing with 14 men for 20 minutes, so maybe we could have won it had we our full complement.

It was a sickening way to end the year after the high of beating Galway in Tuam. But despite the defeat we had proven that this Leitrim team was now a force to be respected.

I could hardly wait for 1994 to come around because I was now more convinced than ever that, together, we could finally deliver the county's long awaited Holy Grail of a Connacht title.

CHAPTER 15

Whenever you come up short you have to identify why you did, and then take steps to make sure it does not happen again.

After the defeat to Roscommon the first thing that needed to be addressed was Gerry Flanagan's sending-off. If Leitrim were to ever win a Connacht title they needed to keep 15 men on the pitch for the duration of the match. We could simply not afford that sort of indiscipline.

Gerry was a mighty Leitrim man and the sort of lad you'd want in your corner in a fight, but his fiery personality had consistently gotten him into trouble on the pitch. He was vital to our plans.

Now, I had to convince him that we needed him on the pitch and not getting into trouble for doing silly stuff. We worked on that a lot over the winter, and in fairness to Gerry, there was a marked improvement in his disciplinary record. He was devastated that he had let the team down, especially because he had done it against Roscommon.

There is a seriously hot rivalry between the two counties, and Gerry was such a proud Leitrim man that he embraced it more than most.

Losing to Roscommon for four years in-a-row in the Connacht championship was a bitter pill to swallow for every Leitrim person.

When I saw the fixtures for the 1993-94 National Football League campaign I immediately circled our match against Roscommon because I knew we simply had to win it. We needed to stop the rot.

When it came around the match assumed even more importance because it was the final game of the league, and if Roscommon lost they would be relegated. We beat them easily enough on the day by five points. It was a seriously sweet victory for all Leitrim fans.

Not only had we struck an important psychological blow against one of our provincial rivals before the championship, we had also managed to relegate them. The night of the match a lot of the players stayed on in Carrick-on-Shannon for a few pints after the game.

They were in a pub playing darts, and there were still a few Roscommon supporters in the place.

Gerry Flanagan would've taken more satisfaction than most from beating their noisy neighbours, and he made sure to apply as much salt to their wounds as he could. When a Roscommon supporter took his turn at the darts, Gerry drew a big map of Ireland on the chalkboard and highlighted where Kilkenny and Waterford were so the Roscommon fella would know how to get there for their Division Three league matches the following year.

That win would've meant very little though if we could not back it up with another one against Roscommon in the Connacht quarter final.

As team manager, I had a duty to make sure we solved the problems that were exposed by the defeat the previous year.

The issue of Gerry Flanagan's discipline had been addressed, but there were areas where we could make gains.

I had gambled by playing Mickey Quinn out of position at full back in 1993. It had worked well in the win over Galway, not so well against Roscommon. He had a hard time of it against their full forward Lorcan O'Dowd, and we also struggled in the middle of the field where John Newton gave a typically powerful performance for Roscommon.

The obvious thing to do was to release Mickey Quinn back out to the middle third, and that decision was made even easier by the fact that Seamus Quinn was blossoming into such a fine footballer. When I met Seamus first he was a young 18 year old and very shy, but his talent was obvious. He was one of the most naturally athletic footballers I ever worked with, and he just lived for the game.

Before every match he'd present himself and ask… 'what do I do here?' He was a sponge who just soaked up tactics and was always endeavouring to improve himself.

The development of Seamus into a first rate full back gave me the opportunity to develop a new system of play because, with Mickey Quinn released from the full back line, I now had an embarrassment of riches in the midfield sector. As well as Mickey, I had Pat Donohue, Jason Ward and Paul Kieran, who were all natural midfielders.

In that era, it was very rare for a team to deviate from the traditional formation of two midfielders, three half forwards, and three full forwards.

But we decided to change the dynamic slightly because we did not have any one marquee forward who was guaranteed to score heavily every day from all sorts of angles and distances. That meant in order for us to build a winning score we would likely have to dominate possession to create plenty of chances, and as many of them as close to goal as possible.

So, we ended up playing one of our natural midfielders as a wing forward who would drop deep as a third midfielder to help us get a grip on the middle third. That required one of our full forwards, usually Aiden Rooney, to drop out to the half forward line.

As well as being a very accurate free taker from close-range, Aiden was also a deep thinker on the game, so he was tactically flexible and knew what I wanted from him in that role. That left Colin McGlynn and Liam Conlon inside as our target men, and basically everything we were doing was designed to get the ball to them as close to goal as possible.

Colin was a powerfully built full forward who, the bigger the day got, the better he got. He was an interesting character and would not have been at all weighed down by Leitrim's history of low achievement.

People often mistook his laid-back demeanour as meaning that he did not care enough about playing for Leitrim. But I knew that he cared deeply.

We once played Derry in a challenge match to open a pitch in Drumkeeran in 1994 and the local band were sitting on the sideline after piping the two teams around the pitch before the throw-in.

One of the lads in the band started abusing McGlynn because he thought he wasn't trying hard enough, so I absolutely went down this fella's throat and quietened him.

McGlynn's body language could make you believe that he didn't give a shite, but it is a mark of the man that he always delivered on the big day for us. He was different, but he was a hugely important member of the team.

Liam was another powerful and direct footballer. He could win the ball in the air, had a bit of pace, and was one of those forwards who would both score and miss goals. He always had a knack for getting himself into the right positions, but occasionally his finishing would let him down.

George Dugdale would usually chip in with a couple of points most days, but his main role was as a ball winner and carrier who would break tackles and create space for others. Padraig Kenny was not an out and out score-getter either, though he was a very intelligent player who would create opportunities for others with his clever movement and vision. He was a natural leader too. When you needed someone with the character to get on the ball in a difficult phase in the game and make something happen, Padraig would usually deliver.

Basically, in order for us to build a winning score, we had to work our backsides off, kick our frees, and have everyone chip in, in some way or another.

We were not a high scoring team, and winning was not an easy business for us, but because of our work ethic and attitude we usually found a way to grind out a victory.

Developing that reputation did us a lot of good. And now the top teams wanted to play us in challenge matches because they knew we always turned up to play. That meant that coming into the 1994 championship we were able to regularly play sides like Derry and Meath in training games which definitely helped us raise our own levels.

In terms of our preparation for the championship we really threw the kitchen sink at the thing and I knew the Connacht title would be delivered in 1994, or it would never happen.

The players must have been confident too.

I later found out that after our pre-championship weekend away in

Castleblayney they all put a few quid into a pot, went down to the local bookies, and laid a generous wedge on us winning the Connacht title at odds of 16-1.

I was feeling confident too because I knew we had prepared as well as we possibly could and had a good insight into what shape Roscommon were in thanks to some typically good sleuthing by my number one espionage agent, Brendan Harvey.

He had watched a number of their training sessions in Hyde Park, and because he was so anonymous he even got away with having a chat with their goalkeeper Brian Morkin while he stood in goal, casually pumping him for information.

We knew exactly how they would set up, what players were in good form, and what players were struggling slightly.

I would say that on balance we were a way better team than Roscommon, but I knew it would probably be a struggle because of the recent history between the two teams.

That struggle did not materialise in the first half as we roared into 1-8 to 0-5 lead. But if our first half was sublime, much of what we did in the second half was ridiculously poor by comparison. We didn't score a single point from play.

And when Roscommon equalised with 12 minutes to go they looked the much more likely victors.

It was then that Declan Darcy produced one of those moments of heroism that would become his trademark when he boomed over a 50 yard free to edge us ahead again.

It was no surprise really that Declan would show leadership at a crucial moment because that was something he always did. As our team captain he was a very important voice in the dressing room and commanded everyone's respect even though he was still in his early twenties.

From a management point of view he was a very positive guy to have around because he very much bought into the mental approach that we were taking to the thing.

He really enjoyed the visualisation techniques that Bill Cogan worked hard on with all the players. Because our captain did, then other players were more likely to follow his lead. We were always telling the guys that Leitrim getting beaten in Connacht for the previous 66 years had nothing whatsoever to do with them.

They would only wear the jersey themselves for a handful of years. Those few years *only* were their responsibility. It was up to them to make their own history, rather than being burdened by the past.

Declan was the embodiment of that ethos because he was the sort of guy who was always trying to make his own history in the way he played the game. He was not reactive; he was proactive.

He was an attacking centre back, who was positive in everything he did. And, even though he was not a 'stopper' of a centre back in the traditional sense, he always worked hard on the defensive side of his game.

The importance of self-improvement was something that we really hammered home as a management team, and Declan was the embodiment of someone who always strove for that. It was no surprise that he had the bottle to kick a late winner like that, because this was as scenario that we had played out in our visualisation sessions with Bill Cogan.

The players had worked through every eventuality, including what you do if you lose a big lead in the second-half?

So that, when it happened like it did against Roscommon, it was no major shock to the system. The players had spoken through this scenario as a group previously, and the attitude was that we simply needed to create one more chance and win the game.

In previous years they might have become overcome with a 'here we go again' type of pessimism, but I had worked hard to weed out all that sort of negativity. I had even gone so far as to arrange a seating plan for our dug-out, so that anyone who was known to be prone to any degree of negativity was seated beside someone who was naturally more positive.

If someone said something negative, he was immediately geed up by the person beside him. Or given a rap across the knuckles if necessary. We had guys specifically tutored to do that job.

I always felt the atmosphere in a dug-out was important, because there's always a good chance you're going to need one of your substitutes to win you the match in the closing minutes.

And, if he has been listening to negative comments for much of the match, then he is going to run out onto the field in a negative frame of mind and is much less likely to make that match-winning play for you. Whereas, if the atmosphere in the dug-out is one of 'we are going to win this game no matter what', then the same man will burst out onto the pitch and really want to be the guy who does win it for us.

I knew the players had bought into that ethos. So even though we suffered a mini-collapse in that second half against Roscommon, I never doubted they would find a way to win the match.

Of course, there are times no matter how well you prepare that you sometimes feel like the universe is out to get you.

When Roscommon got a late chance to equalise the game, when Derek Duggan lined up a long distance free, I confess I let a little negative thought enter my own head.

Duggan had broken my heart in 1991 from a very similar distance and it was hard not to dread he was going to do it again. But, thankfully, his kick went wide and we just about escaped with a one point win.

That was the cue for some wild celebration from the Leitrim supporters who had suffered so much at the hands of their neighbours for the previous four years. But, within the camp, we were not getting carried away. The previous year we had pulled off a great win over Galway only to then be knocked out in the Connacht semi final.

The attitude that we took into the 1994 Connacht championship was that we had to win three Connacht finals by beating Roscommon, Galway and Mayo.

It was the toughest draw possible, but, again, I had done my best to spin it into a positive. I said to the players that it was the ideal situation because this was the best championship possible to win. We would scalp all of the major powers in the province, so nobody would ever be able to say we had ended our long wait for a provincial title by winning a handy one.

After beating Roscommon, I knew Galway would be a tough nut to crack in the semi final because this time they would see us coming. At the same time, it encouraged me to see their forward Niall Finnegan say something like… 'oh no, not Leitrim again', when the draw was made on television.

Once upon a time we had been viewed as cannonfodder. Now teams knew we were coming fully armed.

The game turned out to be a dour draw, but once again the character of the team shone through. In an inch-tight contest, it was an intervention by our substitute, Padraig McLoughlin that enabled us to just about come up to Galway's measure.

Padraig was very much a fringe player at the time. When he came on with a few minutes to go it was the pressure he put on a Galway defender coming out with the ball that earned us a last chance free for over-carrying. Once again, Darcy earned the headlines by kicking it. But it was McLoughlin's effort I was keen to underline in the dressing room afterwards.

His ability to come on and effectively salvage the game for us underlined that importance of having a positive atmosphere in the dug-out. It also reinforced the importance I placed on making sure the fringe players in our panel felt appreciated and sufficiently motivated to make an impact if called upon.

I constantly stressed the point to them that everyone had a big part to play here, and they had to be ready to play it when their time came. Padraig McLoughlin did not play too many minutes for us in 1994 but, were it not for him, we'd have been dumped out by Galway and become yet another forgotten Leitrim team.

By now Galway hated our guts.

There was a huge incentive for them to beat us in the replay in Tuam where we had shocked them the year before.

That was what made our subsequent one point win all the more satisfying. We were confirming that what happened the year before was no fluke, and that this Leitrim team were now serious contenders. The second half of that match was a thrilling see-saw battle that did my heart no good, and the reason we came out on the right side of it was that so many of our players rose their game to new levels.

Paul Kieran, especially, typified how the team had become self-motivated and confident enough to drive itself to new heights.

Paul was a fine athlete. He was also the sort of guy who was totally laid-back and tricky to motivate. I viewed this as an opportunity rather than a problem, because I knew he had huge potential. He normally played at wing forward, but this afforded him the luxury to flit in and out of games, do some good things, but never really grab the thing by the scruff of the neck.

I decided to put it up to him by pushing him into midfield instead where he was always going to be involved in the action and forced to accept a greater responsibility and workload.

That replay against Galway was the first day he moved into midfield, and he embraced the challenge wholeheartedly. His workrate doubled, and now he had more space than ever to showcase the sort of rangy athleticism that made him such a dynamic player.

It was also the day that Seamus Quinn came of age as a full back and announced himself as a special talent.

Others like Declan Darcy, Pat Donohue and Colin McGlynn starred too, but, really, it was one of those days where every player stepped up to the mark when they needed to most.

I had two predominant emotions as I walked down the road to our team coach afterwards. The first was that a win like this was money in the bank from a self-belief point of view. But, by then, my thoughts had also switched to the task of playing Mayo.

We had not played them since I took charge of Leitrim, and I was about to manage a team against my native county for the first time. I knew it would be difficult emotionally.

I had to handle it correctly, but above all else I had to beat them.

Some of my friends in Mayo who felt I had gotten a raw deal there were saying this was my chance to prove they had made a mistake by letting me go, but I was not looking at it like that.

I was in no way motivated by personal revenge. The only thing that mattered to me was that Leitrim would win this Connacht title. We had put too much effort into the thing to fall short now.

CHAPTER 16

I was so confident that Leitrim would beat Mayo in the 1994 Connacht final that before the match I pre-arranged for an open-top bus to bring the team through Carrick-on-Shannon that evening.

Obviously the players did not know anything about that, because as confident as I was I also did my best to shelter them from the massive hype that was building up in the county before the game.

It was not just in Leitrim.

The whole country was aglow with goodwill for us, and media interest in the team had exploded. RTE Radio even brought their outside broadcast unit to Jimmy's of Dromod for a version of *Liveline* that was hosted by Des Cahill. Jimmy's was owned by the eponymous Jimmy O'Connor who was a hardcore Leitrim fan and former team sponsor.

Jimmy lived and breathed Leitrim, and his establishment was very much regarded as the unofficial nerve-centre of Leitrim GAA. There was a live audience in there for the show and they wanted me to go down there and be part of the broadcast.

As much as I'd have loved to have been part of the craic, I wanted to lead by example, and I just did a small bit over the phone with them.

I warned the players not to be getting carried away with things, and it would have sent out the wrong message if I was seeing to be cranking up the hype machine myself.

I had been through this before with Mayo in 1989, and I was better equipped to handle it all this time around. Our County Board chairman, Tony McGowan, was struggling to keep himself on a similarly even keel.

Tony had been the supreme optimist in the county over the years and at various times had also served as County Board secretary as well as a team selector. He was just totally devoted to Leitrim GAA. Even if they had just been beaten by 20 points, he would find the positives in it, so he was revelling in the Connacht final build-up.

He was exactly what a county like Leitrim needed and I had a brilliant relationship with him, but when he turned up to training on night in a car painted in Leitrim colours I had to have a strong word. Some local car dealership had sponsored it for him, but when you are trying to keep a lid on the hype like I was, it was hardly an ideal situation.

Tony must have been a little bit afraid of me, because from then on he'd hide the car in the bushes outside Pairc Sean whenever we had training.

I was laughing on the inside, but I was not willing to let anything interfere with the focus of the players, no matter how amusing it was. It helped that all our midweek training sessions took place in Kells, away from the madness that was brewing in the county.

You could not insulate them from it completely, and I did not want to either because it was important that the players embraced what was happening to a certain extent, rather than try to live in a bubble. The hype was distracting in some ways, but it was a positive development in another because it enabled us to raise money we needed to continue funding our five star approach to our preparations.

In previous years the County Board's fundraising initiatives amounted to little more than a church-gate collection every year. Now, however, they were rolling out all sorts of initiatives.

It had to be done because the travelling expenses to and from Kells for all of our players racked up, and before the Connacht final I also wanted us to invest in another weekend away. The County Board could not have been more helpful in that respect, and it was at times like that our philosophy of keeping them involved and singing off the same hymn-sheet really paid dividends.

Unlike Mayo, I had been trusted enough to pick my own selectors. Tony McGowan, Tommy Moran and the rest of the executive continued to trust me in every other way too, and with backing like that it is much easier to get the job done.

There was no interference. I was allowed to get on with the job. The only question I was ever asked was... 'what can we do to support you?' Two weeks before the Connacht final we stayed in the Slieve Russell Hotel for a couple of nights to finalise our preparations.

Sean Quinn was the contact there, and he made a point of being around that weekend to make sure everything that could possibly be done for the players was done. It's a very luxurious place, so once again the aim was to make the players feel special and associate the team with excellence.

We were taking ourselves seriously, and by now the opposition were taking us seriously too.

Before we had even beaten Galway, our County Board had been unofficially approached by Mayo about potential Connacht final arrangements. Rather than have it in the neutral venue of Hyde Park, they wanted us to play them in Castlebar and were willing to make it worth the while financially for the Leitrim County Board to the tune of a few thousand euros.

I was having none of it, however. I told our treasurer Brendan Gormley to immediately shoot down the proposal.

We had prepared everything so meticulously for our assault on the 1994 Connacht championship that there was no way we were going to sell ourselves at that stage for a few pieces of silver.

For the Connacht final itself, everything was once again planned as thoroughly as possible. The day before, we met in the Bush Hotel in Carrick-on-Shannon for our final debrief like we did before every championship match.

For those meetings I always liked to do one last special thing for the players to make sure they were in the best mental and emotional place possible for the game.

On that occasion I was able to show them a video that Tommie Gorman had put together, like the one he had shot for me when Mayo reached the 1989 All-Ireland final. This time he spent a day going around Leitrim taking scenic shots that captured the mood of the county.

There was footage of all the most historic places in Leitrim that would stoke their pride of place, and a few encouraging words from supporters who worked in a place in Drumshambo that was making green and gold flags. I could see by the reaction of the players that the video hit the mark I wanted it to hit. It seemed as though everything was going perfectly to plan.

That's the time, usually, when a team hits some sort of some speed bump, and, sure enough, one came along that day when our Connacht final jerseys were delivered.

The suppliers, Connolly's, had forgotten to put the No. 26 on the back of one of the jerseys.

I kicked up havoc because as far as I was concerned this was unacceptable. Donal Smith was our 26th man and it would be an awful insult to the massive effort he had made if he was handed a jersey without a number on it.

We were about to make history by winning the county's first Connacht title in 67 years and Donal was going to be winning the same Connacht medal as our captain Declan Darcy. I warned the County Board this could not be allowed to happen.

Tommy Moran went to the factory to get the thing sorted. But, because it was a Saturday, the factory was closed.

In the end it was sorted one way or another, and I think we may even have gotten someone to sew the number on, because there was no way one of my players was going to be treated less equally than any of his teammates

Of course, I was not letting the players know anything about this sort of hullabaloo. You fight those sorts of fires yourself, because you want their environment to be as calm as possible.

On the morning of the game we convened at the Bush Hotel again and travelled together as a team to the match. It was symbolic that we would travel from within the county even if most of the lads lived outside it.

For our pre-match meal we had booked into a Guest House I had previously used with Mayo which is just 500 yards or so from Hyde Park. Because it was on an old estate and down a narrow lane, it was as if the team was totally cut off from the madness around the stadium.

We could hear the crowd building off in the distance, but we were surrounded by serene woodland and it was the perfect atmosphere to get our heads right for the challenge ahead.

The players were encouraged to walk around it in groups to talk through the game plan, so the defenders were hanging out together and the forwards were in another group. The only worry I had about this Guest House was whether our top of the range team bus would fit through the narrow gateway.

The week before the match, I drove to Roscommon and measured it myself to make sure it was wide enough. It was, barely. There was just an inch in the difference, but thankfully we had a good bus driver.

Even though 'The Hyde' was only a short distance away from our Guest House, we insisted on a Garda escort. One of the things I had tried to do when I went to Leitrim was raise their image and help them gather a new respect from other counties.

To do that I knew we'd have to do everything more professionally than every other county, so nothing was skimped on and the image we projected was one of immense pride in the county.

The bus that took us to the stadium that day was brand new, and decked out in the Leitrim colours so everyone could see us coming.

The players were looking sharp too. When I came in first they had all been given Leitrim team t-shirts, but over time we continued building up the gear until the match day attire was slacks and polo shirts.

In those days the best most county teams could hope for were tracksuits, but we insisted on better than that.

And whereas, nowadays, it is common to see county teams wearing neutral colour shirts or polo shirts, we made a point of having everything in the county colours and emblazoned with the county crest.

It was another small way of showing that being a Leitrim footballer was something to be very proud of. Whatever pride the players felt in their hearts must have expanded 10-fold on that drive from our Guest House to the stadium. The place was mobbed with Leitrim fans.

Of the 25,000 who paid into Hyde Park that day, I would estimate that 20,000 of them were from Leitrim.

Most of the county had been deserted, so the banner that hung from the bridge in Carrick-on-Shannon instructing the last person to leave to turn out the lights had as much truth as humour to it.

Despite the feverish excitement in the ground, all was relatively calm in our dressing room. Everyone knew that nothing more could have been done in terms of our preparation, and that knowledge gave peace of mind.

Even when we got off to the worst start possible by conceding a goal after just 18 seconds, nobody panicked.

Seamus Quinn went up to catch a 'half-cross, half-shot' from Pat Fallon, but he uncharacteristically let the ball slip through his hands and into the net. Our goalkeeper, Martin McHugh thought Seamus was going to make a simple catch, so he was flat-footed and powerless to stop it going in.

However, once again, this was a scenario we had gone through plenty of times in our visualisation meetings.

The message was that there is no better time to concede a goal than in the first minute because you have another 69 minutes to make amends. And, apart from the concession of that goal, our first half performance was almost perfect.

Before the game we had rejigged the team and that created all sorts of confusion in the Mayo defence.

In those days it was very rare for teams to name the sort of dummy teams that are par for the course nowadays, so when we made a number of switches in attack and midfield it was something Mayo clearly had not planned for. Padraig Kenny moved into full forward, and he was probably the last player that Mayo expected to see on the edge of the square.

Their players were shouting over to the sideline asking the Mayo manager, Jack O'Shea whether they should hold their ground or move over on to the man they had thought they would be marking?

And after Mayo themselves then made a series of switches to counter ours, we simply went back to our usual formation and once again their players were shouting to the sideline for direction.

It put them on the back foot from the very start, so even though we conceded that early goal we took a firm grip on the game from very early on. Amazingly, that goal after 18 seconds was the only score Mayo would manage in the entire first half, while we kicked six points.

We were winning all the key battles all over the pitch, and it was hugely satisfying from a management point of view to see everything we had talked about being executed so clinically.

At half time the message was that the game was far from won and we would be starting the second half as if it was nil-nil. There was no question of a blanket defence or parking the bus, and trying to hold on for the win.

We kicked another six points in the first 20 minutes of the second half, with just one in reply, so at that stage the score was 0-12 to 1-1 in our favour and we were looking good.

But even though we were much the better team, we typically made life harder for ourselves than we should have.

Mayo kicked two quick points, and then we conceded a penalty. It was saved well by McHugh, but Kevin O'Neill knocked the rebound to the net and suddenly there were only three points between the teams.

Inside I was hugely nervous, but when you are a manager it is important you keep a visible look of confidence one the sideline. When the players look at you out of their peripheral vision it will do them no good if they see you with your head in your hands.

You must continue exuding an air of controlled authority to let everyone know we are keeping this thing on message.

Mayo got one more point to reduce the margin to two as the game ticked into injury time. But, when we then won a free with a late attack, I knew we were home and hosed. As Aiden Rooney prepared to take the free, I had a minute to myself in which I could quietly savour our imminent victory. It was a minute of pure heaven.

The final whistle blew while the ball was in the air and I simply walked away down the sideline. I was so much on message that I was determined not to lose the plot.

Part of it was that I did not want to be seen to glory in Mayo's downfall, but it was as much a manifestation of the self-possessed authority I had tried to show all day. Obviously enough, all hell broke loose all around me. Joe Reynolds, Ollie Honeyman, Tony McGowan and Tommy Moran all rushed to embrace me, but I struggled to immediately switch in to celebratory mood.

All sorts of emotions were churning around in me. For a fleeting moment my mind's eye travelled the journey that had brought me to this place.

When my time as Mayo manager had ended in 1991 it hurt me deeply. I was not taking any sort of dark pleasure from the fact that we had now beaten my home county, but there was definitely a satisfaction that I had proven to everyone that I was a credible and capable manager.

Other people obviously had their doubts about me, but winning that Connacht title in Leitrim was a validation of my own self-belief.

Going through all that hurt had made me a better, stronger manager. I was just thrilled that I had said yes to the opportunity when Leitrim came calling. On a very personal, private level, those were the thoughts that I was immediately processing. Once that was done I could share in the collective euphoria.

It was a very unique sort of atmosphere because even the Mayo fans who came out onto the pitch afterwards seemed electrified by the buzz. Their team had just lost a Connacht title, but they were all genuinely happy for the Leitrim people who were in seventh heaven.

The presentation of the JJ Nestor Cup to Declan Darcy was a marvellous moment. Someone had been thoughtful enough to arrange for the only other man to captain a provincial winning Leitrim team, Tom Gannon in 1927, to lift the cup with Declan.

Tom was 95 years old at that stage, so seeing him up there with Declan made the achievement seem all the more magical.

I was on that pitch for at least an hour after the game, but it felt like just five minutes. It was a wonderfully joyous place to be and my back was slapped raw and my arm almost pulled from my shoulder by the blur of happy well-wishers.

When I eventually started making my way back to the dressing room, Mickey Quinn and I crossed paths and made the journey together.

That was nice, because Mickey was the spiritual leader of the team. He had soldiered through plenty of bad days, but still earned national renown because he was such a good footballer.

I asked him how he felt now?

'Jesus… I didn't think it would be so easy!'

'Didn't I tell you all,' I replied, '… that you would write your own script.'

Mickey was still clearly getting to grips with the whole thing. Yes, we had beaten Mayo more easily than most people predicted. But, when you took a step back, there was nothing all that easy about what we had just achieved.

We needed a last minute winner against Roscommon, a last minute equaliser in the drawn match against Galway, and then came out on the right side of the result by a single point in that semi final replay.

So, really, it was a victory of narrow margins. And it would never have happened at all had everyone involved not striven so hard to tick every box with meticulous diligence.

That is what it took to change a county's culture.

I can remember being at the 1967 Connacht final when Mayo hammered Leitrim. That day it was as if they were simply going through the motions and waiting to be beaten.

Their team of the 1950s that included really talented footballers like Packie McGarty, Cathal Flynn and Josie Murray, was regarded as their greatest ever, but lost four Connacht titles in-a-row to Galway.

Those men had been heroes in Leitrim for even coming that close to the Holy Grail, but now this generation had finally got their hands on it and it was an overwhelming feeling.

When I finally got to the dressing room, it was absolutely nuts. The place was packed with people who wanted to share the moment. GAA President, Jack Boothman, and Connacht Council secretary, Johnny Mulvey led the charge, and there were even two Bishops in the middle of the mayhem congratulating all and sundry.

But even though the place was mobbed, you could still look around the room at all the players, make eye contact, and share a powerful moment.

When Tommie Gorman had made that video for us before the final, part of his commentary said that this would be an achievement that would not just bond us together for ever, but also be something our children and our children's children would also have in common.

So when we looked at each other with the smiles bouncing off our faces, we really were sharing the enormity of the occasion.

The dressing room was so crammed and its surroundings so choked with people that you couldn't get in and you couldn't get out.

At one stage I spotted George Dugdale hanging out a window. His father was outside and wanted to make contact. If George had gone outside there was no way to get back in, so the two of them shared a special moment through the open window.

Everyone in that dressing room had their own personal story and I can only imagine what people like Tony McGowan, Tommy Moran, Ollie Honeyman and Joe Reynolds were feeling like when they surveyed the scene around them.

One of the things I always do in a winning dressing room after a match, when the mayhem subsides, is to get everyone to sit down together for a chat. It was then that the joyous sense of togetherness we had as group really felt like a warm glow.

We had lived in each other's company for two years to get to this moment, and we had gotten what we deserved.

The message then was that we were going to really enjoy the next couple of nights, but also that our achievement had made us ambassadors for Leitrim so we also had to be aware of the responsibilities that went with that.

By then the overwhelming feeling was that everyone wanted to get back to Carrick-on-Shannon to share in the party we knew must be building.

On the way to our coach I spotted Bill Cogan in the big field outside Hyde Park where the old dressing rooms were.

He was just about to get into his new car that was a big, black, stately thing. He was wearing his dark glasses and there was a real air of mystique about him. I winked over at him, and he nodded back at me. Very few people outside of our camp knew just how important a role he had played in our triumph, but I certainly did.

When we got to Carrick we boarded the open top bus. That was a nice surprise for the players, and it proved to be a masterstroke because Carrick was crammed with thousands of people and it was a great way for the players to interact with the supporters.

One moment that really resonated with me was when I caught eyes with an elderly man in the crowd.

He looked like he was from rural Leitrim and had put an awful lot of preparation into going to the match because he was kitted out in his Sunday best and was waving a little Leitrim flag.

He wasn't in company.

He was on his own. But he couldn't have looked happier. He was holding that little flageen like it was a badge of honour and you could see his admiration for the team shining from his face like a beacon.

I waved down to him and I'd have loved at that moment to have gotten off the bus and spoken to him because there was just something unique about him. It really hit home to me at that moment just how much this all meant to the people of Leitrim.

It took us ages to get through the town and when we got to The Square we all climbed up onto the trailer of a lorry and there were a good few speeches that had the crowd cheering themselves hoarse. After that we finally got around to our team meal at the reception in the Bush Hotel that seemed to be thronged with hundreds of people.

One of my most special memories from the whole night was of my father dancing his socks off at around three o'clock in the morning with Stephen Sheridan.

The music was blaring. There was carnival-like atmosphere of joyous mayhem. My father was absolutely revelling in it all. Like any son would, I felt a deep sense of satisfaction that came from making my father feel proud.

I stayed going until five or six in the morning myself, and the party was still in a good old swing by the time I finally left.

The agreement was to meet the following day in Jimmy's of Dromod at 1.0 pm. That was another amazing experience because the place was mobbed with supporters as well as local and national media. From there we went on a tour of the county and everywhere we went there was a massive party organised.

Leitrim is a long, narrow, quite rural county. As we travelled through it every house we saw, even the ones halfway up mountains, had Leitrim flags flying out of them. I think that was the moment it really begun to sink in with the players just what it was they had achieved.

Every place a player on the panel called home was visited, until we finally finished in Ballinamore at about three o'clock in the morning. Even though the weather was bad, the place was still mobbed and there were kids in peoples' arms.

Seamus Duke from Shannonside Radio was the MC and commentary of the Connacht final blared out from speakers until after four o'clock in the morning. After Ballinamore the bus went back to Dromod to drop off lads who left their cars there. By then dawn was breaking.

It had been a hell of a party.

But my mind had already turned to the challenge of playing Dublin in the All-Ireland semi final.

CHAPTER 17

After the high of winning a first Connacht title for 67 years, my first challenge was always going to be getting every player's feet back on the ground.

I did not want them to be happy with simply winning a provincial title and go into the All-Ireland semi final believing themselves to be no-hopers. That is what Sligo had done in 1975 and they ended up losing to Kerry by 17 points.

The first way to get everyone re-focused was a simple one; get them back to the refuge of Kells and run the shite out of them.

That was a quick-fire way of letting the players know the party was over and that we were back to work again. People outside our camp viewed the challenge of beating Dublin an impossible one, but we did not.

We knew it would obviously be difficult because we were playing a side that had won four Leinster titles in-a-row and had been serious All-Ireland contenders in the previous three campaigns. However, I did not want our players going to Dublin feeling in any way inhibited by an inferiority complex, so once again we made a big effort to ensure they only had the best of the best for the All-Ireland semi final.

The team polo shirts were upgraded to shirts and blazers. And after the Connacht final I also got in touch with someone in Puma through the Meath footballer Colm O'Rourke.

I went up to their offices in Meath and struck a deal for new boots for all the players that were wedged into my car for the journey home. Another way we tried to lift the thing before the All-Ireland semi final was to bring in Mick Byrne as a physiotherapist.

He was a household name at that stage because of his long-standing involvement with the Irish soccer team, and in 1994 he was only just home from the World Cup in the USA. Getting him on board was another way of showing the players that we only wanted the best of the best for them.

The first evening he came in, there was nearly more of a queue for him out on the pitch than there was for me. He was always throwing out Irish socks and gear to them, so they were delighted with him.

He was almost as much a psychologist as he was a physio because he was such a positive guy, and surrounding the Leitrim players with positivity had always been a big part of my approach.

Our preparations for the semi final went well apart from one minor blip.

I had expected we would be provided with another brand new 1994 coach for the journey to Dublin, like the one we had used for the Connacht final. So when an older model turned up on the day, I was livid. All year we had done everything to the highest of standards, but now those standards had dropped.

Just like I had with Mayo in 1989, I decided the best place for us to stay in Dublin was the Grand Hotel in Malahide.

And even though a lot of the lads were living in Dublin, I insisted they all return to Leitrim first on the Saturday so we could travel together as a team. When we got to the Grand Hotel the owner, Matt Ryan must have noticed my displeasure with our mode of transport because he said he would get us a top of the line bus if we wanted?

And, in fairness to him, by the following morning there was a massive luxury coach all set to go that had been bedecked overnight in the Leitrim colours.

The hype before the Connacht final had been massive, but now it went to a new level entirely. Leitrim people exiled in every corner of the World made it their business to return home for the match and, on the day, there were more Leitrim people in Croke Park than lived in the county at the time.

It was always going to be impossible to completely shield the players from the excitement that was building, and there were little signs that some of them were being distracted.

Declan Darcy was asked by RTE to be an analyst on *The Sunday Game* for their coverage of the Leinster final between Dublin and Meath which took place a week after our win over Mayo. I was not happy about it because I knew it was an unnecessary distraction, but I did not want to cause any sort of a rift by telling Declan he could not do it.

After the Connacht final Seamus Quinn came to us and said he went into that match fitter than he had ever been before, but his legs still turned to jelly as soon as he ran out onto the pitch and heard the massive roar. He thought that was maybe why he uncharacteristically let the ball slip through his hands for the goal Mayo scored in the very first minute.

Naturally, he was now worried how he would cope mentally with the prospect of playing in a packed Croke Park and marking Dublin's danger man, Vinny Murphy.

In the weeks coming up to the semi final, Bill Cogan worked with him a lot on positive visualisation to make sure he was in the best frame of mind possible. Credit to Seamus, he ended up winning his battle with Murphy and was one of our very best players against Dublin.

The fact that he needed to be, unfortunately reflects the fact that much of the play was flowing towards our goal. Because even though we started well, Dublin eventually took control.

We scored the first point of the match through Noel Moran, and when it went over the bar the place erupted.

It was the first point that Leitrim had ever scored in Croke Park because the 1927 team had not played their All-Ireland semi final there, and the Leitrim supporters could not have celebrated it in more style. They were shouting themselves hoarse by the time we went 0-3 to 0-1 ahead, but after that the wheels slowly started to come off our wagon.

Dublin got two goals at critical moments in the first half, but an even bigger blow was the torn cruciate ligament suffered by George Dugdale that forced him off.

We showed plenty of heart, kept battling throughout, and had fine individual performances from men like Seamus Quinn, Gerry Flanagan, Pat Donohue, Fergal Reynolds, Mickey Quinn and Colin McGlynn.

But ultimately we just weren't good enough for them on the day and they ran out comfortable winners in the end by 3-15 to 1-9. That final score stuck in my craw. I had come to Dublin convinced we would not just be more competitive than that, but capable of beating them.

Even though we had lost the match, the atmosphere at our team reception in The Burlington Hotel afterwards was still one of celebration rather than despair.

It was best summed up by a priest I spoke to who had come home from America for the match and approached me to tell me he had a picture that he was going to treasure for the rest of his life.

Early in the first half he had photographed the scoreboard when it read... Leitrim 0-3, Dublin 0-1.

In October, we had a team holiday to America to reward the players. We were based in New York and Connecticut where there is a huge Leitrim diaspora.

We played a match in Gaelic Park against a New York selection, and there were big Leitrim crowds wherever we went. Yonkers in New York especially was like a Little Leitrim, because every bar on MacLean Avenue seemed to have Leitrim patronage. Many of our functions took place in one of them – the Mike Carty owned pub, Rosie O'Grady's – and after one of them myself and Ger left the place at around three o'clock in the morning. We had barely set foot on the pavement when a car pulled up beside us.

'We can't have the Leitrim manager walking home like this.'

It was yet another Leitrim native, Frankie Dwyer, who drove us all the way to where we were staying in the Pennsylvania Hotel across from Madison Square Garden.

It turns out that in the city that never sleeps, you'll usually find a Leitrim

Showing off my first pair of football boots as I pose in front of my father's travelling shop.

Making hay with my parents, Stephen and Brigid at my grandparents' house in Muinhin, Bangor Erris. I'm with Stephen and Dan, but I'm the one with the controls ready on the radio for the big game of the day. And (right) heading off to the Connacht final in 1966 with my Dad, Dan and Stephen. I'm hatted and have a flag at the ready.

A proud captain of St Nathy's junior football team in 1970 and (bottom) I have the ball in the front row on the college's senior team 1971.

Mayo's All-Ireland winning minor team in 1971. I'm in the back row, seventh from the right, and (below) I'm on the right on the back row of the county's All-Ireland winning under-21 team in '73.

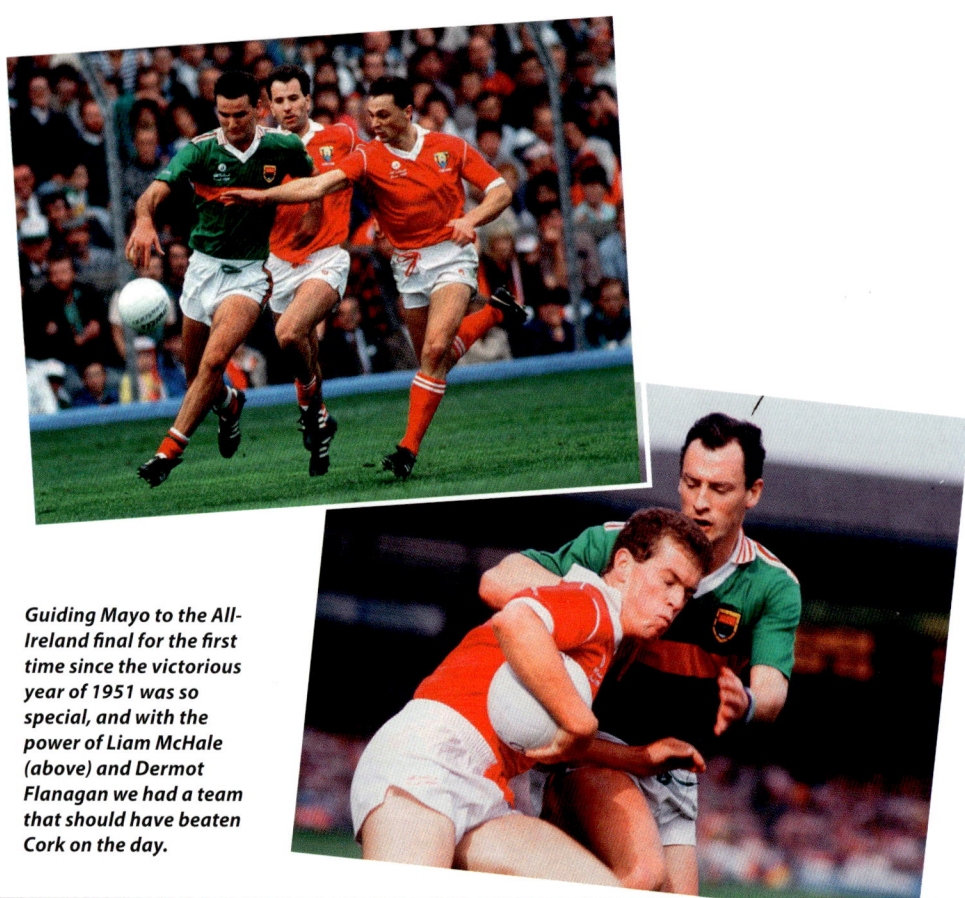

Guiding Mayo to the All-Ireland final for the first time since the victorious year of 1951 was so special, and with the power of Liam McHale (above) and Dermot Flanagan we had a team that should have beaten Cork on the day.

The Mayo team that lost to Cork in the 1989 All-Ireland final.

Anthony Finnerty scores our second half goal in the 1989 All-Ireland final that might have set us up for an historic win.

I can only watch on as Dinny Allen collects the Sam Maguire Cup for Cork but the people of Mayo were still 'Keeping the Faith'.

Jack O'Shea congratulates me after Leitrim had defeated Mayo in the 1994 Connacht final and (below) Declan Darcy lifts the Nestor Cup on the proudest of days for the people of Leitrim.

I had great support from my selectors in 1994, Ollie Honeyman and Joe Reynolds (below). The scenes outside the Leitrim dressing room in Dr Hyde Park were so manic that George Dugdale had to reach out the dressing room window to shake the hand of his father, Joe.

The Leitrim team that proudly met Dublin in the 1994 All-Ireland semi final and (below) the entire squad and team management met up for a memorable 20th anniversary celebration in 2014.

Galway's 1998 All-Ireland final victory over Mick O'Dwyer's Kildare was built, amongst many things, on the strength of Kevin Walsh (top) and Sean O'Domhnaill in the middle of the field.

Getting Ja Fallon back with the county helped pave the way to Galway's historic victory in '98 as there was no more intelligent footballer in the country. The scenes on the field (below) after the final whistle were incredible, as Niall Finnegan is just one of the men carried shoulder high by the county's fans.

After getting so close with my native Mayo nine years earlier, I had a long wait before finally lifting Sam Maguire after Galway's victory in 1998 (top), and then myself and our team captain, Ray Silke got to make the memorable journey with Sam as we crossed the Shannon.

The Galway team that defeated Kildare in the 1998 All-Ireland final.

There can only be one winner and one loser on the biggest day of the year, and what a difference it makes! I shake hands with Sean Boylan (right) after Galway had defeated Meath in the 2001 All-Ireland final, which was a whole different world to congratulating Kerry's Paidi O Se after the final 12 months earlier.

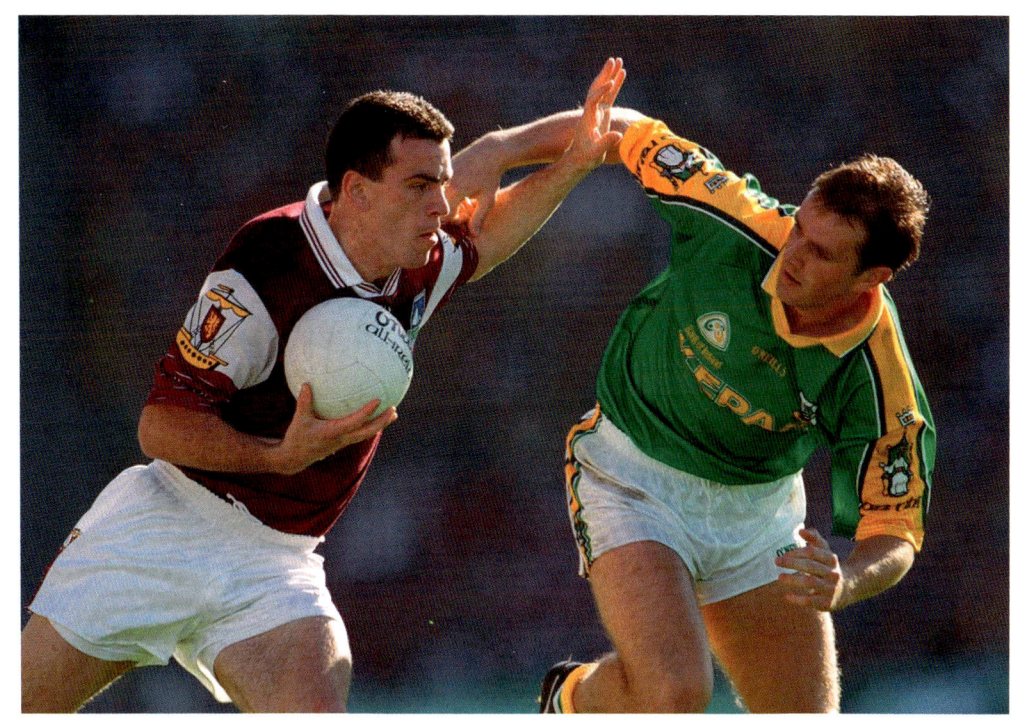

Pádraic Joyce, who led the way with a sensational performance in the 2001 All-Ireland final, rounds Meath's Darren Fay.

I board the train for home the day after beating Meath in the 2001 All-Ireland final with our team captain, Gary Fahey and Sam!

I celebrate our 2001 All-Ireland victory with my Galway management team (from left) Gay McManus, Pete Warren and Stephen Joyce.

Exalted company: At a charity fund raiser in 2001 with Warren Gatland (Irish rugby coach), George Best, and Mick McCarthy (Irish soccer manager)... and Sam, of course!

My wife, Gerardine (front) and I have a spontaneous family celebration in Croke Park after Galway's 2001 All-Ireland final win over Meath with (from left) our girls, Cliodhna, Grainne, Rhona, Niamh and Deirdre.

The Galway team that defeated Meath in the 2001 All-Ireland final.

I returned to manage my native Mayo for a second time in 2007 and had four fond years as we sought to build a team for the future, but the loneliness of the sideline is always a formidable place for any man to walk.

man up later than most.

It was a tremendous trip, heady times, really. But, towards the end of it, I was already getting my game-face fixed again. Back then, the National Football League started before Christmas, and when we came back we had just five days to recover for our first match of the campaign against Tyrone.

There had been great celebrations in New York. But I said to the lads that if we went home and shit on the eggs against Tyrone, then people would say we were losing the run of ourselves. And, despite the exuberance of our exertions in America, we beat Tyrone on our return which told me that the players were still motivated enough to keep pushing themselves.

Despite that positive start I knew it was going to be a challenge for us to hit the same heights in 1995 that we did in 1994.

When you achieve success you almost forget how hungry you had to be to get it in the first place, and in '94 Leitrim had sated 67 years of hunger. The players were all local celebrities now, and even fame on such a small scale can distract you if you are not mentally strong.

It was probably most difficult for Seamus Quinn. His heroics in '94 earned him what was Leitrim's second only Allstar so that put him on a platform all of his own. A bus-load came up from Gortletteragh for the function and he got engaged the same night. It was a great occasion, but the new-found fame was always going to take some sort of toll.

He was only 20 years old, so when everyone is suddenly telling you that you're one of the greatest things since sliced bread it can be hard to cope with. Especially when you're the sort of quiet, shy character that Seamus was.

Eventually he decided he wanted to go to America, and I wouldn't be surprised if was because he had enough of living in a goldfish bowl.

There were some serious negotiations to persuade him to stay, and eventually it was only thanks to the intervention of his parents that we managed to hold onto him. Even with everyone on board it was going to be difficult to go up another level because it had felt like we had maxed everything out in '94.

Another challenge for us coming into the 1995 championship was that now we were being talked up as favourites for the Connacht title and there was a big red X on our backs.

Galway had more reason than any other county in the province to want to bury an axe into that X, and we were drawn against them in the Connacht semi final.

It's a testament to how far Leitrim had come that it was the first live televised game of the year and took place at the unusual time of six o'clock on a Sunday evening. Once again it looked like we had the hex over them as we scored a point near the end of normal time that put us two points up.

It was scored by one of our new players, Ciaran McGovern, who ran forward from right wing back and was put clear through. He could have shot for a goal, but took the right option given the circumstances of punching it over the bar.

We looked home and hosed, but for some reason the referee Pat Casserly allowed four minutes of injury time and Galway scored three unbelievable points through Ja Fallon, Sean Óg de Paor and Niall Finnegan to snatch the win.

There was stunned silence in Pairc Sean Mac Diarmada when the final whistle blew.

The dream of back-to-back Connacht titles had died.

Even now, 20 years later, it's hard not to think about what might have been? George Dugdale missed out on that Galway match because he was still rehabbing the cruciate ligament he had torn in the semi final against Dublin. No stone had been left unturned to get him right, and he was nearly there. He'd have been fit for the Connacht final, so it was that close. Had he been fit for Galway, I'm certain we'd have beaten them.

Galway subsequently hammered Mayo in the Connacht final. I was doing a bit of analysis for Midwest radio and Galway fans were coming up to me and saying, 'Ah Jaysus… if Leitrim were here at least ye'd have given us a game.'

I have no doubt we'd have beaten Mayo too had we come through against Galway, so it really felt like a missed opportunity.

The one regret I have from my time with Leitrim was that we failed to win the Connacht title again in 1995 and have a really serious tilt at reaching an All-Ireland final.

I sincerely believe it would have been possible because we learned a lot from the previous year and we'd have been playing a Tyrone team we had beaten already in the league that year. Obviously there are no guarantees, but 1995 was definitely a great chance for Leitrim to reach an All-Ireland final for the very first time.

People might scoff at that, but those were the targets we were setting for ourselves by then.

After 1995, I knew in my gut that the law of diminishing returns would probably apply to the team. We had put in a massive effort for three years, and the veterans on the team like Mickey Quinn were getting older. It didn't help either that Tony McGowan had stepped down as County Board chairman.

Des Quinn won the subsequent election for the position ahead of Eamon Tubman who I had previously worked closely with on our extended management committee. I wouldn't have known Des as well, and alarm bells rang when I then heard that the executive wanted me to freshen up my backroom team.

I met them and told them straight that if they wanted new selectors they'd have to get a new manager too.

I didn't want anyone pointing the finger at Joe Reynolds and Ollie Honeyman for our defeat to Galway in 1995 because they had contributed hugely to everything good we had achieved. That loss was in no-way down to anything that went wrong on the sideline. It was simply one of those days when a team suddenly gets a run on you in the closing few minutes and you don't have time to respond.

I was disappointed there would even be a suggestion that there needed to be changes. In a county like Leitrim you need complete unity to be successful, but now little cracks were beginning to appear.

It wasn't that I wanted to be a control freak, but the bottom line is that you need everyone to fully buy in to what you're doing, because if they don't then you're in trouble.

We came into the 1996 championship off a below par league campaign and I knew it was going to be difficult to beat Galway in Tuam. It looked like we were going to go out with a whimper when we trailed by nine points with just seven minutes of normal time remaining.

But then the players displayed the sort of character I had come to admire so much by launching an incredible comeback.

Two goals in quick succession helped us reduce the deficit to a single point, but a last gasp attack for an equaliser was intercepted by Ja Fallon, and Galway broke down the field to kick an insurance point.

The final whistle blew, and I knew my time as Leitrim manager was up. It was a sad moment, but I had weightier things on my mind than that.

Around that time my father was dying from cancer and was very much on his death bed.

But he insisted that I not miss the match under any circumstances. A few months earlier a check-up had revealed that he had cancer tumours throughout his body, which was a massive shock. It was difficult, but I never allowed that personal situation to distract me from the job of preparing Leitrim as well as I possibly could.

After the defeat to Galway, Ger was waiting for me with a car to bring me straight to Swinford where my father was in hospice care.

In a way, it broke my heart that I was not able to go back on the team bus with the lads because I knew it was going to be our last journey together. I had to be by my father's side though, and the following evening he passed away. It was a tough time. My father and I had a few battles and arguments over the years, but that was possibly because we were so alike.

Deep down, I knew he was hugely proud of me. Even if like most Irishmen he did not quite know how to express it.

There was never an arm around the shoulder and a quiet word telling you he was proud, but in hindsight I knew for sure he obviously was.

I sourced an awful lot of satisfaction from making him proud. The image of him dancing with sheer joy in the Bush Hotel after Leitrim won the Connacht title is one I will always cherish.

We had the wake in the house on the Tuesday night, and the Leitrim team to a man were there which meant an awful lot to me. The remains were brought to the church and when we went to a local pub afterwards the players and the Leitrim County Board officials all came there too.

It was a poignant moment, because that sort of unity was a recognition of the journey we had gone on together for four years and the fact that we were now one big Leitrim family.

To this day that sense of family is still there.

In 2014 the players organised an unofficial 20th anniversary of our Connacht title win in Paddy's Bar across from the Bush Hotel and it was a lovely occasion. I brought them all Leitrim crested polo shirts to mark the occasion, and it was nice to throw out the jerseys to the lads like I had in the good old days.

I could immediately see that the old camaraderie and magic was still there. It was a very happy night. The *Leitrim Observer* photographer, Willie Donnellan was there to snap the occasion just like he had back in the day too, so it was a great walk down memory lane for everyone.

The fact that it was so informal made it a really intimate occasion. But I do hope that the Leitrim County Board arranges something to commemorate the 25th anniversary. I have only great memories of my time with Leitrim. I am blessed to have been part of something really special.

But the competitor in me means I will always regret we did not win a second Connacht and become the first Leitrim team to play in an All-Ireland final.

CHAPTER 18

When I left Leitrim my plan was to take a total break from football to recharge the batteries, but it was not long before I found myself back in a dressing room again. I was asked to take charge of the St Brigid's senior club team in Roscommon, and couldn't say no.

It was a really enjoyable experience because they had not won a county title for 29 years, and we managed to end that long famine in 1997.

While I was travelling to training with St Brigid's one evening I happened to turn on the radio and there was a report on the sports bulletin that the Galway County Board had set up a committee to appoint a new senior football team manager.

I remember thinking to myself that here is a team with massive potential ripe for the picking for whoever got the job. I never imagined I might be in the frame for it myself. Galway, I always felt, were one of those super-power counties like Dublin, Kerry and Cork, who would never consider looking outside their own borders for a manager.

Not long after I got in touch with Pat Egan, the Galway County Board chairman, because he was from Corofin who were going well at the time and I wanted to arrange a challenge match against them for St Brigid's. He mentioned they had set up a committee to find a new manager and asked me would I be interested? I only put it down as a passing remark, rather than a serious question.

A few days later though, I got a phone call from Tom McManus, from the Milltown club, who asked me would I be willing to let my name go forward if they proposed me for the job?

I was pleasantly surprised.

After thinking about it for a short while, I agreed to let him propose me as a candidate. They may have been one of the super-powers, but I also viewed Galway as the biggest sleeping giant in football, and when my hat was thrown into the ring I said to Ger that if I got this job we would win the All-Ireland championship. The reason I was so sure that it was an achievable goal was because I had a really good knowledge of the impressive array of talent that was in that Galway dressing room. I had massive respect for people like Kevin Walsh, Ja Fallon, Seán Óg De Paor, Gary Fahey, and Tomás Mannion, both as men and as footballers, and I could not understand why they had not had more success.

The previous year I had been working at the match for Midwest Radio when Mayo had beaten Galway in the Connacht quarter final. Mayo won in the end by four points, but Galway gave them a great game and were clearly a coming team.

Michael Donnellan played that day and served notice of his massive potential, but I knew there were other young footballers in the county like Pádraic Joyce, Derek Savage, John Divilly and Tomás Meehan, who were all really promising talents too.

I saw them play at schools level because of my own involvement with St Nathy's, and it was clear to me that they were a gifted generation of young footballers. St Jarlath's won the All-Ireland colleges final in 1994 with many of those players, and they were widely regarded as one of the most gifted teams the competition had ever seen.

I had been worried how taking charge of Leitrim would be perceived in Mayo. Even though Galway were bigger rivals, it was not as big a factor this time around.

With John Maughan as manager, Mayo had been in the All-Ireland final in 1996 and were on the way to the final again in 1997. There was not going to be any demand for me to manage my own county any time in the near future, and I wanted to take this opportunity because I now knew that management was my special calling in the GAA.

I had managed a small county like Leitrim and done relatively well considering our resources, but this was a chance to test myself in a very different environment.

Galway's potential was greater, but that also brought greater pressure. I wanted to embrace that challenge and be successful which meant winning an All-Ireland. The Galway County Board decided to undertake an interview process for the job rather than just headhunt a candidate, which was a little off-putting.

'Listen, you don't owe me anything,' I said to Pat Egan.

'And I don't owe you anything,' I continued. 'But I don't want to go for this job and not get it.'

Pat explained that he couldn't tell me one way or the other, whether or not I'd definitely get it. But I decided to go through the interview process anyway. I wanted to respect the Galway tradition.

There were four other candidates. Val Daly had been player-manager the previous year and was in the running again along with Eamonn Coleman of Derry, Mattie Kerrigan the former Meath star who was managing Westmeath, and Galway's Brian Talty.

The interview took place in Hayden's Hotel in Ballinasloe and lasted about 45 minutes. Sitting at the other side of the table were Pat Egan, Jack Mahon, John Joe Holleran, Brendan Colleran and Francis Roche.

I haven't done many interviews in my life, but I approached it as professionally as I could. I wanted this job. So I made sure I was well dressed and projected the right sort of image. I had a file that detailed how I would do the job and the structures that I would be insisting upon if they decided to go with me.

I wanted to show them that I had thought very seriously about this, and that I was going to put in place a highly professional set-up.

At one point someone asked me bluntly why they should give the Galway manager's job to a Mayo man?

Jack Mahon gave the question short shrift on my behalf, and said that was not relevant. But I also replied and said they should give the job to this Mayo man if they wanted to win an All-Ireland title. I suppose that showed how much potential I saw in the team.

The big thing I emphasised in the interview was the importance of everyone working together to achieve our aims. And everyone meant players, management, and the County Board as one big collective.

Nobody would own the thing. Everyone had a part to play. They all had to buy into it totally.

A week later I was told I was being recommended for the job by the committee, and after the County Board delegates ratified my appointment I immediately set about putting my plans in place and getting a management team and panel together.

I met all the players who had been involved in the 1997 panel at the Sacre Coeur Hotel three weeks before the All-Ireland final. It was quite early to be having a meeting like that, but I wanted to send out a message and let the players know that I meant business. Persuading all of the best players in the county to be part of my panel was always going to be the first task, and I had mixed results.

Alan Mulholland told me at that meeting that he would not be available because of work and family commitments. He was still in the prime of his career and would probably have been a key player for us, so losing Alan was definitely a blow.

Ja Fallon had already told me he couldn't commit and that was a bigger blow again. He had a part-time contract with the Connacht rugby team that earned him a few bob, and he could not financially afford to just drop that and come with us instead.

The unavailability of Fallon and Muholland were negatives, but there were positives too. Seán Óg de Paor rang me from America to let me know that he was coming home and was mad for action.

Kevin Walsh had not played in the 1997 championship because of injury, but when I spoke to him he was keen to get involved again and that was a massive boost because I knew he would be a key player for us. Niall Finnegan was after recently getting married, was based in Dublin, and wanted to take some time out from football. So I met up with him in the Lucan Spa Hotel for a meal on the evening of Mayo's All-Ireland semi final win over Offaly and he agreed that he would return to the panel after Christmas.

I was getting my ducks in-a-row in terms of the panel, and my management team had also come together nicely.

I wanted selectors who had been through the mill in Galway in every sense, with both club and county, and felt Stephen Joyce and Pete Warren ticked those boxes. Stephen had won multiple Connacht championships with Galway, had played in the infamous 1983 All-Ireland final, and was someone I knew fairly well. He had been a top class forward himself and would have a very big input into our forward play.

Pete Warren had been player-manager of Tuam Stars and everything I had heard about him was positive. He was very good at dealing with people on a human level, and became a very popular figure amongst the players. Gay McManus was also an important member of the backroom team because he trained the players who were based in Dublin.

I chose well. We developed a very tight bond and they would all play a huge part in the team's future success.

When I had managed Mayo and Leitrim I had done the bulk of the team training myself and made a big effort to always look for new methods and keep pace with whatever was best practice.

But, by the time I took charge of Galway, strength and conditioning work in the gym was becoming hugely important and I knew I needed an expert in the field. So I got in touch with Eddie O'Sullivan, the rugby coach.

Eddie was living in Monivea at the time, and even though his rugby coaching career was taking off in a major way, he agreed to help us out.

He drew up a strength and conditioning programme for the team, and he impressed me so much that I then tasked him with developing our entire physical training regime. The traditional GAA practice of running players up and down hills and across beaches was an archaic one to someone like Eddie, who was positioning himself at the cutting edge of professional rugby.

Instead, he drew up a programme for us that was based around interval training, and shorter and sharper runs and drills.

He was not around much because at the time he was also coaching the USA rugby team, so I was getting faxes from all over the world detailing what we should be doing for our next month of physical training.

Stephen, Pete and I devised the ball drills, but now they too were based on the interval training philosophy where everything was done as quickly and as intensively as possible. Whenever Eddie was home he would do fitness testing with the players and measure their body-fat and all of that stuff, so he really was a massive help. Because we were putting such a big effort into it, there were no soft excuses ever accepted for missing a training session.

Very early on, Kevin Walsh contacted me one day to tell me he would not be able to make training because of some commitment he had. I told him that was okay, that I would still be there at ten o'clock that night and we would do an individual session with him then.

Kevin turned up at the normal scheduled time!

It was an early test. You respect the commitment that players are making, but if you start absolving them of any of that commitment then you will quickly lose the respect of the group. It's all about the visuals, and there were plenty of occasions when I went ahead with individual sessions late at night with players who could not make training at the appointed time for a good reason.

And if a player had some issue that prevented him from training altogether on a particular evening, I would let the rest of the group know why he could not make it.

The worst thing a player can feel is that some of his teammates are not making the same massive commitment that he is. Kevin was a hugely important player for us and in later years we gave him some leeway when it came to training because he was always managing a degenerative knee injury.

In my first year, however, I had no option other than to treat everyone equally, and that included Kevin.

Shortly after I was appointed, a well known GAA person said to me, 'I see you have Kevin Walsh back… that fella wouldn't train to keep himself warm.'

It hurt me that anyone would think that about him. Kevin gave lie to that statement by giving me a massive commitment throughout my time with Galway. Because he had missed the '97 campaign, he had to improve his fitness and lose some weight. He was really gung-ho about doing both.

He went on the NuTron diet that was in vogue at the time, and worked his socks off in training. That was an inspiration for everyone else because Kevin had massive respect in the dressing room. He had it all as a midfielder in terms of his skill set, and that was complemented by a powerful personality that made him a natural leader of men.

From very early on I could see a really positive chemistry in the dressing room. The likes of Walsh, Mannion, de Paor, Finnegan and Gary Fahey were all one age group, and then we had the likes of Joyce, Donnellan, Savage, and Declan and Tomás Meehan who were a few years younger.

But, despite that slight generation gap, there were no clans or cliques. Rather than feel threatened by the younger players who were emerging, the elder statesmen did all they could to encourage them to express their talent.

In fairness to the young lads, they did not need much mollycoddling or cajoling.

Most young and inexperienced players shrink the bigger the occasion, but I would find out that the emerging players on the Galway panel were born for the big stage and inspired rather than cowed by it.

Someone like Pádraic Joyce had no inhibitions or hang-ups whatsoever even though he was new to senior county football. He knew he was talented, and he wanted to show everyone just how much. No matter how talented a young footballer is though, consistency is usually the last skill he masters.

And my problem was that I could not afford the team to be inconsistent. I was conscious that we would need to start off our league campaign positively and win over the doubters who would not have been too happy to see an outside manager appointed.

We were motoring along nicely until we hit a speed bump and were beaten by Offaly in the league quarter final. It was a poor performance and made me doubt whether things were as healthy as I had previously thought they were. After the match, I spoke with Pat Egan and told him we needed to somehow persuade Ja Fallon to return to the fold, because the defeat highlighted how much we badly missed his physicality and class.

We had a lot of good forwards already, but Ja offered something different and I was convinced he was the missing piece of the jigsaw.

I had never given up completely on him, and he knew that the door was always open. I had met him once when I brought my daughter, Gráinne out to the Dangan athletics arena in NUIG to help her prepare for an athletics competition that was coming up.

I was digging up the long jump pit for her when I saw a group of players come out on to the track for some fitness testing.

It was the Connacht rugby team with their Head Coach, Warren Gatland. So, when my digging was done, I edged over to the fence and managed to have a word with Ja in between sprints.

We had planned a weekend away with the team three weeks before our Connacht quarter final against Mayo, and I knew if we were going to get Ja back then we needed him by then.

It was not going to be possible to parachute him back into the panel any later than that, and three weeks was the minimum he would need to knock the ring-rust from his game.

I'm not sure how Pat Egan persuaded Ja to eventually make the commitment, but at the 11th hour he agreed to make himself available for the championship. He had a rugby match on the Saturday of our weekend away, but I told him that we had a meeting that night and the best thing he could do would be to just walk into it, and that's what happened.

Ja was so highly respected there was no issue with him coming back into the fold that late in the day. It was the complete opposite. Fellas were delighted to see him there and it gave everyone a big boost.

We spent that weekend in The Glenroyal Hotel in Maynooth, and it was a really positive experience that provided the perfect launch pad for the championship. All the players came there thinking they were going to have the legs run off them, but I knew the hard work had already been done.

Instead, our time in The Glenroyal was all about honing their minds for the challenge ahead.

For the first time since I had become Galway manager I brought Bill Cogan into the fold, and he organised some really positive debates and discussions about what our goals were, and how we were going to achieve them?

We showed the players some highlights from the fly-on-the-wall documentary, *Living with the Lions*, which chronicled the Lions rugby team's tour to South African in 1997.

Keith Wood, the Irish rugby player, featured a lot in the clips we played, and the themes of hard work and team unity that were explored in that documentary became the main reference points of our weekend too.

This sort of psychological exploration and toughening was new for the Galway players. They had never been exposed to anything like it before and I knew it was hugely important that everyone was there to take part in it. Galway had won just one Connacht title in the previous 11 years so their traditionally deep reservoir of self-confidence had been severely diminished.

We went to Maynooth early on the Saturday morning, but the day before a relative of Pádraic and Tommy Joyce passed away and the funeral was going to take place over the weekend.

They came to me about it and it was a difficult situation. I told them by all means go to the funeral, but we also needed them in Maynooth. It's always like walking a tightrope when you make those sorts of demands. But, in fairness to Pádraic and Tommy, they were both there in Maynooth.

Everyone was passing all the 'commitment to the cause' tests. They were not doing it simply because I asked them to, they did it because we were playing Mayo in three weeks and they sensed the massive opportunity.

The best players are always the most self-driven ones, but as a manager you can help them develop that aspect of their personality. The worst thing you can do is identify a weakness in a player, tell them about it, and then order them to work on it and sort it out.

Players resent being preached to. They are always more critical of themselves than anyone else is anyway, so instead I always used that as leverage.

Regularly, I gave the players sheets with the words 'Stop', 'Start', and 'Continue' written on them.

The players would then have to write down whatever bad habits they thought they had in the 'Stop' section, whatever specific goals for self-improvement they had and how they were going to achieve them in the 'Start' section, and whatever strengths they felt they had in the 'Continue' section.

Their honesty and ambition almost always ensured that they themselves identified the parts of their game they needed to work on most. Because it was self-criticism rather than outside criticism from me, they were much more likely to act positively, rather than resentfully, when it came to addressing it.

On the very few occasions that a player did not identify a specific I wanted them to work on, I could pick up on something else they had flagged and subtly use it to point them in the right direction.

The players made such an effort in our group discussions that we let them go out on the town on the Saturday night and have a few pints.

The following morning we played Dublin in a challenge match and beat them. It might have only been a challenge match, but it felt symbolic that they could do that despite a heavy weekend of mental exercises. I really felt like we were in a good place by the time we headed back west.

I dropped Michael Donnellan to his home in Dunmore.

'You'll sleep tonight!' I told to him, as we pulled in.

'Oh, no... I have to go to the bog now!' he said as he got out of the car.

Michael Donnellan's father, John and his grandfather, Mick had both won All-Irelands so the bar was set high in the Donnellan family and a weekend away training was no excuse to be slacking on the home front.

From a young age, Michael was constantly reminded of the achievements of elders, which must have put an awful burden on his shoulders. But it did not seem to weigh him down. Maybe he was so strong-willed that he was able to use it as a source of inspiration, rather than be overwhelmed by it.

As well as a being a wonderfully talented footballer, Michael was always a born winner.

The bigger the day the more inspired Michael Donnellan would become.

If anything, he was too much of a perfectionist. If he did not have the perfect game, or if an injury was stopping him from playing to his full potential, he could become very frustrated. He never hid on the pitch. He always wanted to lead from the front, and that could make him a challenge at times from a management point of view.

Michael wanted to be at the heart of everything the team did, and he felt that because our midfielders were under orders to let the ball in quickly to our dangerous full forward line of Niall Finnegan, Pádraic Joyce and Derek Savage, it reduced his chances of getting on the ball in the half forward line.

I had to explain that even if the ball was kicked over the heads of the half forwards, they could still get secondary possession by following its trajectory and feeding off the full forward line.

I would point out too that if our full backs and half backs kicked direct ball, then there was a good chance it would come straight to him. I could not just tell Michael that we were doing something and that was that.

I had to explain it, and justify it with him.

I liked that about him because it meant he was passionate about the thing and a deep thinker on the game. It challenged me as a manager, but I always welcomed debate within the group. One of the great strengths of that Galway team was that when we reviewed training sessions or matches it was a no-holds-barred sort of discussion.

I remember someone once giving out to Donnellan for not passing a ball in a certain situation.

'F*** ye,' he replied instantly.

'If ye're free… ye'll get the ball. If ye're not… then ye won't!'

The last time I had heard someone come out with a statement like that was when I played with Kerry legend, Mick O'Connell in an exhibition game in Maynooth in the early 1970s.

Mick was sick of everyone shouting at him for the ball, and he shut us all up fairly lively when he came out with that!

Just like O'Connell, Michael Donnellan had a self-assurance that was rooted in his latent ability. He was probably the most naturally gifted sportsman I ever coached, and I have no doubt that if he had focused on soccer, rugby or golf instead of Gaelic football, he could have made a career for himself in any of those sports.

Watching Donnellan and the rest of the Galway forwards develop so quickly as a unit in 1998 was a joy to behold.

They all had huge natural talent so the challenge for me as a manager was to create a structure that allowed them to achieve their individual potential, but also harness it all within a team ethic.

Having Ja Fallon back on board helped to accelerate that process. Not only did his strength and ball-winning ability complement the speed and skill of players like Donnellan, Joyce and Savage, he also set them a great example in terms of how he applied himself to training. And, when he offered them some sage advice, they had so much respect for him that they always listened.

With six forwards like Fallon, Donnellan, Joyce, Savage, Finnegan and Paul Clancy in the team, I knew we had the firepower to blow any team out of the water.

I was confident too that a powerful midfield partnership of Kevin Walsh and Sean O'Domhnaill would win enough possession in the middle third to supply those forwards with all the bullets they would need.

Our defence was starting to take shape nicely too. Martin McNamara, our goalkeeper, was a very experienced operator but had suffered a crisis of confidence after Galway lost to Mayo in the '97 Championship.

That day it was obviously a tactic for him to avoid the Mayo midfield with his kick outs and instead aim them out towards the wings. But his calibration was off and many of them went straight over the sideline. He was savaged in the press for that, and when I met him after taking over he said he'd be kicking everything straight down the middle.

I told him he wouldn't.

He would do the same thing he did in '97, but this time he would execute his kicks correctly. His confidence had definitely been eroded by what happened the previous year, but it was restored by Corofin's coronation as All-Ireland club champions in 1998.

Martin would give the impression that he was a happy-go-lucky sort of guy and his sense of fun made him a hugely popular figure within the group. I had a good relationship with him, and I knew that much of that casual exterior was a façade. Behind it, he was a hugely focused individual and playing for Galway meant an awful lot to him.

Gary Fahey was a rock at full back and a player I really enjoyed working with because he was constantly striving for self-improvement. Gary is an engineer and a highly intelligent man, and he took the same technical approach to football that he did in his day job.

He would go to every length possible to gain a competitive advantage. He even weighed football boots until he found the lightest pair that would enable him to run the fastest he possibly could.

Mentally, he was incredibly strong. Full back is a very unforgiving position, but, even if his man scored a goal, Gary would never drop his head. He was always focused on the next ball and that is the best quality any defender could ever have.

Gary was a real leader for us, and so was Tomás Mannion beside him at corner back. Tomás would not say much at meetings or even in the dressing room, but he set an example by the way he conducted himself in training and on match days.

Most players need to undertake an extensive weights programme to build the muscle required to survive and thrive at the highest level. Tomás, however, was a hard working farmer who would wrestle sheep or throw bales most days of the week, so he'd have been a serious physical specimen had he never lifted a weight.

I knew all about his steeliness because I had watched him play for Galway for years. He was the sort of fella you'd much prefer to have on your side than against you.

The full back line was completed by Tomás Meehan who was still an under-21 player in 1998. He was a specialist corner back, one of those sticky markers that give corner forwards nightmares. He wasn't a spectacular footballer, but he was very solid. Like many others on that Galway team, he was a really intelligent guy. I have often found that smart men make for smart footballers.

Another of the young guns, John Divilly had forced his way onto the panel after impressing in a challenge match against Limerick before Christmas. By the time the championship came around he had established himself as our first-choice centre back. He would earn the nickname John 'Delivery' because of his ability to drive long range passes into our full forward line.

John wasn't a tight marking, blanket defence, sort of centre back, but his direct style of play and ability to send those deliveries into the full forward line was an important part of our armoury.

Either side of him in the half back line were Ray Silke and Seán Óg De Paor. Ray was our team captain and a good man to talk in the dressing room. He might not have been the most outstanding individual on the team in terms of pure ability, but he was an articulate and positive speaker in team meetings.

De Paor was a hugely inspirational player for us. He was a model professional in terms of his approach to the game. The boys would slag him and say that de Paor wouldn't even suck a mint because he was so focused on eating healthily. That wasn't really an exaggeration either. He had all sorts of diet sheets and was constantly looking for new ways to follow best practice in terms of getting the most from his body.

Some players try to deflect blame when a team loses, or at least duck it. But de Paor was accountable to a fault and would take the blame for things that had nothing to do with him. I had huge time for him even before I joined up with Galway, and working with him only confirmed everything I had thought. Off the field he set an example for others, and on it he was hugely inspirational too.

In every match he seemed to make those few runs forward that would produce a crucial score, and as a defender he covered superbly for others. Neither Divilly nor Silke were the tightest of markers. De Paor, on the other hand, had the athleticism and game-reading ability to cover across the half back line for them whenever necessary.

When I looked at the team we had assembled, there was no obvious weak link. I went into that Connacht quarter final full of confidence, but obviously we all knew it was going to be a huge challenge.

When I went to Galway it was confirmed for me that they had massive respect for Mayo for what they had achieved by getting to two All-Irelands in-a-row. There was no need to motivate the Galway lads. They viewed Mayo as the high bar that they would have to strain every muscle to vault over.

As a management team we were keen to show too that we were leaving no stone unturned in terms of our preparation for the match.

I had received a tip-off that Mayo were playing Dublin in a challenge game so I made sure I had it well covered. I was even able to show our players video clips of the match. That sent the message to the players that we were pulling out all the stops, and it was also of psychological benefit to them to believe they had the inside track on Mayo.

Even though Mayo were the top dogs in the province at the time, there was a real sense that something was building in Galway.

The supporters felt it too, because on the road into Balla there's a miniature house that was normally painted in the red and green of Mayo. But, on the Saturday night before the game, one or more of them came down from Galway and painted it maroon and white.

Before a ball was even kicked it was brewing up to be an explosive sort of match, and the media did their best to pour some more gunpowder into the keg.

They billed it as a showdown between myself and John Maughan.

I was doing my best to play down the rivalry between us and was happy to be less visible on the radar than him, which was not very difficult. Even though I was not admitting it, there definitely was some element of rivalry or tension between us.

It went back to the time I was Mayo manager myself. When John injured his knee I kept him involved for a couple of years in the hope that it would come right.

And when it became clear that it wouldn't, I gave him a role in the management team as a physical trainer. Weight training was very much in its infancy at the time, and John took charge of that and also organised circuit training for me.

I felt that I was giving him a good grounding and insight into management, but then he suddenly just upped and left without telling me.

I had to find out from someone else that he had taken the Clare manager's job. I was happy for him that he had gotten that opportunity. However, I'd have appreciated it if he had told me himself. But even though it was true that we weren't exactly best buddies, in no way did I view the match as a personal showdown between myself and John. That has never been my style. The only thing I cared about was Galway winning as a team.

We were determined to bring the game to Mayo from the very first whistle, and that's exactly what we did.

But even though we started strongly, they struck the first decisive blow of the game when we allowed them to score what was a very soft goal. Martin Mac gave the ball way with a poorly executed short pass and Ciaran McDonald slammed the ball to the back of the net.

An outsider might have thought that moment a serious blow to our ambitions, but I knew the Galway players would react positively because we had discussed such a scenario so often.

That is exactly what happened. Even though Martin was at fault for the goal, he made a brilliant save a few minutes later. That proved our players were not going to allow any setback to affect them.

It was a real over and back struggle with both teams having their moments, but just before half time Derek Savage scored a superb goal that I really felt was the decisive moment of the match. As a goal it was an expression of the sort of football we had been working so hard to perfect.

John Divilly picked out Pádraic Joyce with one of those trademark long deliveries, and Pádraic popped a perfectly timed pass to Savage.

Derek still had a lot to do, but he kept his cool and curled an absolutely beautiful finish into the top left hand corner of the net. That was the moment he really announced himself to the country as a special talent. But I already knew he was worth his weight in gold to the team.

Not only was Derek very accurate in situations like that, he was also very much a team player. Even if he wasn't scoring he was always making a contribution because he never stopped working and had a great knack for winning possession.

And once he got his hands on the ball he was hugely difficult to knock off it because he had a low centre of gravity and was much stronger than he looked.

One of the most underappreciated skills in football is a forward's ability to hold onto a ball for the right length of time, and then release it at the most beneficial moment. Derek had that knack. It meant he was able to bring other forwards into the play and create chances, as well as finish them himself.

His goal that day against Mayo gave us the belief and momentum to drive on from there and win the match.

It was still a contest of very fine margins though. Derek's goal went in off the underside of the crossbar, but in the second half Ciaran McDonald unleashed a fierce shot that cannoned off the underside of the bar and back out into play.

Had that goal gone in, then Mayo probably would've won the match. But there is no doubt either that we were very deserving winners of a really exciting game of football.

As a manager you do your best to provide direction and create the best environment possible, but the best teams are always player-driven. That is what happened that day. The players took ownership of their own destiny and simply refused to be second best.

Ja Fallon gave an inspirational speech in the dressing room at half time, and in the second half he really grabbed the game by the scruff of the neck.

He was just one of many leaders who stepped forward to be counted. They were all inspiring each other with their actions and there was constant communication and verbal encouragement throughout the game.

The older lads in the team had only ever won the Connacht title once before and it was as if they decided they were done with being underachievers and it was time to write a new script.

In the dressing room after our 1-13 to 2-6 win, there was a real sense that we had set out on a grand adventure. The supporters seemed to think that too, because a big crowd of them congregated outside the tunnel that led to the dressing rooms in McHale Park and belted out the *Fields of Athenry*.

That was the moment I realised there is a very special chemistry between the Galway supporters and their players.

They were back on board with us now in a big-way. We would source a lot of positive energy from them throughout the rest of the championship campaign.

CHAPTER 19

Leitrim were our next opponents in the Connacht semi final and it was a little strange to be preparing a team to beat them so soon after I had managed them myself.

Even though I knew most of their players inside out, I respected them well enough to take nothing for granted. We tracked all of their practice matches and training preparations so we knew what they were about coming into the match.

My chief spy, Brendan Harvey was out of commission because he was never going to conspire against his own county, so I had to get my own hands dirty in the run up to the match.

I heard they were playing a behind closed doors challenge game against Armagh in Breffni Park, so I went up there with my daughter, Niamh in the hope that she would be able to find a way into the stadium and report back for me. When we got to the ground, however, we were spotted by the Leitrim goalkeeper, Martin McHugh and our cover was blown.

In a way, I didn't really mind. It sent out the message that we had enough respect for Leitrim to go to those lengths, and weren't taking them any less seriously than any other team.

The Galway players were never likely to anyway, because they had suffered so much at Leitrim's hands when I had managed them.

One of the concerns raised in our team discussions was that Leitrim were able to make life hard for them because Pairc Sean MacDiarmada was such a tight pitch. I assured them it was not, and to prove my point I drove up to Carrick-on-Shannon and measured it.

When I told them the following evening that it was actually a yard and a half wider than Tuam, they couldn't believe it.

I felt it was important to bust that myth for them, and it once again sent the message to the players that we were leaving no box left unticked.

We beat Leitrim easily, 1-16 to 0-5, with our full forward line of Finnegan, Joyce and Savage scoring 1-12 between them.

After the match I was very conscious that expectation levels amongst our supporters, and perhaps even the players, were now in danger of escalating out of control.

I did my best to keep the players grounded before the final against Roscommon, but there's no doubt they were slightly affected by the growing hype and we very nearly came a cropper.

We had tried to prepare as best we could, to the point that we even had the pitch in Tuam widened because I felt our forwards needed as much space as possible. When Roscommon arrived on the day and saw how close the sidelines now were to the fence they kicked up a fuss, but I knew the game wasn't going to be called off at that point.

Despite all our plotting and planning, we just never got motoring. It was a really wet, miserable day, and Roscommon tore into us. We just struggled to cope.

Even when their substitute Jason Neary was sent off 30 seconds after coming on as a sub in the 50th minute, we still failed to seize the initiative. It looked like were on our way out when Roscommon took a one point lead with time almost up, but we got out of jail when we won a last gasp free that Niall Finnegan scored to force the replay.

After the match some of our players admitted they had been distracted by all the excitement and hype in the build-up.

We had asked them to visualise being Connacht champions, yet sometimes you have to be careful when you do that that you don't lose sight of the fact that you have to work hard to make that vision a reality.

A quirk of my first year in charge of Galway was that the whole campaign was filmed by Pat Comer, our substitute goalkeeper, as he made the acclaimed documentary, *A Year 'Til Sunday*. When he came to me first about it I gave him the green light even though I knew I'd have no editorial control over it. I suppose that showed the trust that existed between us all by then.

The first day I noticed he had a camera with him was on the team coach the day we travelled to play Mayo. After we won that game we stopped in Mullarkeys in Milltown to have a celebratory drink and I remember saying to him he could have a best seller on his hands. I was half-joking at the time, but it turned out to be exactly that. You wouldn't have allowed someone from outside the group do it so it was a unique piece of work in many ways.

Usually, supporters never find out what goes on behind the closed door of a team dressing room so it gave people the sort of insight they would never have had previously.

Everyone can see what's happening on the pitch and keep half an eye on the sideline, but the GAA dressing room is normally as sacrosanct as the confessional box.

I was happy for Pat to pull back the curtain though because I knew he would never do anything to denigrate me, the team, or Galway GAA. He filmed it beautifully, and made a point of not being too overt or obtrusive. I only found out after I saw the documentary that he had a camera in his gear-bag most nights that was filming away without me realising it.

That made it much more natural because the people he filmed in those moments were in no way guarded or self-conscious.

To this day, when I am asked to give talks to teams, someone will bring up the documentary and quote something from it. One of the most famous scenes was the team meeting we had after the drawn Connacht final against Roscommon. A lot of home truths were spoken and that meeting was the making of the Galway team in many ways that year.

Sean O'Domhnaill had a poor performance by his standards in the drawn match so he was substituted. On his way off the pitch he kicked over some water bottles, which I was not happy about at all. Even when I had a go at him in that team meeting I knew I had not convinced him he had a poor match, or that his actions were out of order.

He said that no one even noticed him kicking over the bottles, so I produced a report from the *Roscommon Herald* where they picked up on the fact that he was not a happy camper coming off the pitch.

If I have a problem with a player or I am going to drop him, I tell him to his face. They might fuck you out of it, but it is very important you do it to their face.

It is the hardest thing you will ever do as a manager and there were nights where I didn't sleep because I knew the following day I'd have to tell a player he was dropped. But, ultimately, the player will have more respect for you in the long run if you are up front about it. Some of the best friends I have are players I gave bad news, and of course they were angry at the time, but they did not hold it against me in the long run.

The honest words that were spoken within the group after the drawn match against Roscommon bonded us together more closely, but so did the criticism that was being directed our way from outside the group.

Eugene McGee described us as 'Fancy Dans' in his newspaper column, and that really grated with me. But I also knew it was a gift, because I could use his criticism as a motivational tool.

I knew that we hadn't played to our potential in the drawn game and here was someone saying it for me in an uncomplimentary fashion. So the newspaper was produced at a team meeting and McGee's words were used to prick a response from the players.

The replay was a cracking match.

We raised our level, but so did Roscommon and there was nothing in it. The match went to extra-time before we eventually won, 1-17 to 0-17, and the reason we came out on the right side of the result was because of our mental strength and the ability of the players to execute what we had worked hard on in training.

We had developed certain set plays, and one of them was a routine we had devised for throw-ins.

There were four throw-ins that day because the game went to extra-time, and we scored three points out of four attempts from that set play. In a game of such tight margins, that was huge.

The difference between the teams on the scoreboard was the goal we scored in extra-time, and it was a hugely satisfying one because it came courtesy of the sort of work ethic we were demanding from our forwards when they didn't have the ball. It was the second period of extra-time, but Shay Walsh and Michael Donnellan still had the resolve to close down Roscommon goalkeeper, Derek Thompson. Shay dispossessed him, and Michael was in the right place to kick the breaking ball to the back of the net.

I was emotional in the dressing room afterwards because the quality and character of our team had been questioned after the drawn match.

There would obviously be an intense rivalry between Galway and Roscommon, and I had my own history with them too, so it was a really satisfying victory. Though I cringe now when I watch what I said after the game on *A Year 'Til Sunday*. But, in moments of great relief, your guard is dropped and your true feelings come pouring out.

It had been a real struggle to beat Roscommon, but one benefit of that was that the expectancy and hype that had been around the team dropped.

Galway was different too than Mayo in the sense that the county would not have the same tradition of losing the run of itself when it came to hyping up one of their teams. There's a culture in Galway that they expect their teams - whether it's football, hurling, ladies football or camogie – to be contesting All-Irelands every year.

You have to win to get noticed, and that's no bad thing. That does not mean they support you any less, it is just that they tend to keep their feet on the ground a bit more. And when Galway get to an All-Ireland semi final or final, they're not surprised to be there because of the county's standing as a traditional power of the game.

That is a real plus for them, and why I always say that Galway have the ability as a county to come from nowhere to challenge for a championship in any particular year.

The lack of hype meant we were able to get on with our preparations for the All-Ireland semi final against Derry without distractions like big crowds coming to our training session. We were underdogs going into the match but I was confident we would beat them because I knew the players were in a really good frame of mind.

Our older players had been through the dark days of being beaten by Leitrim in Connacht, but the younger ones were unburdened by past failings.

They had no baggage whatsoever, and that fearlessness spread throughout the panel as they viewed the All-Ireland semi final as a massive opportunity rather than a daunting task. I was conscious, though, that a match in Croke Park would be a new experience for most of them.

So we brought the team to Dublin to watch the All-Ireland hurling semi final and get a sense of what the place was like, and what the occasion would be like. Picking a suitable hotel in Dublin was another priority, and we were lucky that John Glynn, the MD of the Doyle Group, was a Galway man.

The Doyle Group owned The Burlington Hotel and The Berkley Court Hotel. I came up to Dublin and walked through both with John and settled on The Berkley Court.

It was perfect because we were all able to stay on the one corridor, and it was a short walk down to the back pitch of Lansdowne Road where we went for a kick-about on the Saturday evening and our warm up on the Sunday.

Throughout the Connacht championship we had kicked a lot of wides. I was not worried because at least we were creating chances and I knew if everything clicked we were capable of really destroying a team. Happily for us, that's exactly what happened against Derry.

We got some great scores, and Ja Fallon in particular was on fire. He was kicking them off the outside of his boot, both left and right.

And when Sean O'Domhnaill kicked an unbelievable score from long range, I knew it was going to our day because he was not someone I expected to be raising white flags. Derry still had most of the players that had won the 1993 All-Ireland final, however they were a team on the way down and we were a team on the way up.

They never saw us coming, and we just took them apart on the way to a 0-16 to 1-8 victory.

Perhaps they underestimated us, and that might have been because they had been at the Connacht final replay as part of a team weekend away. They saw us struggle to beat Roscommon and I'm sure the Derry players went away thinking we were not up to all that much. If they did, it ended up playing right into our hands.

After the match, John Joe Holleran, the County Board vice-chairman, turned to me and said, 'Jesus... I can't believe this is happening.'

'We're not finished yet, there's more to come... John Joe!'

Normally when you win an All-Ireland semi final that impressively it raises expectancy levels and heaps pressure on the team going into the All-Ireland final. Not this time, though, because Kildare were our opponents. They had beaten the three previous All-Ireland winners on the way to the final and their county had gone half-mad with hype.

I was well aware how distracting that could be having gone through it with Mayo in 1989.

Kildare were the story everyone wanted to write and read about, whereas, in comparison, we were a side-show.

I couldn't have been happier.

CHAPTER 20

Our championship campaign had kicked off with a team weekend away in The Glenroyal Hotel in Maynooth, and we returned there for our All-Ireland final training camp.

We had used video clips from the *Living with Lions* documentary on our first visit to illustrate the themes of hard work and team spirit we were focusing on at the time. I was keen we revisit that in some way to emphasise the journey we had been on, and how far we had come.

Keith Wood had been the star of many of the video clips we had used, so I thought it would be great if we could somehow get him involved personally in our All-Ireland final preparations.

He was playing for Harlequins in London. I knew he was from Killaloe in Clare originally so I rang the local Garda station there to see if I could track down a contact number for him?

The Garda I spoke to said he would get in touch with Keith's mother for me, and 10 minutes later I had the phone number I needed.

Keith could not have been more accommodating. He was playing a match for Harlequins on the Saturday, but he agreed to fly to Ireland that night and then have a chat with our players on the Sunday morning.

He ended up getting a bad belt in the jaw during the game and his club wanted to send him to hospital for an X-ray but, credit to him, Keith insisted on keeping his word with me and flew home regardless. That Sunday morning we brought the players into a meeting room, turned off the lights, and played some of the video clips from the *Living with Lions* that featured Keith.

While the players watched, we brought Keith into the room without them noticing so that when the video was finished and the lights were turned on he was sitting there in front of them.

There was an audible intake of breath from all of the players.

Our surprise couldn't have worked out any better.

Keith spoke to them about how to best prepare for big matches. He described how Irish rugby teams would almost tear the heads of each other in the dressing room before matches, and he described that as emotional over-arousal. Ireland would stay with teams for 60 minutes before fading away, and Keith was convinced that was because they had expended so much energy in the dressing room before the game.

He really put a big emphasis on how important it was for our lads to stay cool, calm and collected on the day of the match.

He also spoke about his own background in Gaelic games, and his whole talk was really inspirational. He really connected with the players, and stayed on with us for dinner afterwards. The lads were hanging on his every word, and afterwards I had a really positive feeling about how the whole thing went.

Our preparations could not have gone better, whereas I knew Kildare's had not been nearly so serene.

Every house, tree, and statue had been draped with something white, and the hype was at fever pitch. Mick O'Dwyer admitted to me afterwards that he realised things were out of control and considered taking the team out of the county for a week or 10 days before the final.

It was difficult for their players not to be affected by the fact that everyone around them was losing the run of themselves.

Their preparations were also badly disrupted by injuries to Glen Ryan and Ronan Quinn. Ryan pulled a muscle in his thigh while out golfing on the Friday before the All-Ireland. They did their best to keep that under wraps, but I had such good contacts in Kildare that he was hardly off the course before I had been given the news.

I was revelling in the intrigue that you always get before an All-Ireland final. Both teams are always trying to get the inside-track on their opponents, and we definitely did a good job of doing that.

My contacts were on duty at all of their training sessions, including their last one. They had practised penalties that day and the feedback I received was so detailed that I knew who had taken them all and what corner of the net they had shot into.

We were told they had booked RTE's Michael Lyster to be the Master of Ceremonies at what was meant to be their post-All-Ireland celebration banquet. Apparently, a car was due to whisk him to Kildare after the match, and this sort of information was great ammunition for us in terms of firing up our lads.

As well as trying to unearth all the information we could about Kildare, we also made a point of putting out some disinformation about ourselves.

We let it be known that we were staying in The Burlington Hotel and even had the hotel erect a big sign welcoming the Galway football team. We wanted all the supporters and particularly the media to think that was our base so they would congregate there on the day before the match, when in reality we were staying in The Berkley Court Hotel again.

In those years the Sunday newspapers loved getting photos of the All-Ireland teams arriving in Dublin, but we wanted to avoid that, and we did.

The morning of the All-Ireland final was a wet one, but as I strolled around The Berkley Court the mood was good. It wasn't one of over-confidence. But there was security in the knowledge that we had done everything we possibly could to get ourselves right for the match. It's a great feeling when you go into a match knowing that.

We did have one slight upset though when we reached Croke Park. We had asked for the same Canal End dressing room we had used for the semi final, and we were given a guarantee by officials that we would get it.

I had brought the players up for the All-Ireland hurling final for a dry-run of what they could expect for our match. I wanted them to be able to visualise everything they would go through on the day of the final, so we visited that dressing room to give the players a look around it again.

But then when we reached the stadium on the morning of the match the stewards told us that Kildare were now using that dressing room, and that we had to use the other one.

I was furious.

I had drawn up a minute-by-minute schedule of how our day would unfold, and unless you're inside that bubble it's impossible to understand just how frustrating it is when someone messes with that.

Kildare obviously had a man in Croke Park with the influence to switch the dressing rooms without our knowledge. I've pulled a few strokes in my time, but I didn't like being on the end of one. I didn't want the players to know how angry I was, so I did not make a fuss about it there and then.

But once the players had gone into the dressing room I turned on the Croke Park officials and told them in no uncertain language that if we did not get the Canal End dug-out that they'd have no All-Ireland final.

They obviously thought I was serious, because even though we were in the Hill 16 dressing rooms we were allowed take the Canal End dug-out.

In the greater scheme of things, having to go to a different dressing room was no big deal. But when you plan something with military precision, any deviation from that plan is annoying. The players do the business out on the pitch, and it is the manager's role to make sure everything is as well organised as it can be outside of those white lines. So you take these things personally.

I had fallen short as a manager in an All-Ireland final with Mayo in 1989, and deep down I was hugely ambitious to make amends this time around. You put the interests of the team above all else, but any manager who does not also admit that they are driven to satisfy a personal goal is lying. You keep that personal stuff inside and you never express it, though a small part of you wants to win the thing to satisfy your own ambition. I really, really wanted this All-Ireland title.

It was only a small part of what was driving me though, because any manager who puts his own ego first is doomed to failure.

Players have no time for someone who does the thing as a vanity project.

They will only follow you if they know you care about them first and foremost, and are doing all you possibly can to help them become better as individuals and better as a collective. That was definitely the case for me as far as those Galway players were concerned. I took a real interest in their lives, and not simply because I wanted them to do the business for me on the football pitch.

They were a great bunch of lads and they gave such a big effort to the cause that I wanted to help them in every way I could.

There was a natural empathy there, and that fostered a real feeling of family within the group. I got to know the players' parents, wives, and girlfriends, and they were also made to feel part of the mission we were on together. The Galway 'family' extended beyond significant others too. The late, great Dympna Burke helped head up the Galway Supporters Club and was someone I became great friends with. She was very suspicious of me starting off because she was unsure about the merits of appointing a Mayo man as Galway manager, but we eventually got on like a house on fire.

Whenever we'd play a challenge game behind closed doors that was meant to be secret, she'd always work her contacts to find out where it was? She'd even bring a ladder with her to the matches so she could scale a wall if she was locked out of the ground!

It was our own private game to see whether she'd be there or not, and she'd give me a triumphant look if she was.

Pat Egan and herself would pretend to be fighting all of the time, but they were as thick as thieves really. There was such a great sense of camaraderie around that Galway team, and I did my best to be inclusive. I put a big premium on everyone feeling like they were part of the thing. Tommy Kelly was the County Board's assistant-secretary, and on match days he was the man that stood outside our dressing room door.

Usually the men who do that want to be standing inside the door so they can see what is going on, but in our set-up it was a two-man operation and we wanted someone on the outside too so you wouldn't have people knocking at the door and disturbing the calm inside.

I always affirmed the importance of everyone's role, no matter how small it was. Everyone was a link in the chain, and we could not afford a weak one.

It wasn't just the ability of the 15 players running out onto the pitch on All-

Ireland final day that gave me confidence we were going to win the match. It was the fact that we were such a tight group and everyone involved from the top to the bottom had given everything of themselves to help the team lift the Sam Maguire Cup.

I recently read Alastair Campell's book, *Winners: and How They Succeed*. He referenced a story in it about former USA President, John F Kennedy, and the early stages of the NASA moon-landing mission while he was in office.

Kennedy was coming out of Cape Canaveral one day and he stopped to talk to someone who was sweeping the floor.

He asked her what she was doing?

As if there was any need to explain? The cleaner replied, however, that she was helping to get a man to land on the moon. In other words, there was such a sense of a mission about the thing that everyone in NASA, right down to the cleaners, felt a part of it.

If you can foster that sort of unity then it is a very powerful thing, and in 1998 I felt really positive about our prospects going into that All-Ireland final because I knew we were such a tight unit.

My confidence seemed well founded when we surged into an early three point lead that was inspired by some brilliant play from Michael Donnellan.

After that, Kildare got a run on us and our team suddenly lost its shape and conviction. A Dermot Earley goal put them in control, and they should have had another just before half time, which may well have killed us off.

Instead, Pádraic Joyce knocked over a free that closed the gap to just three points at half time. We were still breathing.

The main message in the dressing room at half time was that we hadn't played at all, and yet we were still only three points behind. However, if we didn't now give it everything, we might be left with a lifetime of regrets.

I took the starting 15 into the warm up room and simply told them that this was the biggest day of their lives, and it should be the best one too. After that I left them on their own to talk it out.

There was going to be little I could do for them once they ran back out onto the pitch.

When the players emerged from that room, the corridor that led back to the pitch was lined on both sides by our 15 substitutes. They did that off their own bat. There was no instruction from me. It was a spontaneous gesture, but it could not have been organised better. It just sent out the most positive body-language possible. I'm sure when the lads ran down that corridor with their friends and teammates shouting encouragement they must have been bursting out of their skins.

Our credo all year had been that everyone had something to contribute to the cause, whether they were on the field or not.

This was the perfect illustration that there had been a total buy-in to that mind-set. As the starting 15 ran back out onto the pitch, it was as if they were taking the baton off our subs and were ready to run. There is nothing more satisfying for a manager than to watch your team suddenly click and blow the opposition away.

For it to happen in an All-Ireland final is something very special indeed. The 12 minutes of football that Galway produced at the start of that second half was as close to perfection as you will ever see.

Ja Fallon suddenly came to life when he kicked a brilliant point from under the Hogan stand. That was the first spark. Almost immediately, the whole team just caught fire. The goal that put us in the driving seat was a thing of beauty and a perfect example of the philosophy that our style of football was based on.

John Divilly won a free and immediately launched one of his special deliveries deep into Kildare territory, where the ball was won by Michael Donnellan. He had the presence of mind to immediately put Pádraic Joyce through on goal with a defence-splitting pass. Pádraic's finish was sheer class.

Most forwards in a one-on-one situation like that would've blasted the ball, but Pádraic showed great coolness to sell a little dummy that took him past Kildare goalkeeper, Christy Byrne and allowed him to kick the ball into an empty net.

Kildare were reeling.

We kept landing punch after punch.

Ja kicked an incredible sideline over the bar. Then Sean O'Domhnaill landed a sky-scraper of a point from around 50 yards out.

He and Kevin Walsh were now dominating everything in the middle of the pitch, and they were being helped by Martin Mac who was landing his kick outs near the sideline for them to run on to. A year earlier he had been pilloried for driving his kick outs against Mayo over the sideline, but now they were all hitting their targets which was a testament to his mental strength.

Kildare eventually managed to stop the rot and came back at us. Brian Murphy was brought on and got his hand to a ball that hit the crossbar, so I could never really relax. But when Seán Óg de Paor kicked a point to put us four ahead in injury time, I knew we had it won.

And I enjoyed a couple of minutes of pure bliss on the sideline.

I had been at all the great Kerry V's Dublin matches of the 1970s when Mick O'Dwyer and Kevin Heffernan had pitted their wits against one another.

In the closing minutes of those matches I always closely watched the manager who was about to win, and I tried to imagine how he felt in those moments? It was always my dream to experience that sensation for myself. Now, here it was happening for real.

It was just heaven on earth.

I'll remember it to my dying day.

Football management was what I had dedicated my sporting life to after my own playing career had ended, and winning the ultimate prize was a vindication of all the effort I had put into it over the years. There had been some rocky patches along the way, but I had always felt that I was capable of leading and managing teams to the highest standard. Now I had proven it once and for all.

Leaving Mayo in the manner I did in 1991 had been a really painful chapter, but now all that regret had been washed away and I felt a deep sense of personal justification and satisfaction.

It was a lovely private feeling, and one that I would never have expressed publicly at the time. My primary emotion was pure joy for the Galway players and the county as a whole. Not only had they won the All-Ireland, they had done it in some style.

Some of the younger players, especially Michael Donnellan and Pádraic Joyce, just brought their game to a new level on the biggest day of all. Michael was frustrated earlier in the year because he felt we were by passing the half forward line too much by hitting it in long to the full-forward line. But I had always told him I was not trying to inhibit his game in any way, and the onus was always on him to shape and expand his own role within the team.

Against Kildare he had dropped deep to pick the ball up from our full back line occasionally, and he got the crowd to their feet with some electrifying runs.

To be able to do the things he did in that All-Ireland final confirmed to everyone just how much talent we had, how much our self-belief had grown, and how much empathy bordering on telepathy our team could play with.

Successful teams always evolve over time - just look how much Donegal developed between 2011 and 2012.

But whereas it took them two championship campaigns to develop a brand of football good enough to win an All-Ireland final, our team had evolved to that point over the course of just one. That says a lot about the intelligence of our players. They were the people who drove it.

As a management team we set them targets and did our best to incentivise them, but it was the players who really pushed out the boundaries.

As good as our win over Mayo in the first round of the championship had been, we were a much better team by the time we beat Kildare in the All-Ireland final. When the final whistle eventually blew, all hell broke loose. I was submerged by the crowd and ended up being swept from the Cusack Stand side of the pitch to under the Hogan Stand.

I met Mattie McDonagh and a few more of the former Galway players from the three in-a-row team. They all had tears in their eyes, and were delighted to be finally handing over the baton to a new generation of players. I somehow got over as far as the steps up to where the players received the Sam Maguire Cup, and it was a special moment to embrace them all as they passed.

We had been through a lot together, and now we had realised all of our hopes and dreams. I wanted to freeze that moment forever.

There was footage in *A Year 'Til Sunday* of Robin Doyle roaring crying while the cup was being presented. The previous Wednesday I had to break it to him that he had not made the cut for our match day panel of 24. He was not crying out of sadness because he had missed out on being part of an All-

Ireland final match day panel. He was crying with pure joy. That summed up for me just how much everyone felt a part of the thing, no matter how big or small their role.

The post match banquet was in The Burlington Hotel. When we got there it was as if half of Galway had descended on the place. All of the players' families were there and it was another one of those really special moments.

As you looked around the room you could see that what we had just achieved was starting to sink in with everyone. The place was a sea of happy faces. It was a long night, and I wanted to be everywhere at once. The Saw Doctors played an informal gig and everyone was up on tables. It was a really joyous sort of mayhem.

At some point in the wee hours of the morning I managed to make it up to my bedroom. I brought Sam with me.

I just sat there looking at it for a long time and had a private moment to myself. What I held in my hand was something I had dedicated most of my life towards winning, and now I had it.

I'd love to have won it as a player.

This was the next best thing.

By the following morning the place was still full and there was an endless queue of people looking to have their picture taken with the cup, with a good few babies dropped into it for photographic posterity too.

One of the most enjoyable episodes of the morning was when I met Brendan Coffey, who was the team's unofficial mascot. Brendan has special needs and lives in sheltered housing in Galway. For over 20 years the County Board have been good enough to bring him on the official team coach to matches and make him feel like part of the Galway GAA family.

I had a great relationship with him. He liked to call me 'Boss', and he came with us on all our weekends away as well to all our matches. On those weekends away he'd sit outside the nightclub when the players were out for a few drinks. The next morning he'd come to me with his usual greeting of, 'Boss, Boss, Boss', and give me a first hand account of how they all behaved themselves.

Galway meant everything to him. He worked in Roches Stores where he bagged groceries, and if he spotted someone with a Galway jersey he'd bring them to the top of the queue. He got in trouble for that a good few times! At the end of every campaign he'd present an award to his Player of the Year, and it was usually whoever had given him the most lifts to matches.

He was central to the whole thing, the heart and soul of the group. This was as much Brendan's victory as ours.

When I met him on the morning after the All-Ireland final in the foyer of the hotel, he announced that I was the lucky winner of his annual award, and that he was going to make the presentation live on Galway Bay FM who were broadcasting from the hotel.

He even had a trophy. God knows where he had got it from, but it was just a lovely, funny moment.

There was a reception in the hotel on the Monday for both the Galway and Kildare teams. I'm sure the Kildare lads would've preferred to be anywhere else, but it had been the tradition for decades to bring the two teams together the following day.

We weren't too keen on the arrangement either. We had to be conscious of not hurting Kildare's feelings by being too boisterous with our celebrations when all we wanted to do was head home to Galway and have another big party.

We eventually got going and took the train as far as Athlone before taking two coaches from there to Galway. There were thousands of people in Athlone, and Ray Silke and I got off the coach at the bridge over the River Shannon and walked across it with the cup held aloft. It was a symbolic act.

It really felt like we had won the Sam Maguire for the whole of Connacht, not just for Galway.

The journey through Galway was incredible. Every town we passed through was packed with people going absolutely nuts. There must have been 20,000 people in Tuam alone, and it was 2.0 am before we finally made it to Galway. There, a big reception in Eyre Square awaited. It was 4.0 am by the time we made it to the Sacre Coeur Hotel, and another hour or two before we eventually got our meal. It was a real all-nighter.

It was such a totally different vibe to the homecoming I had experienced with a defeated Mayo team in 1989. Massive crowds had turned out to greet us then too, but it makes the world of difference when you have a cup to celebrate with them.

On the Tuesday morning I visited my wife, Ger's father, Mattie Towey with the cup. He was quite ill at the time and would die three weeks later, so it was great that he got to hold it.

I also brought the cup to St Nathy's College which was decked out in signs of welcome and congratulations. That was a lovely occasion too because St Nathy's was where it had all started for me, both as a player and a coach.

A couple of thousand people turned up that night for a reception in the square in Ballaghaderren, and it was great to be welcomed home by my own in that way. I'm sure they'd have all preferred if I had brought back the cup as Mayo manager, however people still seemed to take a lot of satisfaction from the fact that a Mayo man had brought the Sam Maguire Cup back across the Shannon.

Someone had painted a line from *The West's Awake* on a big hoarding in the town square. They had taken a poetic licence that summed up the mood perfectly.

But, hark! Johnno's voice like thunder spake.
The West's awake! The West's awake!

CHAPTER 21

When you climb up onto a pedestal you are there to be shot down. Mayo were not long taking aim.

John O'Shea from the charity GOAL knew what he was doing when he arranged an exhibition match between Galway and Mayo for the Wednesday after the All-Ireland final. Our lads had been celebrating for three nights straight and thought it was going to be a friendly kick-about, but John Maughan and his players had different plans.

They were hitting hard and determined to win it, which they duly did because the celebrations had taken a predictable toll on us. It was bad form really considering the occasion, and it rankled with everyone in our camp.

It would've been nice to pay them back in the 1999 Connacht championship, but that wasn't to be either.

Our young players had become nationally famous names overnight, and it was inevitable that all the adulation and attention they received was going to have an impact. The same beady-eyed focus and ravenous appetite just was not there. All winter I was trying to set deadlines about when we would draw a line under the All-Ireland win and move on. But it proved difficult.

Everyone wanted a piece of the Sam Maguire Cup and the Galway players, and it was difficult to say no.

There were constantly functions where the cup needed to be and requests for the players to go as guests. There was even some celebration out in Canada that the players were invited to, but I put down my foot and some of our County Board officers went out there instead.

I had a bad vibe about the '99 championship from the very first game. That was a trip to England to face London.

The atmosphere over there was almost like a continuation of the All-Ireland final celebrations because it gave the Galway ex-pats in London a chance to glory in the previous year's achievement. The hotel we stayed in wasn't suitable either. It was more like a budget motel, and there were an awful lot of Galway supporters hanging about which made it difficult for us to focus on the task at hand.

Even though we beat London by 10 points it was far from a vintage performance and I came home thinking we had gotten our campaign off on a poor footing. We had not moved on mentally from 1998, and I knew it was going to be difficult for us to do so.

Sligo were next up in the Connacht semi final. On the way to the game we passed a big chipboard sign. It read...

Galway Championship Exit Seven Miles Ahead

It was very nearly a prophetic sign too, because we were poxed lucky to get out of Markievicz Park with a draw thanks to a late Pádraic Joyce equalising point. I had stopped the bus on the way to the game to take down the sign, and I produced it at training the following week to give the players a little bit of extra motivation.

We beat Sligo easily in the replay. However, as the Connacht final against Mayo approached I was uneasy because I knew we were still not playing to our full potential.

The star of our replay victory over Sligo had been John Donnellan, Michael's older brother. John had missed out in 1998 because of a cruciate ligament injury, so he was keen to make up for lost time. Before the Connacht final against Mayo the *Irish Independent* ran a story that someone had laid a massive bet with Cashman's bookmakers that John would be Man of the

Match in that game too.

Cashman's claimed that £1,000 had been laid on him at 12/1, and then another £1,500 at 10/1. The punter was in line to win £27,000.

At that time, RTE's Man of the Match was decided by public vote, so there was speculation that there was a betting sting brewing.

I smelled a rat. When I was interviewed about the situation I asked that RTE suspend the Man of the Match award for the game. It was an unnecessary distraction, and in hindsight it was a mistake for me to make any comment on it. I was only making it worse by playing into the media's hands and the journalists duly built it up into an even bigger story than it was. It put an awful lot of pressure on John. It was the last thing we needed.

The whole affair summed up just how different the 1999 campaign was compared to '98 when we had no such distractions, flew under the radar, and almost had an All-Ireland final won before people realised it. That's the difference between achieving success, and coping with it. Success brings a whole new set of challenges, and by the time we played Mayo in the Connacht final we looked a drained team.

We started the match quite well, but fell away badly as we scored just a single point in the second half while Mayo hit six in the last 14 minutes.

They were the hungrier team. They did to us what we had done to them the year previously. Maughan was chaired off the after the final whistle and their management, players and supporters all celebrated like they had won an All-Ireland rather than just a Connacht title. Perhaps they put too much effort and emphasis on beating us, because they were subsequently beaten well in the All-Ireland semi final by Cork which was a big disappointment.

They had reached the finals in 1996 and '97, so they should have been able to throw more of a shape at doing it again in '99.

When Tyrone and Armagh emerged in Ulster in the noughties they drove one another on to new heights. It would've been great for Connacht football had Mayo gone on in 1999 to bring the Sam Maguire Cup back to the province again.

Our dressing room after that Connacht final defeat was a very deflated one, though we were applauded by a big crowd of Galway supporters, who had hung around for a long time after the match, as we emerged from the room. That gave us a lift.

That was also a really significant moment. It proved that the relationship the players had built up with the supporters had not been in any way broken by the defeat to Mayo. It was clear to everyone then that our journey wasn't over.

I have no doubt that the seeds for the team flowering again in 2000 and 2001 were sown in that moment.

Throughout my county management career I continued coaching school teams with St Nathy's.

Just like it had been when I was a pupil myself, the dream was to win the school's first All-Ireland title since they brought home the Hogan Cup in 1957. We finally made that dream a reality when we won the All-Ireland 'B' Championship in 2000. I took almost as much satisfaction from that achievement as I did the All-Ireland win in '98, because it was very much a labour of love.

By then St Nathy's was no longer a boarding school so we were effectively operating off five clubs, Ballaghaderren, Kilmovee Shamrocks, Western Gaels, Eire Og and Eastern Harps.

We won the Connacht final after extra-time on the same day that Brian O'Driscoll scored those three famous tries against France in the Six Nations Championship. The All-Ireland semi final was on the same day as the FBD League final, and I was determined to be at both games, even though the St Nathy's game was at 1.0 pm in Longford and the Galway match was at 4.0 pm in Tuam.

Dympna Burke and Paul Hearty of the Supporters Club came to my rescue by hiring a helicopter to take me from Longford as soon as the school game was over. We won the semi final by three points. As soon as the final whistle blew I was immediately whisked to Longford rugby ground where the helicopter was waiting.

We landed on a pitch in St Jarlath's in Tuam, and I got a car from there to Tuam Stadium where I made it in time for the Galway team warm up. Everything went to plan, except the FBD final itself. We lost to Mayo again.

I undertook the same level of preparation for the All-Ireland Colleges 'B' final with St Nathy's as I did had with any major match that Galway played. The final was to be played in Portlaoise so we brought the players down there on the Wednesday before the game to get them used to their surroundings. I was getting a great kick out of the whole thing. Not just because it was my own school, but because we had upset the odds so much to get as far as we had.

Every team we played had more individual talent than we did, but our lads were such a tight bunch and had such spirit that they always found a way to win.

The school still had no pitch at the time. There was just a small piece of ground no more than 30 yards by 20 yards behind the old toilets that had to suffice as a training ground. It was little more than a bog really, but that is where we did all our physical training.

Maybe it hardened the team mentally, because in the final against St Augustine's from Dungarvan they once again found a way to dig out a two point win in difficult circumstances. It was a great occasion. Hundreds of past pupils from St Nathy's went to the final and I know the victory meant a lot to them all.

Of that team, Andy Moran would go on to captain Mayo, Sean Mangan and Barry Regan also played for Mayo, and Eamon Towey played for Roscommon.

It was a huge achievement for the school, something recognised by the fact that we held a reunion for that team 10 years later. From my point of view it was also a nice release from the more pressurised environment of county football.

On the Galway front, everyone came back with renewed appetite for pre-season training at the end of 1999 and that encouraged me. But then injury reared its ugly head.

First Tomás Mannion retired because of persistent problems he was having with his back. I put a lot of energy into trying to persuade him to change his mind, but it was to no avail. He never actually announced he was retiring; he just didn't join up with us again.

Losing Tomás was a blow because he was such a vital pillar of our defence, but worse was to come when Ja Fallon then tore his cruciate ligament. I was on my way out the door to a Galway club championship match when I got a phone call from Pete Warren telling me that Ja had been badly hurt playing for Tuam Stars against An Cheathru Rua and that it looked like a cruciate.

My heart sank. Things had been coming together nicely after the disappointment of the 1999 campaign, so this was a real sickener.

Ja was not just a great player, he was a foremost leader in the group and someone who was hugely respected by everyone. He tore the cruciate at the end of May, just after we had beaten New York in the first round of the championship, and there was never any chance that he would be back for the remainder of the campaign.

The only way we were going to be able to be successful without two crucial players, like Mannion and Fallon, was if every other player in the team raised their level, and that's exactly what happened.

In 1998 and 1999, Declan Meehan was on the fringes of the team and used exclusively as a forward. But in 2000 we moved him back into defence, and he flourished. In hindsight, we should have made that switch earlier than we did. He was a real find for us. He excelled in every game he played, and his emergence meant Mannion's loss wasn't as badly felt as it might otherwise have been.

Joe Bergin was another player who joined the party in 2000. He was only 19 but he was already a strapping athlete as well as being a skilful footballer and he made an immediate impact. Kevin Walsh's dodgy knees gave him a lot of trouble in 2000, so Bergin arriving on the scene was crucial.

Perhaps the most important development of all though in 2000 was the manner in which Michael Donnellan assumed the mantle of leadership.

He did not play for us at all in the league. He decided to take up a part-time contract to play soccer with Galway United instead, and we did not start him for the first round of the championship against New York because of that. But he was back in the team for the Connacht semi final against Sligo and replaced the injured Ja at centre forward.

From there, he effectively had a free role to roam all over the pitch as he pleased. There are very few players you can give that sort of responsibility to, but Donnallan had a massive work ethic and possessed such quality on the ball that it suited him perfectly. He was absolutely superb in that Connacht semi final against Sligo, but so was the whole team.

It was as close to a perfect performance as you could get. We led by the scarcely believable score of 0-14 to 0-0 at half time, and ended up winning by 0-22 to 0-4. Nineteen of our 22 points came from play The full forward line of Pádraic Joyce, Derek Savage and Niall Finnegan hit 12 of them. It was a remarkable return.

The fluency of our score-taking was impressive. Equally amazing was the rabid intensity of our tackling, and the work rate without the ball pleased me most.

It was clear that our appetite for success was renewed, and the scale of the win was all the more pleasing considering it was achieved not just without Fallon and Mannion, but also Kevin Walsh and John Divilly who were both injured.

Watching Galway that day, I really got the sense that this was a good team on its way to becoming a great one.

Leitrim were our opponents in the Connacht final, and we beat them at our ease too. My only worry going into the All-Ireland semi final against Kildare was that we had yet to play a hard championship match.

Kildare had a huge incentive to beat us and gain vengeance for 1998, though that played into our hands because it ensured there would be no complacency. We absorbed a couple of big blows in the match – a poor first-half display, and the concession of two goals at potentially critical moments – but our focus never wavered.

Ja Fallon was still an important part of the group even though he was injured, and he made an inspirational half time talk that really galvanised the team.

We were much superior in the second half, and it was our physicality as much as our skill that ground down Kildare in the end. We had developed that dimension. We were able to mix it with teams, if that's how they wanted to play the game, and the old jibe of Galway footballers being 'Fancy Dans' was very much redundant.

When you can combine sheer class with toughness it is a very potent combination, and that day Kildare had no answer to the quality of Michael Donnellan and Pádraic Joyce. Pádraic really emerged as another leader for us that day. He was a strong character and very much his own man. He could be critical of his teammates in training and after a match, but that was only because he was motivated by the desire for the team to be better.

What was especially impressive about those Galway players was that they could have fierce arguments without every losing respect for each other. Of course, as manager I had to make sure that it never became personally insulting or that cliques developed in the dressing room.

That was never a worry.

A culture of constructive criticism, something every outstanding team needs, was definitely driven by our players.

Kerry was going to be a tough nut to crack in the All-Ireland final. They always are.

And when Pádraic Joyce came down with a nasty virus after the win against Kildare it was a serious blow. I went to Meath manager, Sean Boylan, who is also a renowned herbalist, to get Pádraic a remedy. He was in a bad way and I was extremely worried about whether he would be able to play in the final.

He was able to tog out in the end, but the illness definitely hindered his preparation. Apart from Pádraic's illness, I was satisfied that we had done everything we could to get ourselves in the best possible shape for the match. We stayed in the Citywest Hotel where we took over a whole floor. We were very conscious of keeping the players in a quiet, calm atmosphere, and this way they wouldn't be annoyed by anyone outside of our camp.

They didn't even have to go downstairs. All our food was delivered to our floor, and our meeting rooms and physio rooms were all located there too.

On the Saturday night before the final I got a phone call from Michael Meehan, Tomás and Declan's father.

Their brother, Noel had been badly injured in an accident. He had fallen whilst sleepwalking and had broken his hip. It was a serious injury, but Michael didn't want me to tell the two lads for fear it would affect their focus on the game. We had always made an effort to ensure the families of the players felt a part of the greater collective, and Michael's attitude illustrated just how much they did.

On the morning of the match we used that tight bond that existed between the players and their families to get them in a good place emotionally. Pat Comer and Tommie Gorman had visited all of the families and recorded messages of support which we then played for the players after they had their lunch.

We could see it meant a lot to the players. It was a nice reminder that they were not just playing for themselves, but for their families, and for the whole county of Galway. I felt that the team were in a good place mentally. However, you never really know for sure how a team is going to perform on any given day until the ball is thrown up.

And there is no doubt it took us a little time to come to terms with the aggression of the Kerry players, especially in how they went for Michael Donnellan.

I have great time for Kerry football, but the manner in which they targeted him that day was bordering on the cynical. That year *The Sunday Game* had a player-cam that focused on one particular player, and in our All-Ireland semi final win over Kildare that player happened to be Michael.

My information is that Kerry got their hands on the DVD, and it was very obvious in the All-Ireland final that they specifically looked to nail Donnellan. They had studied his style, and it was done in a methodical way. By my count, four different Kerry players got booked for flooring him with overly aggressive tackles.

When we found ourselves trailing by 0-8 to just 0-1 after 25 minutes, we had to make some serious recalculations on the sideline.

One of the tougher calls we made with our team selection was to pick Joe Bergin ahead of Kevin Walsh at midfield. Kevin had been struggling with his knees all year and Joe had done brilliantly for us. But Joe failed to hit the same heights in the final, and we called him ashore after just 19 minutes. I did not like doing that to him, and he told me afterwards he felt harshly treated, but there is no place for sentiment when your team is struggling in an All-Ireland final.

Kevin caught the very first kick out after he came on, and his presence on the field sent a surge of electricity through the rest of the team.

Moving Pádraic Joyce from full forward to centre forward made a big difference too, and by half time we had reduced the gap to just three points.

We drew level with 12 minutes to go in the game. At that stage we looked the most likely winners, but it had taken such an effort for us to drag ourselves back into the contest that we were just not quite able to finish Kerry off and the game ended in a draw, 0-14 apiece.

We had our opportunities to win it. The best chance fell to Derek Savage but his shot felt short into Kerry goalkeeper, Declan O'Keeffe's hands. There was a lot of criticism afterwards that Derek should have passed that ball to Pádraic Joyce who was on his shoulder, but I would not blame him for taking the shot on.

The great thing about those Galway forwards was that they all had super confidence in their own ability. I will happily go to my deathbed insisting that Derek was not being selfish; he was being confident.

There was a two-week gap between the drawn All-Ireland final and the replay, and I found it was a very difficult situation to manage because it was such an unfamiliar place to be. I think it would be much better to play the replay a week later, rather than have such a long wait to do it all again.

The ultimate aim when you reach an All-Ireland final is to have done your preparation so professionally that there is nothing more you could have done. So, when you have to do it all again, even though you are convinced you prepared one hundred per cent for the first day, where do you search for that extra room for improvement?

The replay was down for a Saturday evening at five o'clock. That was also something new. It was a dank, wet October evening too, and by throw-in it was almost dark already.

Declan Meehan scored one of the greatest team goals the game has ever seen early in the match. It confirmed his greatness as a player, but unfortunately it did not give us the momentum to go and win the match.

Kevin Walsh started the replay in place of Joe Bergin, but he only lasted 17 minutes before he was forced off with a knock to the knee. Joe did well when he came in, but Kevin's loss was still immense. We ran running repairs on him on the sideline and sent him back in midway through the second half.

By then, the game was already running away from us. Kerry outscored us by 0-8 to 0-3 in the final 18 minutes to win by 0-17 to 1-10 in the end.

That Kerry team was stacked with some really great players, and we could have no complaints about the result. We had actually done well to be so competitive against them over two games when you consider we were missing two of our best players in Ja Fallon and Tomás Mannion, and that Kevin Walsh was not one hundred per cent.

Had we won the All-Ireland title despite those circumstances then it would have been our greatest achievement of all.

It was not to be.

We gave it everything we had. My only regret is that we did not find a way to win the drawn match having come from seven points behind. It was easy to convince myself too that we'd have won it had we started Kevin Walsh rather than held him in reserve.

That winter, I gave a lot of consideration to walking away from the job. I had given it three years, and I did not want to overstay my welcome.

Pat Egan, however, was a very shrewd County Board chairman, and it was an intervention from him that persuaded me to stay on, and also possibly gave the panel the impetus to win the All-Ireland in 2001.

After the 1998 All-Ireland final we had decided not to go on a team holiday. In retrospect, that was a mistake. Instead we gave the players holiday vouchers and let them all do their own thing. I thought a team holiday would only be a distraction ahead of the 1999 campaign. But I was wrong.

After our 2000 All-Ireland final defeat to Kerry, Pat came to me and said, 'We'll give these fellas a holiday they'll remember for the rest of their lives!'

We went to South Africa. It really was a fantastic bonding experience for all of us. It healed any slight divisions that might have been there between the players themselves, and possibly between the players and management.

We came home from South Africa a tighter unit than ever before. I had a feeling in my gut that we would give the 2001 All-Ireland Championship a really good rattle.

CHAPTER 22

Winning the 1998 All-Ireland Championship with Galway was pure elation, whereas doing it again in 2001 was deep satisfaction.

It is a serious achievement for any team to win an All-Ireland title because it is a difficult thing to do, so when a team wins the Sam Maguire Cup twice it proves they are really something special.

The fact that we had to overcome some serious setbacks along the way in 2001 made the achievement all the more satisfying.

The year started with great promise. Ja Fallon was back in the fold after missing out on the 2000 campaign, we persuaded Tomás Mannion to come out of retirement, and we unearthed talented new players like Kieran Fitzgerald, Matthew Clancy and Alan Kerins.

Things were motoring along nicely until we reached the league final and were beaten by a point by Mayo, after surrendering a three point lead in the closing minutes.

It was a really annoying defeat. I was left convinced that we needed to broaden our attacking options for the championship by having a serious look at Alan Kerins.

Alan was a hurler first and foremost, but he was a very fine footballer too and at the time was in a good vein of form. He had played Sigerson Cup with

Trinity and was beginning to play club football for Salthill.

I sent three people to look at him in a club match, none of whom knew the others were going. They all came back to me saying that he should be given a shot in the championship. When three people form the same opinion of one another independently, it's a very good sign.

I wanted to see whether Alan could cut it at the highest level. I decided to put him into the team for our first match of the championship against Leitrim at the expense of John Donnellan.

I rang John to tell him that Alan would start in his place because we wanted to try something different, but that this wasn't necessarily going to be the team for the rest of the year. Although he was obviously disappointed, I thought he had taken the news well enough.

But when we were about to announce the team I got a phone call from Michael Donnellan. He told me that John and himself were now unavailable for selection.

That came as a big shock.

I had to take the bull by the horns and told Michael that if that was the case then the team would be announced without them.

Michael was absolutely crucial to us, and John was an important member of the panel too. However, if a manager is dictated to by a player then his authority is eroded forever.

Sometimes you have to make hard calls as a manager. But if you can look yourself in the mirror afterwards and know it was *the right thing* to do, then it was the right thing to do.

It was a very difficult time. The one saving grace was that Michael never gave an interview to a newspaper or radio about the situation. If he had done that and castigated the management then it would have been all over. It would have been much more difficult to resolve the situation had it become public knowledge, and people had taken sides.

As long as he kept his own counsel there was a chance something could be worked out. All sorts of efforts were going on behind the scenes to try to ensure it was. Thankfully, common sense prevailed in the end and there was a meeting set-up where Pete Warren and I met with Michael and John in Pete's house.

I made it clear that I wanted both of them back in the panel but that there were no assurances about places in the first team for either of them.

I have always said that members of the same team should only ever argue about the issue; never make it personal. I have had plenty of blazing rows with players about dropping them, and with selectors about who we should or shouldn't drop. But it is never personal. That way you can always move on afterwards without the relationship being damaged.

My disagreement with the Donnellans was never personal, and that is why when we resolved it we were able to quickly consign it to the past without the relationship being poisoned for good.

We picked the team for Roscommon and Michael was in it, but John wasn't. Michael ended up having a quiet game, but so did almost everyone else on the team and Roscommon hammered us with Frankie Dolan scoring two goals.

Of course the talk after the match was that Michael didn't try for us. That was untrue. He had tried, but like the rest of the team he fell short of his usual standard.

I went into the Roscommon dressing room afterwards to congratulate them. The late Jimmy Murray, who captained Roscommon to the 1943 and '44 All-Ireland titles, was up on a bench singing *The West's Awake*. The joy in that room only deepened my own sense of despair.

I was convinced we were out of the championship. It was the first year of the Qualifiers, but I had thought the back door was just for teams beaten in the preliminary rounds of the championship.

I was so focused on winning a Connacht championship I had given little or no thought to the alternative. When Pat Egan told me we were still alive, it did not really feel like much of a reprieve.

The consensus was that we were finished.

That the wheels were off the wagon and the only way out of the rut was to be hauled into the ditch. It was hard to disagree.

I gave the players the following week off. I told them we would not be contacting them, but that if they wanted to try to turn the thing around that there would be training on the Tuesday week.

After our post match meal in the Cre na Cille in Tuam I decided I might as well face the music. Myself and Pete Warren went down the town for a few drinks. I went into Loftus's Pub, and who was there only John Tobin, the Roscommon manager.

He was over the moon and my heart was on the floor.

Once again the emotional difference between winning and losing was stark, and it stung. That night I went home in a deep depression. I was struggling to see how there could be any way back for us.

The next morning I was woken by a phone call.

It was Pat Egan.

'Look… I know there's a lot of flak flying,' he began. 'But the people who count in Galway football are totally behind you.

'You'll have another year after this regardless of what happens… go do whatever you have to do. We're fully behind you…

'… we'll back you one hundred per cent.'

I immediately jumped out of bed.

That phone call from Pat was exactly the tonic I needed. Instead of feeling sorry for myself, I decided to put my shoulder to the wheel once again. I give Pat huge credit for what he did. In Mayo I had experienced the situation of people wanting to distance themselves from me after a defeat, but Pat's support was unstinting.

I rang Stephen and Pete and told them we were going to give this thing one more lash.

My enthusiasm was bubbling up so much all of a sudden that I was dying to ring the players too and really rally the troops. But I had told them I would not be in touch so I had to hold fire until that training session the following week.

It was set for eight o'clock.

I went there earlier than usual to see what my fate would be? Even though it was not long after seven, Tomás Mannion was already there. He would never have been one of the first at training because of his farming commitments. I immediately knew this was a good sign. The few words he said to me before the session also gave me huge encouragement.

The defeat to Roscommon had been an especially sore one for him. Frankie Dolan had scored two goals off him and people were saying he was finished, and should never have come out of retirement.

But he was not throwing in the towel, and that was hugely affirming. No one else was quitting either.

Every single player was in the door by half seven.

We did a few quick drills.

But I wanted to test the waters. So we quickly just let them at it in a training match. They took lumps out of each other. I turned to Stephen and Pete.

'This is looking good!'

I blew the whistle early and brought them all back into the dressing room where we had a really soul-searching discussion.

Every issue was addressed. Everyone was brutally honest with one another. We all had to face up to the performance against Roscommon. The message from everyone was that it was just not good enough, and could not be tolerated. There was no point playing the blame game, though. The focus had to be on turning the thing around because if we kept bitching then every one was a loser.

I was part of the chat for the first 20 minutes but after that I left them to it. All the players stayed in the dressing room for a good while longer having a heart to heart.

That was all very encouraging. However, we were still a very vulnerable team travelling to play Wicklow in Aughrim in the first round of the All-Ireland Qualifiers.

The players were visibly tense on the team bus on the way down to the match, which made me nervous. It was also a very windy day. Perhaps it was a stroke of luck that we won the toss and were able to play with it at our backs in the first half.

That helped us get off to a fast start. After Alan Kerins scored the first of our three goals the self-belief drained from Wicklow and we coasted to a fairly comfortable nine point victory.

It was hardly a vintage performance, but I was satisfied that two of the big calls we had made with our selection had worked out well.

Tomás Mannion had been moved from corner back to centre back, and immediately looked at home there. And our goalkeeper, Alan Keane had made an assured debut.

Martin McNamara had opted out of the squad during the league and the original plan was that he would return for the championship. He had been in the stand for the league final against Mayo, but afterwards decided that he could no longer make the commitment and was calling it a day. Padraig Lally was his initial replacement, but he had a tough day in the Connacht semi final so we decided to take a punt on Keane instead.

He had not been part of the panel during the league, or even for the first round of the championship against Leitrim, but after that win I gave him a ring to ask him would he be interested in playing in a challenge match against Clare?

I only contacted him on the morning of the game and he initially said he couldn't make it because he was working down in Cork at the time. But he rang me back 10 minutes later and said he was on his way. He was a big, strapping man, who had a great physical presence between the posts. It says a lot about his mental strength that he was able to come in for that Wicklow match and immediately look at home.

When the draw was made for the next round of the Qualifiers and we were pulled out of the hat with Armagh, it looked like a bad one for us. We might have won well against Wicklow, but I knew our self-belief was still fragile and that Armagh would represent a seriously tough test of our credentials.

They had taken Kerry to a replay in the All-Ireland semi final a year previously, and had already beaten Down and Monaghan in the Qualifiers after making an early exit from the Ulster Championship.

What worried me most though was that we had played them in a challenge game two weeks before the match against Wicklow and they gave us a serious beating. My friend Frank Kelly settled me down by pointing out we would be genuine contenders again if we beat Armagh, and that was the message I started driving home to the players too.

Even though I knew we'd be up against it, I told the players this was the best draw possible for us. Luck was on our side, because on the day of the game Armagh had a delay getting to Croke Park and were unable to complete their usual warm-up.

That worked out in our favour. We started strongly and went 0-7 to 0-1 ahead. With just 17 minutes remaining we were seven points up and seemingly coasting to victory, but then Armagh summoned a comeback that illustrated just how vulnerable a team we still were. They drew level in the final minute of normal time and looked like the team with all the momentum.

When our need was at its the greatest, the team showed some real grit and character. Michael Donnellan had been our best player throughout the match, so it was fitting that his intervention should lead to the winning point.

Armagh's defender Justin McNulty came charging forward with the ball. Michael read his intentions and blocked down an attempted hand pass which diverted the ball into Paul Clancy's path.

Paul had been out for us all year because of injury and was making his first appearance as a sub that day. He reminded everyone of his quality by slotting over the winner from 40 yards out. After the game I met the Armagh joint-managers, Brian Canavan and Brian McAlinden in the Croke Park players' lounge and they told me that their time in charge of the team was up.

Had we lost the match, then I have no doubt that it'd have been me rather than them deciding to call it quits.

We had shown some fragility in that second half, but the manner in which we had still dug out the win did wonders for the team's self-confidence. Our momentum was building, and I could sense that the players were really driven again to be the best team in the country.

I think it had dawned on them that if they did not win another All-Ireland they would be quickly forgotten. There was a real desire within the group to show the country that they were a special side.

Our round four Qualifier against Cork was another roller-coaster of a match. We went 1-7 to 0-0 up after 20 minutes. They then rallied to within one point of us with six minutes to play. Just like we had against Armagh, we somehow managed to regain the initiative, and outscored Cork by four points to one over the closing minutes.

It wasn't good for the heart to be winning matches in that fashion, but at least it made it very easy at our team meetings to put the players under pressure to eradicate their inconsistencies.

We were on the train home to Galway when we got the news that we were drawn to face Roscommon in the All-Ireland quarter final.

By that stage we always travelled to and from Dublin by train rather than coach. We had a good relationship with Myles McHugh and his staff from Iarnrod Eireann, and all the stops were pulled out of us. We'd ring them early in the week to arrange a food menu and fellas were delighted to eat on the move and get home early rather than hang around Dublin and not get home until late at night.

And, if there was a gap between matches, we would also let them have a few beers on the train so the journey home would become a bonding session as much as anything else.

That evening the atmosphere in the train was a hugely positive one as soon as we got the news that Roscommon were our next opponents.

We had let ourselves down when we lost to them in the Connacht semi final in Tuam, and the body language and excited chatter of the players told me they were hugely motivated to set the record straight.

It was the perfect draw for us and the worst possible one for Roscommon. We blitzed them, 0-14 to 1-5 and afterwards there was a really good feeling that we had wiped clean our mistakes from earlier in the summer.

I was quietly confident of victory going in against Derry in the All-Ireland semi final, yet it looked misplaced when we trailed by five points with just 15 minutes to go. Once again, the players proved they had the character to fight their way out of a tough corner, and possessed the sheer quality to absolutely destroy a team when they got a run on them.

Between the 57th and 70th minutes we outscored Derry by 1-6 to no-score, and the game was won in spectacular fashion.

Mattie Clancy scored the decisive goal and it came courtesy of a tactical ploy that worked just before I was about to abandon it.

Tommy Joyce made a huge contribution for us as a roving forward in that

2001 campaign. We would start him at corner forward, but he had the licence to move all across the forward line. That year he was extremely fit, and he was probably the best distributor of the ball on the team so his vision really gave us an extra dimension.

By pulling him out of the corner forward position, the idea was that whoever played at wing forward on that side of the pitch would have a lot of room to run in to and exploit.

Mattie Clancy was operating there in the second half against Derry after coming on as a sub. But wasn't making the impact in that space that we wanted him to. I ran around the back of the Derry goal to get word into Mattie to go back out the field and play like a more traditional half forward.

Just before I got to him, he banged home the goal that clinched the victory.

The tactic had worked in the end, but I was seconds away from abandoning it, which goes to show you need luck on your side as well. The following weekend I watched Meath unexpectedly hammer Kerry by 15 points in the other All-Ireland semi final. For the last few minutes the Meath supporters in Croke Park 'Ooohed' and 'Aaahed' every pass as they kept the ball from Kerry and toyed with them like a cat with a ball of wool.

Ger and I walked back to Heuston Station after the match and we met some Kerry supporters who wished us luck in the All-Ireland final, but assured us that we didn't stand a chance against that Meath team.

I remember smiling to myself because this was the best scenario possible for Galway.

Meath had been so brilliant against Kerry that they were going to be hyped up to the last, whereas we could come in under the radar again just like we had in 1998.

It really played into our hands and incentivised us big time.

My message in the weeks coming up to the All-Ireland final was that the bigger the challenge, the greater the opportunity. And the players totally bought into that mind-set.

We had a fully fit panel for the All-Ireland final and that made my job of picking the team a hugely difficult one. Alan Kerins had made a big contribution to our journey to the final, but in the end we decided to pick Paul Clancy ahead of him.

It is always tough breaking that news to a player, but Alan made it easier than usual because he took it so well and said he understood.

And, as hard as it was to leave Alan out, I was delighted that Paul was getting his opportunity because he had missed out on starting in the 1998 final because of an injury he suffered earlier in the year against Leitrim. The team we picked was very much based on what we felt would best counter Meath's strengths.

We put a lot of thought into our match-ups. Especially the decision to man-mark Trevor Giles with Declan Meehan, and give Richie Fahey the job of tagging Ollie Murphy, who had been the best forward in the country that year.

What was really encouraging was that when I went to Declan and Richie with this plan, they made it clear they had been hoping to get those jobs.

Darren Fay had been another hugely important player for Meath on the way to that final, and we also devised a plan for him. We figured he'd have prepared himself mentally for the challenge of marking Pádraic Joyce, so we decided to start Derek Savage at full forward instead.

No one would see that coming. Least of all Fay, and we hoped it might sow enough confusion to unhinge what had been a very solid Meath defence until then.

All of our match-ups worked well. Just like in 1998, we saved our best performance of the year for last. The teams were level at six points apiece at half time, but we absolutely blew them away in the second half to eventually win, 0-17 to 0-8.

Declan Meehan completely obliterated Trevor Giles. It was a performance that won him the Player of the Year Award for 2001.

Ollie Murphy was forced off injured, but even before that happened he was struggling to get any sort of change out of Richie Fahey.

Derek Savage's speed and movement made life uncomfortable for Fay, and when we then pushed Pádraic Joyce into full forward he cut loose in the second half and scored five points from play to finish with an incredible personal haul of 10 in total.

KEEPING THE FAITH ■ CHAPTER 22

After our defeat to Roscommon we had played some brilliant football through the Qualifiers, but only in short bursts. Whereas in the All-Ireland final we sustained a high-quality performance for most of the second half and Meath just could not cope with our quality.

The night before the match I had watched a DVD of the drawn 1996 All-Ireland final between Mayo and Meath.

That day Mayo opened up a six point lead midway through the second half but when they then sat back and tried to defend it, everything unravelled for them. On the morning of our match I emphasised strongly to our lads that if they were to find themselves in a similar sort of position they had to go for the jugular.

So it gave me a lot of personal satisfaction that one of the last points we scored came from great interplay between Sean Óg De Paor and Declan Meehan, who had both bombed forward from their defensive positions.

It was the first year of the back door in the championship, so we became the first team to win an All-Ireland title without first winning their province.

The back door system was meant to be designed to help weaker teams improve their standard, but we had shown it ultimately benefited the stronger teams more to have a second chance. Kerry and Tyrone would later do the same.

I learned an awful lot through that championship campaign and felt I became a better manager as a result. The harder you have to work to get to where you want to go, the more rewarding it is when you get there. I know everyone in the group felt the same way, and there was a real sense of achievement afterwards.

We were definitely a more experienced team in 2001 than we had been in 1998. Tactically, we were more flexible and astute, and players like Michael Donnellan, Pádraic Joyce and Declan Meehan had blossomed into bona fide stars of the game.

Michael had started out as a wing forward, but by 2001 he had developed into a hugely effective midfielder. His driving runs, accurate kick passing, and ability to take a score were all hugely valuable to us. We would not have won the All-Ireland without him, so the fact that we nearly lost him for the year underlines the extent to which we lived on the edge of a cliff.

Michael has a strong personality, however I always regarded that as a positive rather than a negative because who wants a team of sheep?

You want people to stand up for what they believe in and give their views, even if those views are contrary to your own at times. I have never had an issue with players like that. My job is to channel that strength of character in the right directions.

We never discussed our dispute in the aftermath of the win, but I suppose the pictures taken of us embracing on the pitch after the final whistle spoke volumes.

Another important factor in 2001 was our decision to persist with Tomás Mannion, when the easy thing to do after the defeat to Roscommon was to drop him. Instead, we moved him from corner back to No.6 where he was absolutely inspirational.

His performance in the All-Ireland final was his best of the year. When I coach centre backs I always tell them to have a look at the video of his display that day because it was perfection. He made about five or six runs up the field at crucial moments in the game, and all of them brought some sort of dividend. He was also rock solid defensively, but had such good judgement that he always picked the right time to leave his base and give the team some forward momentum.

That day, Tomás Mannion wrote the script on how to play as a centre-back. The standard he performed at was all the more laudable when you consider he had gone a year and a half without playing at the very highest level before he decided to come out of retirement in 2001.

But he was always physically very fit because of his work on the farm, and he was also one of those natural sportsmen who was gifted at whatever he tried.

He won a Railway Cup hurling medal with Galway and was also a very talented rugby player. I sat beside him for a while on the train home after the All-Ireland final and asked him which sport he loved above all? He surprised me by saying it was actually rugby.

Had he diverted all of his energy into that sport, I have a feeling he'd have been winning Triple Crowns rather than All-Irelands.

That train journey home on the Monday was a really enjoyable experience.

We all had a great night with the fans after the game in the Citywest, but it was nice to just have a couple of hours in our own company on the train home.

It's another symbol of success when the Executive train is put at your disposal because it always went to the winning team.

The first class lounge is laid out like a room where you can all sit around together side by side. The Monday newspapers were there for us to read. We had a few drinks. It was a great way to unwind and relive the memories of the day before.

Players and management alike had put in a huge effort all season. The pay-back that makes it all worthwhile is when you can sit in a room together like that, look one another in the eye, and feel that warm glow of satisfaction that comes from having achieved something truly special together.

CHAPTER 23

They say you should get out at the top, but that is easier said than done because the view from up there is a nice one.

Perhaps I really should have walked away from Galway after winning the All-Ireland in 2001. The thought did briefly cross my mind.

But the team was still relatively young and I thought we could continue to be successful. We did manage to win two more Connacht titles, in 2002 and '03, but with the benefit of hindsight it is now clear that we were in a slow, but steady decline. You really do have to be maxing out your potential to win an All-Ireland title, so if you even drop your standards slightly then you will fall short.

We were still a very competitive team in '02 and '03, but a number of factors combined to dull our edge ever so slightly and that is all it takes to separate All-Ireland winners from also-rans.

Injuries to key players hurt us more than anything else. Michael Donnellan required treatment after the 2001 campaign for a knee injury I believe had its genesis in the rough treatment he received from Kerry in the 2000 All-Ireland final. Michael was a driven character who always strived for perfection, and while he worked his way back to full fitness he was overzealous in his dedication to the rehab.

As well as doing the training that had been laid out for him, he also took it upon himself to do his own individual sessions in the gym. When he told me that he had done 50 sessions in an eight-week period over February and March, I was impressed by his work ethic. But what we did not know at the time was that by making short-term gains in terms of his fitness, he was actually sowing the seeds for a long-term injury that I believe ultimately cut his career short.

Michael trained so hard in the early months of 2002 that he developed Osteitis Pubis, which is basically an inflammation of the pubic bone that comes from over-exercise. It was still a relatively unknown injury at the time so it was initially misdiagnosed as a pulled muscle in his stomach, and it was some time before our medical team got to the bottom of it and sourced the best treatment for him.

Michael based his game on pace, swerving runs, and a constant work rate. In his early 20s he could rip through teams with his ability to solo run at top speed and play little give-and-go balls that would blow a defence wide open. But the injury restricted his ability to do that, and he found that hugely frustrating.

He knew exactly what he wanted to do in a match, but his body would not always enable him to do it which killed him, because he had such high personal standards. He was still one of our best players in my final three years in charge, from 2002 to 2004, and produced some moments of absolute brilliance.

But he could never quite get back to the level of fitness that he knew he needed to be at to do all the things he wanted to do on a pitch.

I think that is why he eventually retired from county football at the relatively young age of 28 in 2006, when he should have been at the peak of his powers. He was obviously an awful loss to Galway football first and foremost, but he was a loss to the game as a whole too because talents like him do not come along very often.

Michael wasn't our only key player who was never quite able to get back to his very best physical shape after injury.

Ja Fallon had returned to the team in 2001 after rehabbing from the torn cruciate that wrecked his season in 2000. But the knee did not heal as well as he'd have hoped, and he struggled to hit the sort of form that had made him the best player in the country in 1998.

The weakness in his knee led to issues with his hamstring, and he too was hugely frustrated by his inability to get back playing at full-throttle. So much so, that he also retired prematurely from county football after the 2003 campaign.

Injuries to key players was not the only issue we had to contend with in 2002. We also seemed to lack the single-minded focus we had in 2001, and there was an element of friction within the group that had not been there before. That was not too apparent when we beat Roscommon easily in the first round of the championship, but it definitely seemed to drain our energy as the year progressed.

I felt we were well briefed for the challenge that Mayo would pose in the Connacht semi final thanks to a nice piece of espionage that gave us some inside information.

I got a tip-off that a hotel in Boyle had taken a booking from Sean Boylan for a meal for the Meath team. I knew that could only mean one thing!

Meath were up to play a challenge match against Mayo, and the most likely venue was Carrick-on-Shannon, just down the road from Boyle.

I immediately rang Joe Reynolds and asked him to check it out? He called down just as the match was starting, and was able to give me chapter and verse on how Mayo had lined out and performed. Even though we were forearmed with that knowledge, we were still desperately lucky to beat Mayo.

We did not lead until we kicked two injury-time points to win the game, and the result might have been different had Conor Mortimer not missed an easy free just before we scored them.

It was only some typically classy finishing from Pádraic Joyce that dragged us over the line in those dying minutes.

On the one hand I was encouraged that we had shown the quality of champions by grinding out a win in difficult circumstances. On the other, I was worried that we fell so far short of our highest standards.

Around that time the story that dominated every headline on both the front and back pages of the newspapers was the bust-up between Ireland soccer manager, Mick McCarthy and Roy Keane in Saipan that led to Keane walking out on the squad on the eve of the World Cup.

Tommie Gorman had arranged what would become a famous interview with Keane in Manchester. Before he went, he rang me for my opinion on the whole thing, and thought I could help because of what had happened the previous year with the Donnellan brothers.

When he spoke with Keane, he even suggested that if the Donnellan brothers and John O'Mahony could have successfully mended our relationship, then there was no reason why he and McCarthy couldn't.

The irony was that in the summer of 2002 my relationship with my own captain, Pádraic Joyce was not as healthy as I'd have liked it to be.

I think a tension first developed between us because I had dropped his brother, Tommy from our starting team for the championship.

I'm sure it was a source of angst for him, because it was probably all anyone was asking him about back home in Bearna Déarg.

Pádraic took the duty of captaincy seriously and he was very keen to push the thing on. He was a very driven sort of character with high personal standards, and he wanted everyone else to reach those standards too. The problem was that not everyone was going to be able so, simply because Pádraic was such an exceptional talent. When they didn't meet his expectations, he grew frustrated.

He was giving out to his teammates on the pitch which was fine when it was peers like Michael Donnellan or Derek Savage, who had played with him all the way up and were able to give it back as well as take it.

But he did not realise that it was having a negative impact on younger players who would not have been so self-assured.

My instinct has always been that if you want to hold someone accountable for a mistake, the best thing you can do is gee them up by telling them they'll get it right next time, rather than fuck them out of it. Pádraic and a couple of the other lads who had strong personalities did not realise just how influential they were and how much a negative criticism from them could inhibit the self-confidence of the younger lads.

Pádraic was a perfectionist and he probably tried too hard to be the perfect captain. He took too much on his own shoulders and allowed himself to get sucked into things he'd have been better off steering clear from.

A week before the Connacht final against Sligo there was a round of club league matches in Galway that were supposed to be 'starred' matches. This meant that the county players would not have to play in them. But some of the clubs desperately needed a win in the league so there was pressure put on the players to play in them. And Pádraic came to me to tell me that they would.

I hit the roof, and told the players in no uncertain terms that if they played in the league matches I would not be going to Castlebar with them for the Connacht final.

Sligo were a better team than people were giving them credit for, and I knew if the majority of our team played a league match the week before it would put us at a massive disadvantage. After missing out on the Connacht title in 2001, there was no way I was going to let anything screw it up for us again.

It was definitely a worry though at the time that Pádraic was getting distracted by side issues. I wanted him to realise that all he needed to do to be an inspirational captain was to get himself right and play his own game, because that would get everyone else playing around him.

On the day of the Connacht final there were a couple of other issues that caused unnecessary friction.

It was a really wet and windy day. Pádraic wanted to play against the elements in the first half, whereas I thought it made much more sense to play with them.

Against a team like Sligo you want to take their hope away as quickly as possible. If you let them into the game then they are very dangerous opposition, whereas their heads will drop if you get a run on them early on.

I had also checked the weather forecast and knew the direction of the wind was due to change and that it would probably not be as big an advantage for the team who played with it in the second half. But I did not want to simply veto Pádraic's opinion. Instead it was put to a vote in the dressing room and the majority wanted to play with the wind if we won the toss.

I always liked to have two sets of jerseys on match day so the players have the option of changing if the weather is bad and they are soaked at half time.

The decision was made to play in our long sleeved jerseys because it was such an unseasonably cold and wet day. However, Pádraic and a couple of other lads came to me and said they wanted to wear the short sleeved jerseys.

This sounds like a very small thing. But I did not want any distractions before any match because in that pressure cooker environment everything is magnified a thousand degrees. We ultimately beat Sligo without having to really extend ourselves, and it is a testament to Pádraic's latent ability that he was our best player by a wide margin despite my concerns he was losing his focus.

He was absolutely majestic on the day in terrible weather conditions, and it only emphasised my conviction that all he needed to do to be an inspirational captain was do his stuff on the field.

Apart from his individual excellence, it was far from a brilliant performance by us. Sligo scored the last six points of the match. My chief emotion afterwards was one of relief rather than elation, and it was one that seemed to be reciprocated in the stands because there was an almost eerie silence once the final whistle blew.

Players sometimes have their hunger sated by success, but not to the same extent that supporters do.

Expectation of success can dull the edge of supporters and players alike, and my concern now was that our team was going through the motions a little bit rather than jumping out of their skins every time they played.

I was trying to emphasise to them that they would confirm their status as one of the truly great teams of any era if they put All-Ireland titles back-to-back. But I was not sure I was getting through to them.

We had a five-week gap between the Connacht final and the All-Ireland quarter final. That did us no favours. Our opponents, Kerry had come through the back door and had built up momentum and match sharpness by winning three matches in the same period of time.

To make matters worse, our preparations were also hit by yet another distracting side issue.

Pádraic Joyce's club, Killererin drew with Carraroe in the county championship and were meant to play extra-time, but Killererin refused to. The ball was thrown in without them and the game was awarded to Carraroe.

That caused some serious ructions behind the scenes, and was the last thing we needed when trying to get focused on an All-Ireland quarter final. Another problem we had was that Michael Donnellan's injury was getting worse all the time and affecting his ability to train.

The consequences of that became apparent in the quarter final. He scored a truly brilliant goal early in the match, but his injury caught up with him and he faded from the game thereafter. Michael's struggles mirrored that of the team as a whole. We just could not summon the same intensity we had the year previously and in the end we were well beaten by eight points by a hungrier Kerry team.

It was the first time that some of our most stalwart players began to show the considerable mileage they had clocked up in the previous five years. Michael Donnellan, Ja Fallon and Sean Óg de Paor were all substituted, which would have been previously unthinkable.

It broke my heart to have to do it.

All of them were such loyal servants and had given their all to the cause for as long as I had been manager. Pádraic Joyce was one of our few players who played to his usual high standard on the day, and afterwards he was quoted in the newspapers as saying that the team management needed to take a look at themselves too after the defeat.

That did not upset me unduly. I have always felt that if you are happy to take some of the credit for a victory then you must take a share of the blame for a defeat. The optics of a team captain coming out and having a pop at the manager weren't great though, and underlined that we were not as unified a group as we had been the year previously.

But I did have to consider the possibility that Pádraic was right, that I was largely to blame for our drop in standards and that my race as Galway manager was run.

We had five really good years together, and I did not want to sour the connection with that Galway team in any way.

If there was a chance that I was now a barrier to their success, rather than someone who facilitated it, then it was time to move on and let someone else take over. Whenever there has been a moment in my life where I need to think deeply about something or make a big decision, I have always gone back to our old homestead in Kilmovee and walked the land behind the house.

That little field was where my obsession with football began, and as I walked around it all sorts of memories came flooding back.

I was struck by how quickly life can change. The days when I played football in that field with my neighbours felt within touching distance, and yet here I was now all these years later with both my parents passed away.

For a brief moment I just felt very lonely.

Maybe that is what happens when you have a big decision to make and the people who supported you for most of your life are no longer there to lean on. I realised that I was feeling emotional because I had already subconsciously decided that I had come to the end of an important chapter in my life.

Galway had been great for me and I had been good for Galway. Now it felt like the right time for us both to part ways.

Around this time, Kildare, Laois and Roscommon got in touch to see if I was available to take charge of their respective teams. There was also an approach from the Mayo Supporters Club to see if I was interested in managing my native county again.

But even if I had decided to leave Galway, there was no way that I would immediately jump into another dressing room straight away.

When I told Pat Egan of my decision to call it quits, I was certain that my mind was made up. But Pat was a very persuasive sort of character and told me straight up he didn't want me to go, and put forward a strong argument as to why I should stay.

He worked on me for a couple of weeks, and he was helped by the fact that the county under-21 team, that I also managed, won the Connacht championship. I could see there was another generation of very talented players coming through, and it was easy to convince myself that if they could be successfully blended with the players who had already won two All-Ireland titles then we'd have a very potent mix.

The more I thought about it, the more I persuaded myself that I would regret it if I walked away at that point.

So, when Pat Egan put the gun to my head and told me he needed an answer one way or the other before we played a Kerry team inspired by Colm Cooper and Tadgh Kennelly in the All-Ireland under-21 semi final, I ultimately decided to give it another go.

It looked like I had made the right decision when we subsequently beat Kerry, and then won the All-Ireland under-21 title by hammering Dublin in the All-Ireland final. It was the county's first All-Ireland title in the grade since 1972, and it was a hugely satisfying achievement.

My enthusiasm for driving Galway football forward was renewed.

Deep down, however, I already knew there was a hard road ahead.

CHAPTER 24

The first challenge ahead of the 2003 campaign was to persuade Pádraic Joyce to continue playing for Galway.

The row over Killererin's exit from the 2002 club championship when they had refused to play extra-time against Carraroe had turned increasingly bitter. They even took their case to the High Court and won an injunction to prevent Carraroe's next match in the championship going ahead.

Ultimately, they failed in their bid to be reinstated to the championship, and Pádraic was so disillusioned over their treatment by the Football Board that he let it be known he would not play for Galway in 2003.

There were even rumours doing the rounds that he might declare for Cork because that is where his girlfriend lived. But, as angry as he was, I knew Pádraic would never do that because he was such a proud Galway man.

Obviously I desperately wanted Pádraic to come back on board, but only if he was in a positive frame of mind.

There was an awful lot of speculation in the media about the situation, but the fact that Pádraic kept his own counsel ultimately made it a lot easier to resolve.

And when he decided that he wanted to come back, we played him the following day in an FBD league match against Mayo even though he had not been training with us. The optics of him wearing the jersey again and parading him in front of the neighbours killed all that speculation stone dead, and we were able to move on swiftly.

Pádraic's willingness to come back despite the fact he felt his club had been shafted by the County Board proved that our relationship was still solid.

We had not always sung off the same hymn sheet the previous season, but that in no way eroded the massive respect I had, and still have, for Pádraic. Not only was he one of the most naturally talented footballers I ever worked with, he was also one of the most dedicated.

Another boost was Kevin Walsh's decision to play on for one more year. He and Tomás Mannion had both decided to call it quits at the end of the 2002 campaign, but we were thankfully able to persuade Kevin to change his mind. We made him team captain, and he responded brilliantly. So much so, that he would finish the year with an Allstar award that was a fantastic achievement considering he was in the twilight of his career.

We also finally got a correct diagnosis of Michael Donnellan's pelvic injury, and the County Board were good enough to stump up a few thousand euros to get him operated on by a specialist in England.

He recovered in time to make himself available for the championship. A week before the Connacht quarter final against Roscommon, however, he turned on his ankle in our final trial match. On the following Monday the *Irish Examiner* ran a big headline saying he had broken his ankle and was gone for the year which was absolute rubbish.

When that 'exclusive' about Donnellan's injury broke, I quickly set the record straight with the *Irish Examiner* and also quashed the story by speaking to Brian Carthy from RTE.

It might seem like a small thing, but you do not want the rest of the players thinking a key teammate is injured before a big game or, worse, that you had hid that from them. Michael was only fit enough to make the subs bench for the Roscommon match. Even without him, we won comfortably enough.

One of the highlights was the debut of Michael Meehan who was a huge addition to us in 2003. He was an incredible talent, one of the most naturally gifted forwards I have ever seen.

It is such a shame that his career was ruined by injury to the extent that it was. He was as big a loss to the game as Colm Cooper would've been had his career been similarly blighted. The win over Roscommon was followed by another straight forward victory over Leitrim which set up a Connacht final showdown against Mayo.

John Maughan was back in charge of them. I knew they'd be gunning for us and I was determined to tick every box possible in terms of our preparation. It is always satisfying to strike a psychological blow against your opponents before a match, and we landed a few.

I booked the Glenlow Abbey Hotel for our pre-match and post-match meals. Ten minutes after that was arranged they rang me to say Mayo had also just been in touch in the hope of doing the same. It was nice to know we had just got in ahead of them, and got a head-start on our Connacht final preparations.

Then, at a challenge match against Limerick in Pearse Stadium, we spotted that they had sent a 'spy', Tommy Lally to keep tabs on us.

Tommy was Mayo's goalkeeping coach at the time, so they weren't cute enough to send people we didn't know. I recognised him immediately, and he was quickly shown the road home. Our own attempts at espionage proved more fruitful than theirs.

I had detailed Brendan Harvey to travel to a challenge match they were playing against Kerry, but he rang me to say that his car had broken down. I wasn't going to give up that easily, so I rang John Glynn in the Citywest Hotel and he gave Brendan the loan of a brand new BMW.

Brendan travelled to the game in style. Once again, the big advantage of using Brendan as my chief spy was that no one knew who he was. He went right down behind the Mayo dug-out and got a great read on what the Mayo management were saying to one another, as well as his notes on the match itself.

That was of huge benefit. I got further encouragement when I was driving home one evening and I passed two of my former St Nathy's pupils, Andy Moran and Sean Mangan one the side of the road.

They were both on the Mayo panel and were clearly thumbing their way home from training. So I offered to give them a lift.

They seemed a bit embarrassed by the situation and explained they had called for a cab to pick them up. It was reassuring to know not every box was being ticked in the opposition camp.

We had one last trick up our sleeves to keep Mayo guessing for as long as possible before the ball was thrown in for the final.

Michael Donnellan was still struggling to get himself fully fit, and Michael Meehan was carrying a knock. We decided to hold them in reserve. I didn't want Mayo to know for sure exactly how we were going to line up until the very last minute though, so we sent out 17 players for the pre-match parade.

It was only when the game was about to begin, when Donellan and Meehan ran over to the subs bench, that all our cards were on the table.

It was a tough game and we didn't play particularly well, but we still managed to grind out a four-point victory. I thought there was a lot more in us that would come out when we played Donegal in the All-Ireland quarter final. But it just didn't happen.

We looked like an ageing team when we hit the wall in the second half as Donegal came from four points down to go one ahead. In the end, we needed a last gasp point from Kevin Walsh to snatch a draw.

Michael Donnellan was substituted with a couple of minutes to go. He drew a kick at some water bottles on the way off. It was out of sheer frustration on his part because he was still struggling to get back to full fitness after his surgery at the start of the year and was not doing the things he wanted to on the pitch.

Of course, there were elements in the media who were only too happy to highlight the dissension he showed coming of the pitch. Eugene McGee wrote that there was trouble in the camp, and Martin McHugh had his say on it before the replay too.

Michael gave the best possible answer to that by producing his finest performance of the year in the replay. That's why I always admired him so much. Instead of sulking or feuding with me, he went out on the pitch and made his point there. Unfortunately, his heroics were not enough to prevent us falling to a three point defeat on a nightmarish day that saw us kick wide after wide.

In the immediate aftermath of the loss I was convinced I was finished as Galway manager, and perhaps I should have announced that there and then.

But, instead, I stalled and that gave Pat Egan the opportunity to work on me and eventually talk me around with the help of Tommie Gorman. Ultimately, the main reason I stayed on was that I knew I may never get to work with such a talented group of players again.

Also, when some of the older players like Sean Óg de Paor, Gary Fahey and Kevin Walsh were willing to go for one more year, I thought I should give it one last shot as well.

If they had gone and I was faced with a two year rebuilding job I would not have had the appetite for it, but with them still there and the graduates from the 2002 All-Ireland under-21 team one year older, I felt there was still an All-Ireland in the team.

I knew I still had the backing of those veterans, and the energy and enthusiasm of the younger lads was guaranteed too, though I did have doubts whether some others were as committed to me or the cause as they were previously.

Players like Derek Savage, Michael Donnellan, Paul Clancy and Pádraic Joyce had been listening to me for all their county careers. I was worried that my voice and the message had grown stale to them.

They had known only success. I wondered too whether their appetite for it had already been sated.

I knew it was important that I freshened things up for them and I made two additions to the backroom team. Liam Sammon came on board to help with team training and also to act as an extra pair of eyes in the stand on match days, while the sports psychologist, Liam Moggan was also recruited.

We also started using a cutting edge audio-visual computer package that helped with our statistical analysis of the game, and finally we arranged a team holiday in Lanzarote for January that doubled up as a warm weather training camp.

I was pushing the boat out as much as I could.

It looked like we were sinking fast, however, when we were beaten, 5-12 to 1-7 by Wexford in a league match. We were so bad it was incredible. It was a total humiliation. Mattie Forde scored 4-3 from play and rang rings around our defence.

What was most worrying was that we fielded a fairly strong team that included most of our big name players.

Near the end of the game a supporter came up to Pete Warren and started talking through the wire to him and giving out to him. Pete responded, which was understandable, but not the right thing to do either.

He was so devastated by the whole thing that he took the week off work afterwards.

At one stage I heard someone from the stand shout out.

'Go back to Mayo!'

It was the first time I had ever heard anything negative from a Galway supporter. We met the following Tuesday night for a team meeting to sift through the rubble of the defeat and see if we could salvage anything from the experience?

It ended up being a marathon three-and-a-half-hour session where we all had a bit of a go at each other. By the end of it a lot of important issues were addressed, and I felt a lot more positive leaving the hotel that night than I had when I arrived there.

It seemed to be a turning point in our season. From a position where it looked like we could be relegated in the league, we ended up qualifying for the semi finals. Had we lost our last game to Cavan we'd have been relegated, the league table was that tight. Instead, we showed a lot of guts to come from behind to win it by a point and set up a semi final clash with Tyrone.

I knew that one way or another this match would tell me whether we were serious contenders anymore.

I relished the challenge, because the impression I got from Mickey Harte and his team was that they thought they did everything right, and everyone else did it wrong.

The way they went on, you'd swear they had reinvented the game. So I viewed it as an opportunity for us to remind everyone that we had not gone away and that Galway footballers were still a match and more for anyone.

KEEPING THE FAITH ■ CHAPTER 24

I had watched the rise of the Armagh and Tyrone teams in 2002 and 2003 with interest, and I knew that playing an orthodox formation against them was an invitation for defeat.

The game had moved on tactically. We all had to make adjustments to evolve with it. Brian Dooher was the key cog in the Tyrone machine. He had an incredible engine and the ability to almost always be in the right place at the right time at either end of the pitch, so he would run the game if you let him.

The problem was that if you detailed your wing back to stick with him he would be dragged out of position and a gaping hole left behind that Tyrone's running game was designed to exploit.

We decided to set up a little differently than usual by selecting Tommy Joyce as a corner forward but giving him a man marking brief on Dooher. That left Sean Óg de Paor free to hold his defensive position and sweep effectively across the half back line rather than follow Dooher.

And it also meant that Dooher had to be wary of Joyce's scoring threat so he perhaps could not wander all over the pitch with the impunity he usually enjoyed.

A difficult task for us was made even tougher when we lost a coin toss and the venue for the game was fixed for Omagh. Their home pitch was a real fortress, but we were up for the battle.

So much so, that Tyrone almost seemed to take it personally that we would dare put it up to them as much as we did, and lashed out repeatedly.

Such was the aggression from Tyrone that day, the impression I was left with was that they were an outfit who felt they had the right to win everything ad infinitum.

At one stage I went behind our goal to give Alan Keane an instruction regarding kick outs. When Tyrone forward, Owen Mulligan spotted this he made a bee-line for me, and got into my face.

I didn't react.

Towards the end of the game their midfielder Kevin Hughes banged into Joe Bergin off the ball. We brought the incident to the attention of the linesman, and Hughes got a second yellow card and his marching orders.

Mickey Harte got on my case at this point, accusing me of getting Hughes sent off. Pádraic Joyce had already been sent off earlier in the game, unjustly in my opinion, but after the match Mickey did not leave that incident alone either and said he should have been sent off earlier.

The game finished 1-16 each after extra-time, which was a fair achievement for us considering Pádraic had been sent off in the first period of extra-time and had been comfortably the best player on the pitch until then.

It was a hugely encouraging performance by the whole team. Our tactics had worked a treat, we played some really classy football, and we dug in and showed some great character too when we had to.

On the Monday after the game Mickey Harte had another pop at Pádraic Joyce, so I decided it was time to fight fire with fire and had a go back at him via a couple of newspaper interviews.

Our boys were really wound up for the replay, and it looked like we were going to blow Tyrone away when we raced into an eight point lead by half-time. But Tyrone came back at us strongly in the second half and scored an unbroken sequence of 1-7 without reply.

For the second weekend running the game went into extra-time, however we dug deep and won an absolute classic, 2-18 to 1-19.

The misery of the defeat to Wexford now seemed like a distant memory, and it was easy to convince myself that we were once again a team with serious championship prospects.

Pádraic Joyce had been absolutely outstanding in both games, Michael Donnellan looked like he was getting back to his best too, and Paul Clancy had played well enough to suggest he could fill the gap left at centre back by the retirement of Tomás Mannion.

All three also performed well in the league final against Kerry, but even that was not enough to get us over the line.

We were eight points down with 10 minutes to go before summoning an impressive comeback that just fell short as we were beaten, 3-11 to 1-16.

The size of the score we conceded concerned me, but it was encouraging too that we had the spirit and conviction to fight back in the closing stages like we had. Despite the defeat, we were able to take a lot of positives from the game into the first round of the championship where we hit London for eight goals and won easily.

At that point it felt like we were in a good place, but between the win over London and the Connacht semi final against Mayo we suffered a series of mini-disasters.

Sean Óg de Paor suffered a torn cruciate ligament that ruled him out for the rest of the year. Then, in an A versus B game in training, Kevin Walsh, Gary Fahey, and Nicky Joyce all picked up injuries too. Ja Fallon had retired at the start of the year, so as I looked down from the stand in Pearse Stadium, it was as if the team was breaking up in front of my very eyes.

We had to field a weakened defence against Mayo, and despite racing into a 1-3 to 0-0 lead, the match turned into a living nightmare for us. They outscored us by 0-10 to 0-3 in the second half. It was a devastating defeat really.

We had a team meeting the following day to clear the air, but it was a fairly bad tempered one. People were keen to push the blame around, rather than be accountable.

A number of players complained that we were having too many of these meetings and that they were just an exercise in writing the same old things up on the board all the time. I told them they should ask themselves why we had to keep on writing the same things? And perhaps if they thought about that we would be closer to solving our problems?

The overall tone of the meeting made me apprehensive. Rather than release our frustrations, it seemed to amplify them. For the first time I sensed a resistance among the group to my methods. Many of us had been living in each other's pockets for seven years, and perhaps it was just getting to the point where they were sick of the sound of my voice.

We beat Louth in the Qualifiers the following weekend, but it did little to lift our collective mood because we played so poorly. To make matters worse, Tommy Joyce reacted poorly when I decided to replace him at half time.

He went straight to the showers which I only noticed when he reemerged from them. I could understand why he was disappointed, but I could not stand for someone potentially eroding team morale. I ordered him to put back on his jersey and sit in the dug-out for the second half.

He refused. He didn't turn up for training on the following Tuesday either, and it was just the sort of controversy we didn't need because things were bad enough.

It would've sent out the wrong vibes if it wasn't resolved and became public knowledge. So Pete Warren and I sat down with Tommy who apologised, and things were smoothened over. We also wanted Tommy to stay with us for the simple fact that he was a fine footballer who had made a big contribution for as long as he had been part of the panel. Especially in 2001, when he had a floating role in attack that made the most of his vision and accurate kick-passing.

We needed to have everyone pulling in the same direction because we were drawn out of the hat with Tyrone in the round three Qualifier draw which was always going to be a hugely difficult match for us.

It became even tougher when Kevin Walsh was ruled out after pulling a hamstring in training. We put him in an oxygen tent for a week and sent him to Dublin for laser treatment. All to no avail.

As the Tyrone match approached, I really had the sense that this was our last stand as a team. I think the players did to, and a determination to give it one last lash really solidified within the group.

I was proud of the way they performed on the day, but we were just not quite good enough. There was only a point in it at half time, but when we lost both Joe Bergin and Mattie Clancy to injury a lot of the pace went out of our play and they finished more strongly than we did.

It did not help either that a few poor refereeing decisions went against us. It was not just supporters or pundits who thought we were a team on the way out, I think referees did too.

The margin of the defeat to Tyrone, 1-16 to 0-11, was in no way a fair reflection on the competitiveness of the match. That was not much of a consolation though, because as I walked off the pitch I knew it was the last time I would do so as a Galway manager.

I called Pat Egan aside in the dressing room and told him that was that. I had given the job everything I had.

There was nothing more I could possibly do.

Pat asked me not to announce my retirement publicly yet because I still had to take charge of the under-21s for their campaign, so I didn't.

But I let the players know in the dressing room and it was a very emotional moment. I'm usually calm enough in those sort of situations. But we had been through an awful lot together and it all came flowing out. I didn't say everything I wanted to say. At the same time, I think I got the message across as to just how privileged I felt to have shared those years with them.

Michael Donnellan and Pádraic Joyce both embraced me, and that was a special moment because we had our ups and downs. But despite occasional episodes of friction, I had only massive respect for them as both men and footballers. The only reason we had clashed on a couple of occasions was because they were such strong characters. Were it not for that force of personality, they would never have been driven enough to become the footballers they did.

We were one big family for seven years, and like every family you have rows and reconciliations, highs and lows.

It was a fantastic journey, and I was very lucky to have been given the opportunity to go on it with what was a really special group of Galway players. I still have good relationships with them all, and that means a lot to me. Mayo is my native county, but Galway will always be close to my heart too.

Winning those two All-Irelands has been the pinnacle of my managerial career, and the only regret I have is that we didn't win more.

There have been some great teams in the modern era like the current Dublin side, and the Kerry and Tyrone teams of the noughties. But, for pure talent, I would rank that Galway team right up there with any of them.

They played a hugely positive and skilful brand of football, and that is what made them so special.

In recent years football has become a more defensive and risk-averse sport, but that Galway team kept people on the edge of their seats because their instinct was to always attack and throw caution to the wind.

Not only were they great footballers, they were also great characters. That is why it was such a pleasure for me to be involved with them for as long as I was.

CHAPTER 25

I was exhausted after the seven years with Galway, and when I finished up with them I was in no rush to get back into county management.

But, John Maughan stepped down as Mayo manager in 2005, and I came under a lot of pressure to replace him. At the time I was hosting a phone-in sports show on Midwest radio. Father Peter Quinn, who had played on the 1951 All-Ireland winning team, even rang in one night and urged me to take the job.

I had already been approached by the Mayo County Board and it was difficult to say no to my native county. But sometimes you have to put yourself first and at the time I still felt burned out from my time with Galway.

As well as having a radio show, I was also writing columns for *The Irish Times* and *Western People* newspapers, and doing some work with *The Sunday Game* as a panellist, all of which I enjoyed.

I was able to devote a lot more time to my own club, and also got a good kick from having a backroom role with Ballina Stephenites when they won the All-Ireland Club Championship in 2005.

Their manager Tommy Lyons, who's a friend of mine, came to me after they had beaten Killererin in the Connacht final and asked me to lend a hand. I basically took on a mentorship role by evaluating where they were at and what it might take for them to take the next step and win the All-Ireland.

It was really enjoyable to have an involvement without the sort of ultimate responsibility that goes with being a manager.

I was in no rush to put myself in that firing line again. So when Mickey Moran was given the Mayo job and led them to victory over Dublin in the 2006 All-Ireland semi final, I thought I'd have at least another year's grace before I came under pressure again to take charge of the team.

But then Mayo were well beaten by Kerry in the All-Ireland final and I was suddenly in the picture again.

I knew I couldn't turn down my own county again. But the situation was complicated by the fact that I had already agreed at that point to run for Fine Gael in the 2007 General Election.

I had retired from teaching in May of 2006. When I was approached by Fine Gael it just felt like a great opportunity at the right time. They had previously asked me to run in the 1999 European Elections, but it didn't suit me at the time.

When I was approached by the Mayo County Board a few months afterwards I knew it was going to be a massive commitment to run an election campaign, and also manage a county football team at the same time.

And when I was elected, there was the obvious challenge of managing Mayo even though I was based in Dublin for three days of the week for much of the year.

I felt that potential negative could be turned into a positive. The only night of training I would miss over the winter was on a Tuesday, when instead I could work with the 10 or 12 players who were based in Dublin while my selectors, Tommy Lyons and Kieran Gallagher ran the session in Mayo.

I felt that was of benefit because it meant I was valuing the players who would normally be a little bit isolated from the main group through the winter months. I never missed a training session in Mayo on a Thursday night, even though it was always hectic to get my day's work completed in time to make it.

I never wanted either role to compromise the other, and it was possible to make sure they didn't through sheer hard work and good time-management. I can say with a clear conscience that I kept both roles totally separate from one another, even though I know the perception in some quarters was different.

After I was appointed manager, there was even talk that I was not picking certain players because they did not share my own political persuasion and was instead promoting players who did!

That notion was absolutely preposterous and genuine football supporters would not give it any credence, but there were activists for other political parties within the county who'd have been happy to spin that sort of tall tale. Even before I was elected there were people keen to promote all sorts of conspiracy theories.

Some said it was a political decision to become Mayo manager again, and that the only reason I had done so was to increase my chances of being elected. And others said I had been emotionally blackmailed into accepting the job by the County Board because they knew if I turned it down it would hurt my election campaign.

Both theories were absolute rubbish. It really pissed me off to hear them doing the rounds. I quickly learned that politics is a dirty and absolutely ruthless game.

In football you will occasionally be stabbed in the back, but in politics they will knife you straight through the front.

At the end of 2006, when I got on the nomination papers I spent a few hours every week knocking on doors and introducing myself to people. It was not serious canvassing, just a way of letting people know that I would be running. A lot of people said if they elected me then I'd resign from the Mayo job, so that was another theory I had to quickly knock on the head.

From the very start, I was determined that both roles would be absolutely separate.

For instance, some of my supporters suggested getting some of the Mayo players to canvass for me, but there was no way I would even consider something like that. I also had a situation where I could not canvass on Tuesday and Thursday evenings, Saturday mornings, and Sunday afternoons, because they were sacrosanct from a football point of view.

The profile I earned from football was always going to be a help, but I found out very early it would only bring me so far. In an early opinion poll of the Mayo constituency, my name did not even register on the pie-chart.

I rang up Jim Higgins, who had first persuaded me to run for Fine Gael, and asked him what the hell he had gotten me into?

He told me not to worry. However, it made me realise that getting elected was going to require as much hard work as managing Mayo to success.

I suppose nothing feels like hard work as long as you are passionate about it. That is why football management has never really felt like hard work to me, and I soon found that politics engaged me in a similar way.

My father had been a dedicated Fine Gael supporter, a big Michael Collins man, so that is where my interest in party politics first came from. I remember him bringing me to rallies in Ballaghaderreen when James Dillon was leader, and it definitely left a mark.

Dillon had a big, booming voice and never needed a microphone. He'd stand up on the back of a lorry and the square would be packed with people who had come to hear his message.

I had been PRO of the local Fine Gael branch in Ballagh for years, so I was always politically inclined. Geography was one of the subjects I taught in school, and I especially enjoyed talking to my pupils about socioeconomic geography, the difference between core areas and peripheral areas, and the difficulty that peripheral areas experienced.

Discussing the theory was fine, but deep down I thought that instead of reading it out of a book and debating it with students, I should try to influence it in some way if I could. I suppose I ultimately agreed to run for office for the same reasons that I was first attracted to the GAA, love of my own area.

When you come from the West of Ireland you grow up with a sense that you are often overlooked or even downtrodden, and I wanted to stand up for it and help people achieve.

That might sound a bit idealistic, but if you are not idealistic then I don't think you have any business wanting to get involved in politics in the first place. Ideals on their own will not bring you very far, though. You have to be willing to graft hard, and I was lucky that I had a brilliant campaign team behind me.

It was driven by family members and friends, as well as party supporters.

Ger, all of the kids, and plenty of cousins got involved too. But we pulled people out of everywhere, really. There were personal friends I had been to school or college with, and players I had managed in the past.

We did a massive campaign on the ground because I wanted to meet as many people face to face as I possibly could. I was widely written off as a no-hoper. I knew that if I was to be elected I'd have to win an extra seat for the party, not one we already held.

It was always going to be tough battle for a newcomer like me to get elected in such a competitive constituency, but the closer the election came the more confident I was that we were going to do it. Once the polls closed on the Thursday, everyone around me was very excited, but I was extremely relaxed about the whole thing.

It was similar to the feeling I had on the morning of a big championship match, that you know you have prepared really well for. There's nothing more you can do at that stage, so there is no point getting stressed.

And when the tallies came in and we found out we had done it, it was a really special moment.

I was delighted for my campaign team because I knew just how much work they had put into it. They put their neck on the line for me evening after evening, and this was a just reward for their effort.

It was a real high, and felt all the more so because just five days earlier my spirits had been at rock bottom after Mayo were beaten in the first round of the championship by Galway.

We had played very poorly, and the nature of the defeat confirmed to me something I had already known in my bones, that the Mayo job was going to be a difficult one.

When I took over Galway and Leitrim they were teams on the way up who I knew were ready to challenge for silverware.

Whereas some of the key personnel in the Mayo panel I had inherited, like David Brady, David Heaney, Ciaran McDonald and James Nallen had played in three or four All-Ireland finals and were great players coming towards the end of their careers.

My job was always going to be to build a bridge between a group of players that had gotten very close and a new generation of emerging talent, while all the time keeping the team competitive as it went through a period of transition.

I was quoted regularly as saying that I was laying the foundations for a team of the future. I'm sure people thought I was saying that as a way of lessening expectation, but that is genuinely how I felt. There was definitely a train of thought amongst some members of the County Board, and maybe some supporters too, that Mayo would win an All-Ireland just because I was back as manager.

But that simplistic view abhorred me, and it brought its own pressure.

I told the County Board that if we were to be successful then they'd have to put their shoulder to the wheel, just like the Leitrim and Galway County Boards had when I managed there. Unfortunately, I never got the same sort of total buy-in from everyone on the County Board. There were some awfully good people who did everything they could to support me, but not everyone sung off the same hymn sheet as much as they needed to.

The season had started promisingly enough as a decent league campaign culminated in a final appearance against Donegal. But, after we lost that match, things quickly went into free-fall.

We subsequently lost a challenge match to Longford and, afterwards, I got word back that some members of the County Board were telling anyone who would listen that the team was in an awful mess.

It didn't help to hear that sort of negativity in the background, but it was true that things were not quite gelling.

Injuries to key players did not help our cause. Ciaran McDonald had not played a single game for us during the league because of a back injury, and his first appearance of the year was as a sub in the championship against Galway. Going into that match I still thought we could win it even though I knew we had problems. But two early Cormac Bane goals for Galway meant the game was over as a contest not long after it had begun.

After the match I had to go to a political meeting in Kiltimagh which was the last thing I wanted to do because I was in such a foul humour.

I knew that my election campaign would be used as a stick to beat me with by people who wanted something to blame for the team's defeat. There were so many false accusations floating around that I made the decision to go on local radio the following day to discuss the defeat and make it very clear that my focus as Mayo manager had in no way been compromised by my election campaign.

That night my management team and I met with the players to pick the bones out of the defeat to Galway, so it was a 24 hours I wouldn't wish on anyone. We had pool session in Claremorris, and then sat down with all the players for a heart to heart.

Coming away from that meeting I made the decision that it was time to accelerate the handover of the team from one generation of players to the next by bringing in a couple of new faces. I thought that both Pearse Hanley and David Kilcullen were two players that Mayo could build around for years to come, so they were drafted in for our first Qualifier against Cavan.

We won that game with a bit to spare, but were then convincingly beaten ourselves in the next round by Derry.

The scale of that loss, 2-13 to 1-6, was very sobering, and underlined the scale of the task I faced in turning Mayo back into a team that could challenge for All-Ireland titles.

CHAPTER 26

Jack O'Connor, the former Kerry manager put it well when he said that politicians want to be in the newspaper on a Friday, whereas managers want to be in it on a Monday.

After I was elected I quickly learned there are some other glaring differences between being a member of a political party and a football team. For a start, you just do not get the same unity of purpose in politics that you do in sport.

When you think about it, sport is pure. It is the ultimate public examination of just how well you have prepared for a challenge. To be successful in sport, you have to have every single member of your team buying into the same vision of where you want to get to.

There is an acceptance that if everyone does not buy totally into the concept of a completely loyal and supportive collective, then you will achieve nothing. I naively thought that a political party would operate with the same ethos, but I soon learned that was not the case.

We held parliamentary party meetings every week. The idea of this is that you're able to go into a room with your 51 colleagues, as it was at the time, where you trash out different arguments and develop a common policy on a particular issue.

What I quickly found out was that everything we discussed in those meetings was almost immediately leaked to the media.

With any football team I was every successful with, if even half of what we discussed in a dressing room got out then it would have destroyed our chance of achieving what we wanted to achieve.

After one particularly long parliamentary meeting we broke for a vote. There was an agreement to put out a statement on the result of that vote, but in the meantime the nine o'clock news came on and they already had it.

I just turned to my colleagues and said, 'Jesus lads… ye would never win an All-Ireland with this sort of carry-on!'

But even if the culture of politics sometimes frustrated me, I quickly gained a respect for the job of a politician. I know there is not always a whole lot of sympathy out there, but people have no idea just how much hard work politicians from all parties do.

It never stops, and it is multi-faceted.

You have the big picture politics, the legislative stuff, and also the parish pump politics where you do your best for the people who elected you. There is always some unexpected issue or problem around every corner, and I suppose in that way it is similar to county football management.

Because, as challenging as my new career in politics was, managing Mayo through the 2008 season was an even more stressful and difficult experience.

Before the championship even begun, our preparations were badly disrupted by a very public disagreement between Ciaran McDonald and myself that polarised the county. Ciaran had been disappointed in 2007 that I had only brought him on as a sub towards the end of our defeat to Derry.

He wanted to start that match, but he had no real training done that year because of his back injury and I did not feel he was ready yet.

I'd have loved to have him in the team. I would go so far as to say that Ciaran McDonald is the best individual player that Mayo probably ever had. But he was not fit. I would not make exceptions for unfit players no matter how talented they are.

Sometime after our championship exit he rang me and let me know in no uncertain terms that he was pissed off and would not be rejoining the panel ahead of the 2008 campaign.

That, at least, is the impression I got from what he said to me over the phone. I left him alone at that point but it was always my hope that he would come back into the fold in time for the championship.

I was not bothered all that much about Ciaran missing the league. He was at the stage in his career where he was that bit older and injuries were beginning to creep in. A break during the league would benefit him, and I felt the same about James Nallen, who was also not part of the panel for the league.

Once the league was over, however, I wanted the two lads back in and I wanted it done in such a way that no other player on the panel would feel Ciaran and James were getting special treatment.

So I decided to reintegrate them by asking them to play in a trial match.

It was never a situation whereby they had to play well in that trial match in order to make it back onto the panel. I knew well what they could offer, I just wanted to get the visuals right. So the plan was to give them half an hour each, have them back on board, and then take it from there.

It was just meant to be a public way of showing they were back in the fold, much like what I did with Pádraic Joyce in that FBD league match in 2003. I felt Ciaran could still be inspirational on the pitch as well as in the dressing room. Myself, Tommy Lyons and Kieran Gallagher discussed it ad infinitum, and we all wanted him back in.

From our perspective, we made every effort to make contact with him and to do it as smoothly as possible.

But the reality was that he wasn't answering phone calls or texts and was very difficult to get hold of. We had two trial matches scheduled, and eventually Ciaran did get back to me via text and agreed he would come down and play some part of the second one.

But then he texted me again at the last minute to say he was not available after all, because he was going to be out of the county. At that point I really felt like my mettle was being tested and I had no option but to move on and name a championship panel without him in it.

I had to be fair to everyone and respect the contribution that all the other players were making. That was the priority. It would have done our championship preparations no good if there was constant 'will he, won't he?' speculation about Ciaran's possible return hanging over us.

I'm sure the situation could have been salvaged eventually and a way found for Ciaran to return. All it would've taken was a face-to-face chat. But instead he went to the newspapers and did an interview with Martin Breheny of *The Irish Independent*.

That was not Ciaran's style. Over the years he rarely if ever spoke to the print media, so I am convinced he was acting under bad advice from someone who should have known better. Ciaran suggested in that interview that I had not made much of an effort to get him to return, but the reality is that he didn't return calls and I'd have to send a huge number of texts before I'd get anything in response.

It's very hard to resolve a dispute when it becomes a public issue and people take sides on it.

We solved bigger problems in Galway and Leitrim when I was manager there, but that was because everyone kept their own counsel rather than go public with their grievances. That meant we were able to concentrate on quietly solving the issues, rather than public debating who was right and wrong.

In those situations it ultimately does not matter who is to blame, the important thing is that you eventually come together and resolve it one way or another.

Once Ciaran had gone public with his version of events, I felt I had no option other than to defend the management's decision in the same sphere. I was uncomfortable fielding questions on the issue publicly though, because I knew that everything that was said on it would draw an opposite opinion.

Ciaran McDonald is revered in Mayo. So regardless of what I had to say, a large rump of public opinion would take his side, and that is understandable. The local media were keen to blow the thing up to high heavens as well. The *Western People* even had big pictures of both of us on the front page, to make it look like we were going head-to-head.

I still hoped there could be some way to resolve the whole thing, but that was always going to be much more difficult once such a public issue was created about it.

I don't blame Ciaran for that. In fact, I would defend him, and instead point the finger at whoever it was that advised him to go public. If Ciaran had just rung me instead of speaking to Martin Breheny, there'd have been no major drama. Breheny was not to blame for anything, he was just doing his job as any good journalist does. If he just said, 'I want to play', then I'd have told him that I wanted him to play too.

In an ideal world, Ciaran would've been a central player for us in 2008, but it was not to be. His absence was not the only disruption to my plans.

By the end of 2007 I had decided that Pearse Hanley and David Kilcullen could be two of the main pillars of a reconstructed side. But, unfortunately, I had to go back to the drawing board. Around that time, Australian Football League clubs were taking an ever increasing interest in talented young Irish footballers they thought they might convert into Aussie Rules players.

It was no surprise really that Pearse came to their attention because he was such a naturally gifted player. He was given a serious offer by the Brisbane Lions, but I did everything I could to persuade him that it was a better option to stay in Ireland.

He had already won a scholarship to study PE teaching in DCU. Not only would he have received a fine education there, his development as a footballer would also have been accelerated by their expertise.

But it soon became apparent that both Pearse and his family were keen to take the opportunity presented to him by the Brisbane Lions, and, ultimately, that was the decision they took. It has turned out to be the right one from his point of view because he has done brilliantly there.

As much as I am delighted for him on a personal level, I know too that he has been a massive loss for Mayo football.

I have no doubt that Mayo would've won an All-Ireland in recent years had he stayed in Ireland. He was a brilliant centre forward, the sort of natural attacking talent Mayo really could have done with. I was also convinced that David Kilcullen was the real deal and had great hopes for him.

I was lucky enough to watch and admire the great John Morley play at centre back for Mayo back in the 1960s, and James Nallen in the '90s, and David was the closest I had seen to them in terms of being a natural No.6.

He wasn't initially keen on playing in the position, but when we put him there he fitted it like a hand into a snug glove. His sense of position, his strength on the ball, and his peripheral vision were all superb.

Sometimes talent alone is no guarantee, and ultimately David didn't take the opportunity that was there for him so he never fulfilled all that potential. Thankfully, other talented young players like Keith Higgins, Colm Boyle, Donal Vaughan and Ger Cafferkey were emerging who would stay the course, so bit by bit a new look team started to come together.

I had high hopes of winning a Connacht title in 2008 and we started the campaign well with a 13-point win over Sligo in the semi final.

But in the Connacht final I found out the hard way what it was like to be on the wrong side of a Pádraic Joyce master-class as he inspired Galway to a one-point victory. They hit 2-2 without replay in a 12 minute period in the first half, and even though we fought back bravely in the second half we just came up short.

Morale in the county was low after that defeat, and I could feel support for me and my management team ebbing away. That was vividly illustrated when we decided to travel to Dublin by train for our subsequent Qualifier game against Tyrone. Travelling by train on the day of the match had worked well for me when I was in charge of Galway. It meant the lads got to sleep in their own beds the night before.

The key thing is to have a nutritious pre-match meal for the players to eat while they travel. But, when I asked the County Board to sort that out, I was told it was not possible.

I found this hard to believe, because when I had travelled by rail with the Galway team, Iarnród Éireann rolled out the red carpet for us. Now I was being told that if I wanted food for the train, I'd have to sort it out myself. Left with little option, that's exactly what I did.

Ger prepared all the food herself, but it was outrageous that it had to be done that way.

And when you consider that we lost the match by just a point to a team that would go on to win the All-Ireland final, it just makes it all the more annoying. Sport at that level is all about very fine margins, and it was easy to convince yourself that greater support in terms of our pre-match preparation might have made a difference.

It did not help either that we were the victims of some terrible refereeing calls on the day.

I usually refrain from criticising referees because I have been one myself and I know it is a tough job, but that day Maurice Deegan did us no favours. The worst of a series of bad calls came in the final minute when Trevor Mortimer was absolutely mauled while we went hunting for a late, equalising point.

Instead of giving a free in, Maurice awarded the free to Tyrone instead. Maurice Deegan's brother, Joe is a Fine Gael party member and once told me that his mother had a lot of admiration for me. I told him that if that was the case them maybe she could do me a favour and tell her other son to give us the odd break now and then!

Had I been a rookie manager, then there's a good chance I'd have been shown the door after that defeat to Tyrone.

Expectations had been high when I went into the job, but after two years we had no silverware and had made early exits from the championship in consecutive years. My track record bought me some time, and the message I was sending out was that everyone needed to hold their nerve.

I had known from the start that we needed to rebuild a new team and that there could be some growing pains.

I was still convinced we could develop into a high calibre outfit.

CHAPTER 27

My success in Leitrim and Galway had been based on a total unity of purpose between the management team, the players, and the County Board.

Unfortunately, that same unity of purpose was not there to the same extent in Mayo, largely because the County Board Executive itself seemed divided. That became very obvious when we travelled to New York for the first round of the 2009 Connacht championship.

Those championship trips to New York are always hectic because it is a chance for a county's diaspora to see the Mayo team and renew bonds to the homeland. I knew what to expect having been there with Leitrim, and you make allowances for the fact that the Mayo supporters in the city have to be facilitated.

At the same time, you do not want the players to be pulled this way and that. Ultimately, you are there to win a championship match, and you have to treat that task with some respect. I planned the entire weekend carefully with the County Board and we agreed that the players would attend an official fundraising dinner on the Friday night, but that they would go straight back to their hotel afterwards.

That went like clockwork. But, unfortunately, individual officers in the County Board also promised that players would be available to go to other events that were not part of the official plan, and that ended up causing mayhem. There was even a falling out between some members of the board.

When we came back from New York I called a meeting of the wider management team, which included County Board officers, to thrash the whole thing out.

They were acting as if everything was hunky dory, until Tommy Lyons said, 'for God's sake lads… some of ye weren't even talking to each other!'

Effectively, the end result was that I hammered home the reality that if Mayo were going to win something we needed to all be singing off the same hymn sheet.

That meeting seemed to calm the troubled waters. When we won the Connacht championship just over two months later, the Mayo County Board president, Eddie Cuffe said to me that the most important factor that led to the success was that meeting we had when we came home from New York.

It was definitely an important milestone for us that year, but there were other factors too that helped us get over the line.

By 2009 the team was more settled. Young players like Keith Higgins and Ger Cafferkey were really finding their feet, and Andy Moran had brought his game to a new level. That was also the year that Aidan O'Shea arrived on the scene and made an immediate impact.

He was still doing his Leaving Cert but I wanted to get him in as quickly as possible because I knew he had a massive future and there was the risk of losing him to the AFL, like we had with Pearse Hanley.

I didn't make huge demands on him training-wise because of his exams and the fact that he was playing schools football with St Gerald's in Castlebar and the county under-21s.

But I did want to give him a clear message that he was going to be involved in the 2009 championship, so we put him on a strength and conditioning programme and stayed in constant communication with him. By then he had also been contacted by a couple of AFL clubs. I was on red alert. What made it easier to persuade him that his future lay with Mayo, rather than on the other side of the world, was that his parents. Jim and Sheila O'Shea wanted him to stay.

It helped too that he made an instant impression with the team when we brought him in for the league. We used him as a target man in the full forward line, and he showed incredible maturity on the ball for someone so young.

I told him he did not have to come to New York with us because I didn't want to disrupt his Leaving Cert studies, but he insisted on travelling and ended up scoring 1-3 from play in what was a comfortable win.

I was expecting a much tougher test from Roscommon in the Connacht semi final, but we also ended up hammering them, 3-18 to 0-7.

I had been optimistic about our chances going into the match, but the scale of the win underlined just how much progress we had made as a team. For the first time since I had taken charge, we now had a strong and settled spine to the team and were playing with a real self-confidence.

Morale was high going into the Connacht final against Galway, and we looked set for another comfortable win when we led by five points at half time, and seven with just eight minutes to go. But then Galway came roaring back at us and ended up levelling the game in extra-time, when Michael Meehan scored a goal. I was good friends with him and I thought to myself...'don't do this to me, Michael!'

It looked like we were going to throw the thing away, but it is always a good sign of a team that they can respond positively in the face of adversity and that's what we did. We went straight down the field and scored the winning point, courtesy of the quick thinking and leadership of Andy Moran and Peadar Gardiner.

Andy picked out Peadar in full flight with a quick free, and Peadar held his nerve to stick it over the bar. Ultimately, it was all the sweeter to win a match like that because Galway had no time to respond.

Andy and Peadar were the last action heroes, but Conor Mortimer also deserves a lot of praise for that Connacht final success. He had recovered from a shoulder injury that kept him out of the matches against New York and Roscommon, so he'd have been disappointed not to get the start against Galway.

But he responded in the best way possible by scoring 1-2 after coming on as a sub and having a major influence on the game. I was not surprised, because I never doubted Conor's quality or commitment. He had no shortage of critics, even within the county, but I always felt he was misunderstood because of the bleached blonde hair and the white football boots.

He had a huge love of playing for Mayo and a massive ambition to do well for the county. I have heard people suggest he was not dedicated to the cause, but nothing could be further from the truth because he never missed a training session. Perhaps, though, he did not have the sort of positive influence he should have had considering his ability as a footballer.

Some people had the impression that he had a big head, so one of the first things I asked him when I met him was what perception he thought people had of him?

'What people?' he smiled in response.

I was trying to get him to realise that he could do more to improve his image with his own teammates and with referees, but Conor could be his worst enemy sometimes. His attitude was... 'just give it to the Mort... and I'll do the rest'.

He had the individual talent to unhinge defences every time he played, but he could have made an even bigger contribution had he a better understanding of how a team dynamic worked. He did not realise that a few encouraging words from him could mean an awful lot to another player, or that if he threw his hands up in the air with frustration when they made a mistake it was having a negative impact.

And because his public image was not the most positive, I felt it did him no favours with referees. Fifty-fifty calls usually went against him, and I believe that is because they subconsciously or maybe even overtly did not like the personality he projected. His brashness was more of a front. Deep down, I think he had his own insecurities.

I remember him saying to me one day that the posts in McHale Park seemed wider to him than they did in Croke Park.

It was big of him to actually admit that because when a player is that honest about his inner fears then at least you can work on them and help eliminate them.

Conor was full of ironies. He liked to come across as cocky and confident, but in many respects he was very shy. That shyness might not have been very apparent to others though after he scored that goal against Galway in the

2009 Connacht final and lifted his jersey to reveal a t-shirt emblazoned with a particular message…

RIP Micheal Jackson

The pop singer, Michael Jackson (not Micheal!) had passed away a few weeks before the game and for some reason Conor thought it would be appropriate to show his respect in this manner.

He only meant it as a bit of fun, but I knew the way the media worked and how the image would be plastered everywhere. I wanted people to see Conor as one of the best forwards in the game, not someone who made headlines for something other than his football.

I had a word with him in training the following Tuesday. I wanted the players to know that I was dealing with it rather than just pretending it never happened. It was only a small annoyance though in the greater scheme of things. My overriding emotion was one of relief and satisfaction that we had finally started winning some silverware again.

I knew going into that Connacht final that I was out the door if we didn't win it, so the stakes were high.

We still weren't the finished article as a team. Nevertheless, I was confident that we were building nicely and had the potential to keep getting better and better if we could maintain our momentum. Unfortunately, we came to a sudden stop against Meath in the All-Ireland quarter final in circumstances that still leave a bitter taste in my mouth.

We led by four points with 20 minutes to play, but then lost both Aidan Kilcoyne and Aidan O'Shea to injury. Between them, they had scored 1-4 from play and led the Meath defence a merry dance. The match also swung on a couple of decisions by the referee, Joe McQuillan and his assistants.

Meath were awarded a line-ball that should have been given our way, and directly from it they won a penalty that should never have been awarded. They scored it, and generated a momentum which until that moment seemed beyond them.

The Sunday Game pundits that night accounted for 1-2 of Meath's total that came directly from incorrect officiating, so this is not just a case of me having sour grapes. We were on the wrong end of bad calls from the very start of the game because Meath's first point came from the awarding of a '45' that was clearly a wide ball.

I was furious after the match. But I bit my tongue because at the time there was a Manager's Committee and we had all been asked not to comment on referees just after the heat of battle. But my time as a county manager has convinced me that there has to be some accountability for GAA referees in the cold light of day.

For instance, it would have been very informative for us if we were given an official assessment of the referee's performance a few months later. Players are dropped and managers are sacked every year because of poor results, but it seems as though referees are never held to account for their failures.

I was a referee myself and would acknowledge they have a difficult job, but the GAA definitely needs to be more transparent in how they assess their referees and more proactive when a referee falls short of an acceptable standard.

In the Premier League you have a situation where a referee is stood down for a few weeks or temporarily demoted to a lower league if he has a howler. I think that strengthens the whole system. In the GAA, they seem to think it is a sign of weakness if they publicly acknowledge the fact that one of their referees has performed poorly.

Losing a big match like an All-Ireland quarter final is always tough to take, but it is much more devastating when you feel like you lost it because of circumstances that were beyond your control.

The following day my daughter, Grainne gave birth to our first grandchild, Ciaran in New Zealand.

I had not intended to visit them because I had hoped to be planning for an All-Ireland semi final. But, after the defeat to Meath, I was glad to have an escape route out of the country.

I booked a last-minute flight with my daughter, Niamh.

It was a relief to be able to just leave it all behind me and have a nice personal time with my family, but the long flight to New Zealand was hard because I had a lot of time to think about our defeat.

The sense of an opportunity missed was reinforced when my tenure as Mayo manager ended in fairly disastrous circumstances the following year.

CHAPTER 28

It initially looked like we would be capable of building on the progress made in 2009, when we showed some great form in the league by beating Galway, Tyrone, Derry, Kerry, Monaghan and Cork.

Then, we played Cork again in the league final and they hammered us by eight points which was a massive set-back just before the championship. I don't think we ever recovered mentally from that.

We made a great start and went four points up against Sligo in the Connacht quarter final, however even at that stage I felt we were flat and lacking authority and energy around the middle of the field.

Sligo were playing at home and had a huge hunger that we just could not match on the day. We struggled to get our hands on the ball.

We ended up being well beaten by four points, and it was just soul-destroying as all the progress we had made in 2009 just crumbled away in the space of 70 minutes. In the immediate aftermath I pulled Tommy Lyons and Kieran Gallagher together and asked them what the hell we were going to do here?

I was seriously disillusioned.

You don't run away from a tough situation, though.

We had three weeks to prepare for our first round Qualifier against Longford, but it was a difficult time because everything had unravelled.

I knew I was a dead man walking as far as most of the County Board were concerned. Apart from the chairman and president, I felt I had lost their backing, and was reliving the nightmare of 1991 all over again. Their lack of support was in stark contrast to the backing I had received from the Galway County Board after we had been knocked out of the Connacht championship in 2001.

The essential difference was that I had already won an All-Ireland final with Galway whereas Mayo were still searching for their first since 1951. I did not have the same cushion.

I did my best to rally the troops by doing all I could to exude a positive air, even though the negativity around me was palpable. People were going around with heads down and shoulders slumped. Eye contact was being avoided.

Ciaran Gallagher and Tommy Lyons were absolutely brilliant in those three weeks, but it was very difficult to prevent all the pessimism from seeping through to the players. I knew the mood was all-wrong on the team coach the day we travelled to the match in Longford. We were just very vulnerable.

When there's a chance that you're walking into an ambush, you want to know every detail about your surroundings to make sure you're as well prepared as possible. Unfortunately, I never got a precise 'clár an lae' from the County Board secretary.

That meant I did not know until I got to Pearse Park that there was a hurling match on before the football which meant we had to revise all our plans for the warm-up at the last minute.

The match itself was a slow, agonising death. We led by three points at half time, but when Paul Kelly scored a second half goal for them the writing was on the wall. In the last play of the game Alan Dillon was hauled down and a free was awarded. The referee blew the final whistle rather than allow it to be taken and give us a last gasp chance for an equalising point.

That was a strange one. But, ultimately, we just did not play well enough and the better team on the day won.

I knew that was it as far as me being Mayo manager was concerned, and it was pretty emotional in the dressing room afterwards.

We stayed in there for a long time. I told the players that even though it had been a disastrous year, I was convinced they would someday win an

All-Ireland title.

I was not saying that to make them feel better about themselves. I was confident that the younger footballers we had brought through like Aidan O'Shea, Donal Vaughan, Keith Higgins, Kevin McLoughlin, Colm Boyle and Alan Freeman were a very special generation.

They have since proven that by becoming the first team to win five Connacht titles in-a-row, and the dream of bringing the Sam Maguire back to Mayo for the first time since 1951 is still very much a realistic one.

My second spell as Mayo manager might be considered by many to be a disappointing one, but my priority was always to bring through a new generation of footballers. I knew all along there was a chance that it might be another manager who would benefit most from that, and that is what came to pass.

I'm not taking any credit for what they achieved when James Horan was manager or what they won in 2015 with Pat Holmes and Noel Connelly at the helm. I just saw the regeneration of the panel as something that had to be done.

Noel and Pat had little option but to resign their position when the present squad told them they had lost confidence in their management. The two lads, who have given so much of their lives to Mayo football, put the interests of their county above themselves in deciding to go after that, and they also saved Mayo football from a situation where dirty linen was going to be aired under the public glare.

They simply shared the same ambition as the players – to bring Sam Maguire to Mayo. But obviously there was a desperation, and deep frustration, amongst the players at the failure to capture the ultimate prize in the game. In deciding by a majority vote that they did not want to work with Pat and Noel anymore they immediately placed even more pressure on themselves, however.

Of course I wish I had been more successful in my second period, and there are always regrets when you fail to reach your targets.

Perhaps I started the surgery on the team prematurely after we were beaten by Galway in the 2007 championship. Maybe if I had taken a step back and given some of the veterans another chance to prove themselves, we might have gone on a run through the Qualifiers that year.

We didn't have much luck with injuries over the course of the four years, and luck is very much an underestimated commodity when you're a county football manger.

Perhaps the saying that you should never go back is a true one.

I had my time with Mayo from 1988 to '91, and maybe I should have left it at that.

But I would die a very happy man if I was to manage the Mayo team that brought the Sam Maguire Cup back to the county after such a long wait, so I was never going to turn the opportunity down.

I've no doubt that it will eventually happen, sooner rather than later, and when it does people will say it wasn't as difficult as we all thought it would be. I had grown accustomed to success in Galway so it was very frustrating that my second spell in charge of Mayo did not go as well as I or anyone else would've hoped.

But I do not regret taking the risk because you do not do the thing for your own glorification, you do it because you want to help a larger group achieve something meaningful.

You have to take the bad with the good, and even the very best managers like Mick O'Dwyer, Sean Boylan and Mickey Harte have probably had more bad days than good ones.

For most managers, the thing is going to end in tears. But, overall, my two spells in charge of Mayo and my years managing the Galway and Leitrim teams were very rewarding experiences. The most valuable thing I took from all my years in management were the friendships I made, and the loyalties I earned.

Sharing a major commitment to a common cause is a powerful way of bringing people together and bonding them for life. I think that is the true reward that anyone who is involved in the GAA takes from the experience.

I couldn't possibly mention all the people who helped me along the way and are now good friends of mine, because there are just too many of them. But when I think back on the great days, they are always personalised by a moment shared with someone else who had travelled some portion of my journey with me.

There were 20,000 people to greet us in Tuam the day after Galway won the All-Ireland final in 1998, but Mary O'Haire is the one I'll always remember most.

Her late husband, Christy has been a selector with me on the Mayo under-21 team that won the All-Ireland in 1983, and there she was banging on the side of the bus to offer her congratulations as we came into Tuam. You can't buy that sort of friendship and loyalty, and there were many other incidents like that throughout my years in management.

The Tuesday after that 1998 All-Ireland final win I brought the Sam Maguire Cup to Ballaghderreen for a function in the town square, and a huge number of people I had known through football down through the years made the effort to be there.

Joe Reynolds, one of my selectors in my time at Leitrim was there, as was Fergal Reynolds who played corner back on the 1994 team. My other Leitrim selector, Olly Honeyman made a point of meeting me outside the Galway dressing room after we won the 2001 All-Ireland final, and Gerry Flanagan waved me off as the Galway team bus left Dublin the following day.

Another Leitrim man, Benny Guckian was a panel member who did not get as much game time as I'm sure he would've liked, but he too made the effort to be there when I brought the cup to Ballaghderreen after both All-Ireland wins with Galway.

Paddy Henry played football with me in St Nathy's and Maynooth, and remains a life-long friend even though I joke with him that he ended my own county playing career because he played on the Sligo team that beat us in that fateful 1975 Connacht final.

Tommie Gorman gave very generously of his time throughout my time in management as an unofficial video-analyst and hugely influential confidant. He played a bigger role in any success I had than anyone would realise, and is another who has become a very good friend.

It's the human element that made my time in county management so worthwhile. But, of course, the success was sweet too.

I'll always hold the joy and sense of accomplishment of winning two All-

Ireland senior titles with Galway especially close to my heart. But it would be nice if I also had the physical memento of an All-Ireland medal to dust down and look at now and again.

In most team sports the manager of a championship winning team also gets a medal for their efforts, but not in the GAA. The referee even gets one, so why shouldn't the manager and his selectors get one too?

You will not win an All-Ireland without a group of really talented players. But, equally, you will not win one unless you have a competent manager. He is the leader who puts the pieces together behind the scenes that enables a team to unlock its potential, and there should be some recognition for the part he plays too.

The cynics will say we get rewarded enough, but half of the rumours about under the table payments to managers are not true.

I accept that none of them should be true. I was never in it for the money, only the satisfaction you get from helping a group of footballers unlock their potential and achieve something worthwhile together

I could never put a price on how much joy I got from winning the two All-Irelands with Galway, or the Connacht titles with Mayo and Leitrim.

Sometimes young managers ask me for advice because they have been asked to manage a certain county. One of the most common questions they ask is, 'how much should I ask for?'

I tell them straight out that they are asking the wrong question. What they should be asking themselves is, 'how much can I win?' If you are in it for the money then you are in it for the wrong reasons, and I doubt you will have much success.

There's no doubt that some county managers are being paid and that will always continue to happen as long as County Boards and Supporters Clubs are willing to stump up the money to do so. The GAA will never be able to eradicate that culture, but they could control it by legitimising it.

We already have full time coaches and administrators in the GAA, so why not full time managers?

Their role could extend beyond merely managing the county senior team.

They could also oversee high performance structures that extend down to the underage level and develop links with clubs and schools.

The GAA moves slowly when it comes to changing their traditions, but when they do move they usually get it right and that is why I think we will eventually see full time managers being part of the fabric of the association.

I'm out of the county game five years now, but at times I still miss it an awful lot. It's a tough gig, but I loved the cut and thrust of it, the raw tension, the public examination of all of your hard work when the championship comes around.

County management is a much different job now than it was for most of my time doing it. I tried to do everything as professionally as possible, but I was largely relying on people to give me their expertise voluntarily.

My wife, Ger, was the team nutritionist for many years, and Tommie Gorman spent countless hours over the years doing video analysis work for nothing more than a heartfelt thanks. Nowadays, the successful counties have management teams of over 20 people, many of whom are well paid specialists in their fields.

I always endeavoured to be at the cutting edge of team preparation and to leave no stone unturned, but it has gone to an entirely new level now in terms of the sort of money that is being spent on teams. There's nothing wrong with that if a county can afford it, though I took a lot of satisfaction from having professional standards and out-thinking our rivals in an era where the game was more true to its amateur ethos.

I had a great innings.

I doubt I'll be back.

Certainly not as long as I'm a TD. Now that there are Friday sittings of the Dáil it would be an impossibility to make the required commitment. In a way, my political career seems to be echoing my time as a county manager, because I now face the tough challenge of seeking election in a new constituency, Galway West.

The reconfiguration of Mayo from a five-seat constituency to a four-seater means I now have to win over a public beyond my native county. A unification of Mayo and Galway worked well in 1998 and 2001, so hopefully we can repeat the trick.

My achievements with the Galway footballers and knowledge of the county should be some help, but there's an intelligent electorate out there who will base their judgement of me on my political performance more than anything else.

There's a big risk in moving constituencies, but I've been taking risks all of my life.

This is just one more.